Lexical Variation of an East Midlands Mining Community

Lexical Variation of an East Midlands Mining Community

NATALIE BRABER

EDINBURGH
University Press

Edinburgh University Press is one of the leading university presses in the UK. We publish academic books and journals in our selected subject areas across the humanities and social sciences, combining cutting-edge scholarship with high editorial and production values to produce academic works of lasting importance. For more information visit our website: edinburghuniversitypress.com

© Natalie Braber, 2022

Edinburgh University Press Ltd
The Tun – Holyrood Road
12(2f) Jackson's Entry
Edinburgh EH8 8PJ

Typeset in 10/12 Times New Roman by
Cheshire Typesetting Ltd, Cuddington, Cheshire

A CIP record for this book is available from the British Library

ISBN 978 1 4744 5554 1 (hardback)
ISBN 978 1 4744 5555 8 (paperback)
ISBN 978 1 4744 5556 5 (webready PDF)
ISBN 978 1 4744 5557 2 (epub)

The right of Natalie Braber to be identified as the author of this work has been asserted in accordance with the Copyright, Designs and Patents Act 1988, and the Copyright and Related Rights Regulations 2003 (SI No. 2498).

Contents

List of Figures   vi
Acknowledgements   vii

1   The Linguistic Heritage of East Midlands Mining Communities   1
2   The History and Geography of the East Midlands Coalfield   23
3   Methodology   62
4   Analysis   83
5   Conclusion: Preserving Pit Talk   149

References   168
Index   179

List of Figures

2.1	Map of the UK coalfields	26
2.2	Leicestershire coalfield	37
2.3	South Derbyshire coalfield	38
2.4	North Derbyshire coalfield	42
2.5	North Nottinghamshire coalfield	45
2.6	South Nottinghamshire coalfield	46
2.7	Thoresby trip to Skegness	52
3.1	Sense Relation Network 1	73
3.2	Sense Relation Network 2	74
4.1	Miners having snap in Clipstone in the 1960s	89
4.2	Snap tin and water dudley	91
4.3	Drilling at Shirebrook Colliery in the late 1970s	104
4.4	Different shovel shapes	106
4.5	Faceworker cleaning up with a shovel in Pleasley Colliery in the 1960s	107
4.6	Onsetter taking identity tags from miners arriving underground	111
4.7	Miner hand-loading large pieces of coal onto a face conveyor	116
4.8	Shaft sinking at Bevercotes Colliery in the late 1950s	118
4.9	Circular tunnelling machine being assembled in a roadway in the early 1980s in Cadley Hill Colliery, Leicestershire	123
4.10	Props	125
4.11	Shearer on 93's face (Thoresby) in 1976	127
4.12	DOSCO roadheader	128
4.13	Loaded conveyor belt at Gedling Colliery	129
4.14	The Hunt Rider cable cars at Babbington	130
4.15	Underground manriding train at Thoresby	130
4.16	Double-decker cage at Mansfield	132
4.17	Motties, tallies or checks	133
4.18	Headstocks and winding gear at Clipstone	138
4.19	Coal preparation plant at Mansfield Colliery	140
4.20	Testing for gas	141

Acknowledgements

This research would not have been possible without all the miners who took part in the interviews and questionnaires and answered all the questions asked of them. Thanks also to the mining heritage groups (Bilsthorpe Heritage Museum, Bestwood Winding Engine House, Pleasley Pit Trust, South Derbyshire Mining Preservation Group and Coalville Heritage Society) which put me in contact with many miners who wanted to take part in this work.

My thanks also go to Alice Cope, Chris Dann, Suzy Harrison and Claire Ashmore for their work on the project over the years. I am also very grateful to David Amos, both for his work on the interviews and for answering all my coal mining related questions! I would also like to thank Helen Simpson and the Coal Authority as well as the Mansfield and Ashfield Chad for allowing me to use their photos throughout the book. Also thanks to the Northern Mine Research Society for the use of their maps and to Brian Morley for allowing me to use his work on the front cover of this book.

I would also like to thank Ben Braber for reading through earlier drafts of this work and always giving helpful and constructive advice.

Finally, many thanks to Leon and Finn who are always there to support me when I need them.

1

The Linguistic Heritage of East Midlands Mining Communities

1.1 Introduction

In July 2015 the last deep coal mine in the East Midlands of England closed. That was the Thoresby pit, near Mansfield. Although in decline for many years, the final contraction of deep coal mining in the United Kingdom had been rapid, including in the East Midlands. In this region, the number of pits fell by a third in the 1970s and by a further 70 per cent in the 1980s. This had a heavy impact on local communities in spatially very diverse locations. For many years, coal mining had been a central aspect of local industry; the mines employed large numbers of workers and many communities relied on coal for their economic survival. Mining also gave these communities a sense of identity and belonging. For example, miners used specific words in their daily work, which can all be classified as 'pit talk' but which varied from region to region, and these words had become part of local everyday language. Now that the coal mines have all closed, this linguistic variety is used less and is in danger of being lost. With the ageing population of former miners still present, we have a short window of opportunity to preserve and investigate these words. This book takes the opportunity to examine the lexical variation of mining communities. It reviews to what extent these words were and are used around the East Midlands, and it investigates the effects of migration on this vocabulary as miners moved around the country in search of work. The sections in this introductory chapter discuss the background, research questions and aims, structure of the book, language in the East Midlands in general, dialect attrition, lexical variation, and industrial languages and heritage.

1.2 Background

Barbara Freese has written: 'Coal was no mere fuel, and no mere article of commerce. It represented humanity's triumph over nature – the foundation of civilization itself' (Freese 2003: 10). Thesing has added: 'In its encyclopedic definition, it seems both simple and sublime in a biblical fashion: Mining is the process of taking minerals of coals from the earth ... People have mined the earth for thousands of years ... What distinguishes the industry of coal mining, however, is its enormous scale and its terrible human costs' (Thesing 2000: xi). In this way, coal mining was a crucial part of Britain's industrial power for many years. However, the year 2015 saw the 'end of an era' for deep coal mining in Britain when the last three deep coal mines finished production. Overall, deep coal mining in Britain had been in decline for just over a century, from its peak year in 1913 with the production of 287 million tons of coal. Significant colliery closures occurred after the Second World War, especially from the late 1950s through to 1970 and again in the decade following the 1984–1985 Miners' Strike. In 1960 around 600 collieries were in production in Britain, this halved to around 300 collieries by 1970, and by the start of the 1984–1985 Miners' Strike just over 170 were still producing coal.

The sudden closure and demolition of mines and pit equipment was particularly traumatic for the East Midlands. Many people realised that almost nothing would be left to remember the industry in the region unless some significant structures were listed and preserved. As a result of this realisation, structures belonging to collieries such as Pleasley Colliery in northeast Derbyshire and Coalville in Leicestershire (held by Snibston Discovery Museum) were retained and preserved. Nevertheless, Snibston Discovery Museum has since closed, the headstocks at Clipstone are in danger of being demolished and many other former pit sites have been built over, either with parks, housing or industry. Moore has commented: 'Today the casual visitor to the Erewash Valley would probably find it difficult to envisage the events described here. The decline and virtual disappearance of the British coalmining industry is here indeed an accomplished fact. The last working mine closed after the 1984–5 strike and the transformation of the physical geography is largely complete' (Moore 1995: 81).

The demise of the mining industry had drastic effects on employment, causing widespread job losses and local deprivation in the East Midlands. This is similar to other de-industrialised areas around the UK, but there are also marked differences. A report on the state of the coalfields in 2019 (Beatty et al. 2019) has shown that former mining regions display a distinctly higher incidence of ill health, lower rates of population growth and further ageing of the local population due to younger people moving away for work, because of high unemployment, low job density and poor levels of higher education. The report has also revealed that the former coalfields of the East Midlands make up a high proportion of the most deprived areas of the UK.

Many local community groups are dissatisfied with these circumstances, and this may have contributed to recent changes in political leanings. Some of these areas are no longer seen as 'safe' Labour seats, as they had been historically, and they have shown tendencies towards support for anti-immigration

Linguistic Heritage of East Midlands Mining Communities 3

and pro-Brexit policies. For example, Mansfield in north Nottinghamshire, voted by almost 71 per cent to leave the EU in 2016 and elected a Conservative MP for the first time in 2017.

1.3 Research questions and aims

Despite a burgeoning body of research on the life and language of miners in north-east England, North and South Wales, Scotland and Staffordshire, the pit talk of the East Midlands has received relatively little interest. This is perhaps surprising as well as worrying given that for a very long time coal mining was one of the industries that formed the bedrock of the regional economy, with historical records of local coal digging dating back to the thirteenth century.

Pit talk has contributed to the identity of many mining communities. The National Coal Mining Museum states that there are many words and dialects unique to the mining industry and that these are regionally distinct – a legacy that continues to date but which is now dwindling and will disappear in the near future if nothing is done to conserve it.

This raises the question: what, if anything, can be saved of this important aspect of local culture and heritage in the East Midlands? This variety of language is now in danger of disappearing fast following the last deep mine closures. A further challenge is that the industrial and recent nature of coal mining places it outside of traditional, and popular, understanding of 'heritage', while, as it stands, there is in general relatively little nostalgia for our lost industrial past. Consequently, the coal mining heritage is at risk of being lost forever.

Pit talk is an essential part of the coal mining heritage. This linguistic variety should be also preserved because it is an important indicator and reminder of local identity. Many community groups are losing their in-depth knowledge of coal mining. One of the reasons for this loss is that local heritage groups have usually focused on tangible heritage, such as mining memorabilia, within their projects. As a result of this focus, pit talk has so far received little or no attention.

This book wants to correct these shortcomings. It scrutinises East Midlands pit talk in order to identify, classify and record the words used, and to critically examine the contribution of this usage to regional and local identity. It takes account of the movement of miners to determine how and where its influence has spread. And it analyses data gathered in the East Midlands in comparison to data from other regions to discuss similarities and differences between different coal mining areas.

However, this book also offers more. Miners' language expresses their whole culture and their lives below and above ground. Examining such a specialised register can enable us to inspect local language variation more generally. Douglass (personal communication) has stated that examining language used by coal miners allows linguists to examine features of language that may have disappeared 'above ground'.

1.4 Structure of the book

In this book, I examine the language of coal miners in the coalfields of the East Midlands. In order to do so, I use extensive data collected from many miners around Derbyshire, Leicestershire and Nottinghamshire to discuss variation within the region as well as to make a comparison with other mining varieties to determine whether there is a sharing of industrial language. The main focus, however, remains on the East Midlands, which is so frequently overlooked within linguistic research. In this chapter, I first briefly look at the linguistic research which has been carried out in the East Midlands more generally; there is relatively little known about language variation in the East Midlands compared to other regions of the UK. I then consider issues around dialect attrition and lexical variation which are relevant to the linguistic variety of this book. Industrial languages, including that of coal mining, do not frequently feature as the subject of linguistic study. However, such language is a crucial part of both identity and local heritage.

The second chapter outlines the history and geography of the East Midlands coalfield as well as considering the movement of miners and miners' culture and language. Chapter 3 describes in detail the methodology applied in all the different stages of this project. Chapter 4 analyses the language used by the miners who were interviewed as part of my research project, examining words used for different machinery, job descriptions, tools and processes to determine variation. Examples of such language are provided and evidence of these words in other sources is added. The final chapter draws together the findings and highlights work still to be done.

1.5 Language in the East Midlands in general

It seems that the East Midlands does not form an important region in the mental maps of people outside the area and is seen as being 'neither here nor there' (Wales 2000: 7–8) and as a 'no-man's land' (Montgomery 2007: 352). Traditionally, the East Midlands has been somewhat neglected in linguistic research; recent work by Braber and Robinson (2018) was the first in-depth linguistic analysis of this region. Much of the research on language in the East Midlands has come from a historical angle, where the dialect has been studied in relation to the development of Standard English (see for example Baugh and Cable 2002; Fennell 2001). The *Survey of English Dialects* (*SED*) in the 1950s (Orton et al. 1962–1971) was the last regional survey which included the East Midlands. More contemporary varieties of East Midlands English have received little attention, and more recent localised studies presenting an overview of regional speech in the UK either lack up-to-date research data from the East Midlands or simply ignore the region (e.g. Britain 2007; Kortmann and Upton 2008). There are some publications which focus on individual areas within the East Midlands, for example Docherty and Foulkes (1999) and Milroy (1996) who look at Derby, and Braber and Flynn (2015), Flynn (2007, 2012) and Jansen and Braber (2020) who examine Nottingham, Derby and Leicester. There have also been a few non-academic pieces which examine language in the area, such as Scollins and Titford (2000), Wright (1975, 1979), Stennett and Scollins (2006) and Beeton (1999). We will return to these non-academic sources in section 2.6, where they discuss language used by coal miners.

Trudgill has distinguished between traditional dialects and modern dialects (see also Hughes et al. 2005: 33 for a description of traditional dialects). In this, traditional dialects are split into 'North' and 'South' branches and are then further sub-divided. In this classification, 'Leicestershire' and 'Lincolnshire' are both labelled as 'Eastern Central' from the 'Central' branch which comes from the 'South' branch (Trudgill 1999: 35), whereas in modern dialects (which according to Trudgill are what most people speak now) the 'East Midlands' is still part of the 'Eastern Central' and 'Central' branch but this now comes from the 'North' branch. As part of these branches, 'Derbyshire' is in the 'Northwest Midlands' group, whereas Nottingham and Leicester are in the 'Central Midlands' (Trudgill 1999: 74).

The East Midlands is considered by some linguists to belong with the northern varieties of English and Wells has explained that the varieties used in cities such as Nottingham and Leicester are similar to those used in cities in the middle north, which include Sheffield, Manchester and Leeds, but different to those used in the far north which includes Tyneside and Teesside (Wells 1986: 350). Wells has also added that the language of the East Midlands shows significant differences to that used in the West Midlands. The region differs from areas to the north by having diphthongs in 'gate', it fluctuates from the Northwest Midlands as it lacks the velar nasal plus in words such as 'singer', and it diverges from areas to the east and south because of the /ɛ/ in 'coffee'. Trudgill has added (1999: 75) that both Nottingham and Leicester have diphthongs in 'made' and 'coat' but that these are wider in Leicester than Nottingham, with regions in the middle showing intermediate variation.

For a full description of East Midlands features, see Braber and Robinson (2018) or Braber and Flynn (2015), but, to summarise, speakers in this region usually have northern [a] for BATH and [ʊ] for STRUT (see Jansen and Braber 2020 for ways in which this might be changing). However, speakers may also show increasing forms that are associated with more traditionally southern features, such as t-glottalling, l-vocalisation and th-fronting. The region is also generally yod-dropping, not only in words such as 'news' but also 'student' and 'tuna'. A particular point of interest which Wells points out is that in Nottingham the happy vowel is even more open than other regions of the north and is almost approaching the /ɛ/ of DRESS (Wells 1986: 262).

Linguists have frequently considered the north/south divide when examining language variation in the UK and the linguistic features that separate the two regions (such as Trudgill 1999; Wells 1986), but it appears to be not always a straightforward division. For example, the question can be asked as to where the East Midlands fits in. This has raised questions as to whether there is a clear partition boundary or whether the East Midlands should be seen as 'an essentially unstructured transition zone' (Upton 2013: 190; see also Upton 1995, 2012) and Stocker has argued that the East Midlands is not north or south but a 'third place altogether, with its own distinctive landscape and history' (Stocker 2006: 9) which would suggest a tripartite division instead of the more traditional binary division.

1.6 Dialect attrition

Much has been written about the historical perspectives of dialect (see for example Beal 2018: 166), which often consider awareness and evaluative attitudes towards 'other' varieties of language. This is also a current issue as we are being told that dialects are dying out and there may be dialect levelling, but at the same time it appears that many people, including non-linguists, are very interested in regional dialects (Beal 2010: 1). Recent experience at the British Library has confirmed that there is presently significant popular, media and academic interest in regional speech. This has been demonstrated by the impact of the Library's online dialect archive, Archival Sound Recordings (www.bl.uk/sounds) and its interactive educational website on contemporary spoken English, Sounds Familiar (www.bl.uk/soundsfamiliar). These sites are highly valued and widely used by their target audiences and popular and media interest has proven the wide appeal of this material. Furthermore, the British Library's 2010 exhibition 'Evolving English: One Language, Many Voices' was the most popular winter exhibition ever held in the Library (see Robinson 2015: 4).

Dialects have often been perceived as being threatened by present-day superdiversity (Beal 2018: 165; see also Britain 2005), whereby the upheaval of two world wars and improved travel, transport and education opportunities were destroying variation, after the Industrial Revolution had altered many agrarian lifestyles (Pearce 2020: 487) and brought people to the cities en masse. In fact, Millar (2016: 143) has stated that traditional dialects are dead, although urban ones can still be found. Britain has commented that dialect death is 'inextricably linked to dialect contact' (Britain 2009: 122). Beal (2010: 2) has argued that many urban dialects are the result of the diffusion and levelling of these traditional dialects (for full details on dialect contact and diffusion, see Trudgill 1986). In addition, it seems that dialects need to be protected, as stated by Beal '… dialects are like crumbling castles: not practical for everyday use, but in desperate need of shoring up in order to preserve the nation's sense of its own history and identity' (Beal 2018: 168). Such language varieties can be an important link to social identity when speakers represent their identity linguistically (Millar 2016: 144, see also Agha 2003: 22). Johnstone has mentioned that:

> dialect levelling and dialect awareness in fact have exactly the same origins – namely in social and geographical mobility and in the discursive practices that arise in its wake. The noticing of linguistic difference that can lead to celebrations of, or conflicts over, linguistic localness can also lead to the eradication of difference, and the conditions that make dialect awareness possible are the same as those that make levelling possible. (Johnstone 2010: 386)

Some of the earliest dialect studies were carried out to record and preserve these 'pure' and traditional dialects, often by members of the English Dialect Society, founded in 1873, which resulted in Joseph Wright's *English Dialect Dictionary* (1898–1905) and *English Dialect Grammar* (1905). These studies aimed to preserve dialects spoken in English villages (for full details see Beal 2010: 2–3). Ellis's work on language variation in the late 1800s has shown huge variation to language used today (Britain 2009: 121). Such studies allow us to see the erosion of traditional, rural dialects, although Britain (2009: 123) has commented that we rarely get to see such attrition in action, which may be possible in our mining communities.

Britain has claimed (2005: 23) that research focuses more on the distribution and spread of linguistic features than on the obsolescence of local structures. Indeed, few studies examine lexical attrition (see also neglect of lexical variation in section 1.7), but those which do can use data collected from the *SED* in the 1950s and the *English Dialect Dictionary* to examine which words are still recognised by contemporary speakers (for more details on studies see Britain 2009: 124–125). The *SED* was a nationwide survey of the vernacular speech of England, undertaken by researchers based at the University of Leeds under the direction of Harold Orton. It aimed to make a systematic record of significant linguistic features (mainly pronunciation and lexis) before these dialects disappeared or were in even more contact with Standard English (Beal 2010: 4). From 1950 to 1961 a team of fieldworkers collected data in 313 localities across England, initially in the form of transcribed responses to a questionnaire containing over 1,300 items. The informants were mainly NORMS (non-mobile older rural males) as the aim of the survey was to capture the most conservative forms of dialect and it was believed that these speakers would fulfil that category. Almost all the sites visited by the researchers were rural locations, as it was felt that traditional dialect was best preserved in these isolated areas. It was initially the intention to include urban areas at a later date, but this plan had to be abandoned on economic grounds. As Durkin has stated, this study took an onomasiological approach, whereby it collected the words that speakers used to realise particular meanings (Durkin 2012: 7). Such sources allow us to underpin lexical variation and change in contemporary English (Beal and Burbano-Elizondo 2012: 11). The work from the *SED* has also been turned into visual dialect maps, such as in Upton and Widdowson (2006) who provide a visual result of the data, showing where in England certain words and pronunciations can be found.

On the whole, these studies confirm that dialectal words are recognised by a much smaller proportion of younger speakers and that those which are recognised are the most local words, rather than those which have regional or national currency. This has also been found by Lawrie (1991) who examined the familiarity of Scottish dialect items and found that dialect terms were being used less than more general alternatives by younger speakers. She has added that increasing mechanisation has meant that many dialect terms have become obsolete and that the standardisation of English, added to increased individual mobility and the advent of mass media, has led to an acceptance of Standard English to the detriment of local terms. Furthermore, Britain has commented (2009: 142) that intra-regional mobility reinforces supralocal structures, so that the mobility of speakers must be taken into consideration. Beal has added that as well as thinking about the loss of words, we also need to consider the impact of change (Beal 2010: 6).

The type of community of which a language is a part can also affect the way language changes and whether it becomes moribund. Trudgill (1989: 228) has stated that geographically peripheral areas tend to be less innovative and linguistic change is slow when populations are well established, which is likely linked to less contact with outside communities. For example, certain mining communities in the north-east are real strongholds of traditional dialect (Beal 1993: 189) and older variants are found there that are not found in Newcastle. However, there is also evidence which shows that certain phonetic changes can be greater in relatively closed communities, as internally driven (evolutive) changes easily take place there (Kerswill 2018: 14). These changes are different to adaptive changes which involve changes that come from another contact community. Linguists may not look at a dialect area if the standard language is not vanishing (Wolfram and Schilling-Estes 1995: 697). However, dying dialects of thriving languages do need to be documented as they may exhibit features that are not found in the standard language, and these may thus disappear. Such loss of language is part of the loss of cultural and intellectual diversity (Wolfram and Schilling-Estes 1995: 698 and see also page 701 for relevant case studies) and therefore must also be documented. Frequently, non-standard dialect may be seen as unworthy of study and may therefore be neglected. Although dialect includes many linguistic features, the focus of this book is on the lexical variation of the mining communities in the East

Midlands, bearing in mind that, historically, lexical variation has not been examined in as much detail as other types of variation.

1.7 Lexical variation

The words people use are influenced by many factors: family heritage, educational background, environment, friends, audience, purpose and sense of identity (Robinson 2015: 7). All languages change over time and vary according to place and social setting (Wales 2006: 195). We can observe lexical variation, which consists of the different words and phrases used by speakers, by comparing the way language is spoken in different locations and among different social groups.

The interest in the geographical nature of some lexical variation has been indicated by the earliest dialectological studies. As Millar (1999: 55) has noted: 'It is a commonplace but entirely reasonable assumption that the further you travel from your place of origin, the less likely you are to understand what local people are saying. A large part of this sense of similarity or dissimilarity must be lexical in basis.'

Furthermore, lexical variation is an important way for people to identify themselves and is a way of allowing them to differentiate themselves from others (Boberg 2005: 52). Despite the belief that dialect words are disappearing, there remains a great deal of lexical diversity in the UK. As noted in the previous section, there is great public interest in local vocabulary and regional differences. Despite the fact that lexis is probably the area of linguistics that is most accessible and salient to non-academics, it presents 'some uniquely difficult challenges for systematic scholarly linguistic analysis' (Durkin 2012: 3). Upton has commented that '... lexical ordering and analysis are not necessarily straightforward, and the messages coming from careful research are certainly not clear-cut: words, never easy to gather in the mass in an orderly, structured way, are unruly and hard to codify once collected' (Upton 2013: 180).

Although lexical variation is a crucial aspect of dialect and language variation, there is a lack of studies, particularly contemporary ones, which focus primarily on the lexicon, particularly when compared to phonetic/phonological and morpho-syntactic variation (discussed by Beal and Burbano-Elizondo 2012: 11; see also information about lexical studies in Millar 2016: 150). Vocabulary has frequently been omitted in linguistic studies and Beal (2010: 53) has commented that the study of regional lexis is the 'Cinderella' of academic dialectology of recent years; few new studies use lexical criteria for the comparison of dialects and have instead focused on typology. Dent has stated that 'any conscious notion of dialect is defined by its sounds' and that 'academic study has concentrated largely on morphology and pronunciation at the expense of lexis' (Dent 2013: 110). Adams has argued that vocabulary has rarely been the favourite subject of sociolinguists and tends to have a place 'in the corner' rather than as a main focus (Adams 2014: 164), because, according to him, it is hard to measure and results from different studies are not easily comparable. Robinson has noted that one of the areas of linguistics which does not include lexis in theoretical or epistemological considerations is sociolinguistics (Ju. Robinson 2012: 38) and that sociolinguists tend to avoid investigating meaning as 'semantic variables do not "fit" into the notion of a variable proposed by sociolinguists' (Ju. Robinson 2012: 38). Traditionally, a main focus of lexical studies has been etymological in nature, examining where words have come from, providing clues about historical contact with and the influence of other speakers (see Beal 2010: 55).

In fact, it is lexis which really allows us to witness moves away from local dialects; for example, words may be given up for more standard varieties. This phenomenon has been described by Millar (Millar 2016: 151) in his study on fishing communities in Scotland which is discussed in section 1.8. Another study which has used lexis to examine usage of such items in relation to identity is Sandow (2021), which examines the change and social meaning of certain Anglo-Cornish words in relation to a sense of local and regional identity, and Lee (forthcoming) which investigates lexis and identity in Gypsy, Roma and Traveller communities in the East Midlands. Such studies exemplify that lexis is the feature of language that is probably most accessible to the non-linguist (Durkin 2012: 3). Even changes to phonology are often linked in the public's eye to vocabulary, as these changes may be associated with particular 'totemic' words (Durkin 2012: 4). Durkin has explained why lexis is a difficult topic for linguists: the lexicon is not a fixed entity and individual lexicons are unique. Furthermore, lexis shows variation in different dimensions – onomasiological and semasiological – meaning that there are different ways of saying the same thing, and that the same word can mean different things (2012: 6).

This lack of attention to lexical variation is not unique to English; for example, Beeching (2011: 25) has commented that this neglect is also the case for French. Boberg has discussed lexical studies carried out by North American dialectologists (see Boberg 2005: 22) who have used lexical variation to establish regional boundaries, adding that these historical studies are of great importance, but it has been a recent challenge to 'find new variables that reflect the continued vitality of regional variation in North American English and new methods for analyzing them' (Boberg 2005: 23).

Despite the availability of Dialect Topography, used by Chambers (1994) with postal questionnaires to gather and analyse data, using semantic domains such as modern technology, school life and fast food, many contemporary studies do not always focus on lexis, even when they would be able to do so. The English Dialect App, launched in 2016 to collect online data from participants about the words they use and the way they pronounce them, has been used mainly for phonological variation (for more information see

Leeman et al. 2018) and, to date, little analysis has been carried out on the lexical variation found within the data.

However, lexical variation is particularly interesting when used to identify regional boundaries (Boberg 2005: 23). Dialectology studies have used isoglosses and maps to plot such variation. Unfortunately lexis is complicated, and such isoglosses tend to capture the bigger picture and cannot capture the 'interplay of style, ranges of meaning, collocations and context' (Dent 2013: 111), so they cannot necessarily capture accurately who uses particular words (categorised by age, gender, ethnicity, for example). On this Upton has written:

> County and national boundaries, like isoglosses, *contain* nothing. Lines on a map, and their respective labels, might help to direct our focus onto what, from time to time, is the object of our interest, a linguistic form that has a particular resonance, say, or a localized identity for which linguistic manifestations are sought. (Upton 2013: 194, emphasis in original)

Probably more worthwhile is the examination of the social meaning of vocabulary (Sandow 2020: 78), where speakers can use language to show their affiliation to certain geographical (and other) groups. This sense of regional identity tied to lexis is noted (Durkin 2012: 4) and often seized upon by commercial enterprise, where towels, mugs, T-shirts and other objects are produced with local words and expressions printed upon them. Beal (2018: 170) has commented that such commodification presupposes enregisterment, as people associate particular linguistic features with personal qualities or social factors.

Wales has suggested that even though some dialect words may be lost, a certain number of these words will be retained by speakers as they hold positive associations and memories of their pasts (Wales 2006: 197). It can also occur that certain words (or pronunciations or grammatical structures) can be used as 'a proxy for place' as they become associated with a particular region and, as speakers, 'we can deploy linguistic resources to index non-linguistic information about our geographical provenance' (Watt and Llamas 2017: 194). Beal has stated that the upsurge in interest in dialects at a time when they are perceived to be disappearing is not surprising as this rise could be seen as a similar reaction to aspects of globalisation (Beal 2010: 1; see also Johnstone 2010: 390; Pearce 2020: 488).

The previous section explained that there is a concern that dialects are being levelled due to traditional dialect words going out of usage due to changes in society. One of the most well-known studies to consider lexical variation is the *Survey of English Dialects* and other studies have gone on to use some of this data (see examples given in Wales 2006: 196). Studies such as Upton and Widdowson (1999) and Simmelbauer (2000) have been mentioned in Beal

(2010: 66) as indicating that the diversity of terms is lessening. However, there are also studies which consider regional patterns and lexical variation and have used innovative means of data collection (the difficulties of collecting data for lexical studies will be discussed in section 3.1). One of the most recent methods which focuses on lexical variation is known as the Sense Relation Network (SRN) sheet, which was pioneered by Carmen Llamas, under the supervision of Clive Upton and John Widdowson at the Universities of Leeds and Sheffield. This method is like a 'web of words', and encourages participants to record all the words they know in a particular concept (such as 'appearances', 'body'). These can be adapted to all different kinds of lexical fields and have been used in this study (see section 3.4.1, where the benefits of such a method of data collection will also be discussed). Since this innovation, other studies have gone on to use such methods to collect various lexical data, including the Voices study carried out by the BBC radio stations at the start of the 2000s (for a full discussion of this project, see Upton and Davies 2013). Robinson has commented that this survey differed from most post-*SED* studies because of its focus on lexical data. The interviews were about the usage of different words, but the public's interest in the regional variation of words can be seen by the demand for slang and dialect glossaries and online forums (Jo. Robinson 2012: 25).

Examining linguistic attrition from a lexical point of view – where language is lost from a region or industry – is important (dialect attrition was discussed in section 1.4). There has been some work carried out on fishing communities in Scotland (Millar et al. 2014) and this needs to be extended to other communities. A more detailed look at particular work communities can be found in section 1.8. One of the aspects we can investigate is whether lexis is likely to survive rather than be lost over the years. Pearce (2020: 449) has suggested this is most likely when it belongs to either domestic or informal usage. This particular study has also looked at lexis from an innovative viewpoint, using social media to investigate active knowledge and use of particularly local words by particular communities of practice, and how such usage can flourish as a result. This is relevant as one of the criticisms of earlier studies (see more detail in section 3.5) has asked whether questionnaires can distinguish between passive and active vocabularies, and what the difference is between words that a speaker knows (passive) and those they actually use (active). This allows the examination to question to what degree certain traditional terms may be in the process of being lost to younger speakers (see also Beal 2006: 55). This can be due to changes in the social mobility of speakers, changing industries and technology, and the influence of standardisation (Wales 2006: 195).

Notably, Durkin (2012: 5) has suggested that the shared core vocabulary in communities may be quite small and words may have different meanings to different groups. Speakers' active and passive vocabularies are affected by a large number of factors, including their occupation and this is going to be the case particularly for miners and their mining vocabulary, where some of these words may also be used by the wider community but the meanings may be different – either narrower or broader or apply to different semantic fields. Such words may also be shared by other industrial groups – such as electricians and people working in the navy and military. Certain words might remind people of a particular time or place which can keep them in usage (Wales 2006: 198). In the next section, languages in certain workplaces are examined in order to investigate what is already known about them.

1.8 Industrial languages

Now that coal mining in the UK has come to an end, we are at risk of losing much of our knowledge about pit talk, as those who speak the language are no longer passing it on. Beal (2006) has said that many industrial terms are in decline and such vocabulary may be lost. In the current post-industrial society many 'traditional' jobs are disappearing, as is the culture that lived alongside them (see also Millar et al.'s 2014 monograph on Scottish fishing communities), and for many of these communities, identity can be closely linked to such language usage, which is increasingly at risk of disappearance. 'The 20th century has seen unprecedented changes in the regional speech of the British Isles. The industrialisation of Britain in the 18th and 19th centuries led to the establishment of new, urban varieties of English in all its cities and large towns' (Kerswill et al. 1999: 257–258). Obviously, all the different ways of working and the replacement of more traditional working practices must also have been affected by these changes. Occupational dialects refer to specific ways of speaking that certain groups of people in particular jobs might use. It tends to allow for clear and economic communication between people talking for a particular purpose who have a shared understanding of such terms. Many occupations may develop their own specific language features. The most identifiable feature of occupational languages is the vocabulary, the words that are used to talk or write about particular aspects of these jobs. As Drew and Heritage have written: 'Lexical choice is a significant way through which speakers evoke and orient to the institutional context of their talk' (Drew and Heritage 1992: 29). They have explained that there are numerous studies which examine technical vocabularies in areas such as law and medicine and their edited collection contains many examples that look at language usage in the workplace. However, such occupational language (sometimes referred to as 'jargon' or 'trade argot') occurs in many more workplaces.

Agriculture and traditional industry supplied the English language with a rich stock of dialect vocabulary. Farming, for instance, produced many words to describe local landscapes and agricultural practice that differ across the country. Until relatively recently, different breeds of livestock and traditional farm practices ensured a strong localised vocabulary (see for example Braber

2015). Due to the increasing mechanisation of farms and the automation of heavy industry, many of these words are now no longer as widely used, as either the objects to which they refer have become obsolete or the practices they describe have become outdated. Like the implements themselves, words may be disappearing from language use, but there may remain a small number of people working in traditional industries or in rural communities who continue using these words in their daily vocabulary. Some of these terms are distinctly local; words such as 'gimmer' (female sheep) are used in Nottinghamshire and Derbyshire, as confirmed by the *SED*, while Leicestershire is more likely to use 'theave'. Fox has suggested that the variations found within the East Midlands show that there is a clear transition zone between Leicestershire and Lincolnshire, more so than between Nottinghamshire and Lincolnshire even though the border is longer (Fox 2012: 177). Fox has added that these differences between working vocabulary are also supported by an analysis of the routes taken by carts in the nineteenth century, which suggested that Leicestershire and Lincolnshire operated largely separate economic systems. In this, Fox has used evidence from Orton et al. (1978) who show that isoglosses of regional variation were more likely to divide Leicestershire and Lincolnshire than Nottinghamshire and Lincolnshire.

There are links between post-industrial heritage and language (see more about heritage and language in section 1.9) and some of them have formed the focus of sociolinguistic studies – some of these have focused on particular linguistic features rather than occupational language, but the connection between occupation, identity and locality is important. There is very little research about such industrial dialects. Several research projects started when it was believed that such varieties were in danger of disappearing or had disappeared. An extensive study of the language variation and lexical attrition of Scottish fishing communities was, as mentioned earlier, carried out by Millar et al. (2014). As fishing practices changed, the language used within the community also changed and some of the traditional vocabulary is no longer used (see also Millar 2016: 155). Some of the patterns which Millar commented on were the 'thinning' of lexical use, where previously a semantic field had multiple lexical items which showed subtle distinctions in meaning and association were becoming lost (Millar 2016: 156), as well as the 'broadening' of meaning, where words which originally had a precise meaning now had meanings that were broadened to include a wider range of states (Millar 2016: 158). Some vocabulary moved from active knowledge to passive knowledge – where speakers are aware of terms that the older generations used, but that they no longer use themselves. Furthermore, Millar has argued that words tied to particular industries may disappear more quickly or earlier than other dialect words: 'In the Fisher Speak research it is probably understandable that words and phrases connected to the fishing industry, moribund in most communities and altered considerably through technological and cultural innovation where it continues, should have suffered most from attrition' (Millar 2016: 162).

Dialects typical of fishing villages also feature in the study of Cromarty, a Scots dialect that was particularly specialised for certain nautical techniques and contained culture-specific terms for the tools and nets used for fishing (Rosetta Project 2012). This project's blog mentioned that this dialect was in the process of being lost due to the industrialisation of the industry and the loss of traditional fishing practices. Two of the last remaining speakers, a set of brothers, were recorded as part of the project and the blog has been updated to say that the last native speaker of this variety died in 2012. The blog explains that this unique linguistic knowledge is now lost with the passing of its speakers, something that was reported internationally (BBC News 2012). The blog went on to explain that the change of industry also eroded the strong connections of the village's cultural, economic and linguistic identities, and it referred to another dialect in the US, the Tangier Tidewater dialect, which is similarly connected to fishing heritage, where the variety used by the local population is said to sound similar to the original colonists who arrived centuries ago (YouTube Tangier Tidewater Dialect). The blog finished by saying that we should use the example of the Cromarty dialect to ensure that such varieties are recorded and documented.

Petyt has published a study on accent and dialect in 'industrial West Yorkshire', in which he mentions that this region was the capital of the wool trade and is an 'identifiable unit' (Petyt 1985: 6), but his study looks only at phonological features and some grammatical features and does not touch on the wool trade or its lexicon. The study used a random sample, so many of the speakers involved may not have worked in the industry. However, he has also said that if language changes in such a location, then vocabulary is likely to be one of the first features to disappear due to overt pressure, before other phonological variables.

Sandow (2021) carried out work in a similar post-industrial society, examining local vocabulary related to a sense of local identity in Cornwall – a former tin mining area. Again, in this work there is no study of lexis associated with the tin mining industry, but instead it uses local terms that have gained a sense of belonging to the region. Similar to many other regions, Cornwall struggled to adapt to the post-industrial world and this affected how younger and older people view the region. Sandow has distinguished two communities, 'the Industrial Celt' and the 'Lifestyle Cornwall', where the first group is more likely to retain pride in the former industrial power of the region and the second is more focused on its tourist aspect and is more outward looking. This is also reflected in the usage of words which have particularly strong local associations, with the Industrial Celts more likely to use local words to signal this sense of local affiliation.

Leach (2018) has carried out research on the pottery industry of Stoke-on-Trent, using previously collected oral history interviews to examine particular sociophonetic features. As part of this study, certain lexical items pertaining to the industry – including words for job descriptions and particular processes – are explained. The pottery industry in this region is similar to the coal mining industry in the East Midlands in that the advancement of technology mechanised the industry and led to the loss of particular jobs and work processes. Historically, many jobs remained in the family and sons could take over jobs from their fathers. Both industries contained more skilled workers and those with more general skills were paid less and had less prestige. In the case of coal miners, those working below ground had higher pay and more prestige than those working on the surface, and this difference could also be reflected in language usage, where specific words would be used by specific workers. We can also see that the rise of a post-industrial society in both the pottery and coal mining industries (which also applies to other de-industrialised areas) resulted in similar developments. Increasing mechanisation resulted in higher unemployment, high levels of deprivation and a frequent swing in politics from Labour to more right-wing parties. In the potteries, UKIP and the BNP have achieved popularity, and rising anti-immigrant beliefs among some people mirrored the fact that some mining regions were areas that strongly supported Brexit and have recently voted in Conservative MPs. This occurred in regions which 'were seen as amongst the last bastions of support for labourism and the collectivist values of social democracy' (Hudson and Sadler 1990: 435). A fascinating aspect of Leach's work is an analysis of two features, /h/ and /i/, which has found that for some of the speakers there was variation between these variables depending on whether they were being used within a work or home environment conversation. This is something that was also found in a study by Devlin in a north-east mining community which will be discussed shortly.

A further study which involves particular occupations concerned mill workers and farmers in the American South. This study has suggested that local dialects are patterning and that this is linked with 'cultural contours' (Du Pree McNair 2005: 1) that reflect the different occupations of speakers. The study has correlated social behaviour and language and has shown that as contact increased between the communities, cross-cultural diffusion developed. Similar to miners, these mill workers lived in villages which supplied their own education, culture activity and shops. Many had to migrate for job opportunities and DuPree McNair has highlighted that dramatic linguistic changes can take place following changes in living and working environments (there are some references to other studies with similar communities, DuPree McNair 2005: 5). She has stated that occupation is pivotal, and that these dense networks can be used to examine language change. As with some of the aforementioned studies, particular lexical items are not discussed in her work.

There are some studies which specifically consider mining communities and language change, for example Devlin (2014), Devlin et al. (2019) and Burland (2017). These studies have focused on particular phonetic forms which are used by speakers who are from mining communities. In the studies of the miners of the north-east, carried out by Devlin, it appears that certain recessive forms may continue to be used by such speakers. It is suggested that certain phonetic forms index allegiances to particular communities (in this case, former miners) and that this can result in different forms being used to other speakers in the region. We know from previous research (see Devlin et al. 2019: 305) that certain topic-specific words, which may be used in restricted senses by speakers, can be the last to change in phoneme shifts. This research has shown that older speakers often shift to the more local [ɛʊ] forms, while they may otherwise use the more non-local form [aʊ] when discussing mining topics. Devlin's work has shown that ex-miners are more likely to use more regional variants of vowels when talking about topics related to mining (Devlin 2014: 233), and the author has said that miners have suggested that the pit influenced their language, adding that 'traditional pronunciation might be preserved or stored in speaker memories to be reactivated with the trigger of a traditional conversational topic' (Devlin 2014: 234), and that this might trigger the use of phonetic features that are usually linked to older, more traditional speakers. Burland has noted that the understanding of local historical contexts, social experiences and tensions is crucial as these may impact upon the use and perception of linguistic variables (Burland 2017: 235). Burland has also shown that in Royston, a former mining community, speakers appear to be resistant to supralocal norms and are continuing to use diphthongs in FACE and GOAT.

Another study on mining communities, but this time in the Unites States, has looked at the merger of COT and CAUGHT words and how linguistic changes are different between mining towns and non-mining towns (Herold 1997). The area of eastern Pennsylvania, where the merger is found, was largely confined to a coal mining region. There are other towns in the region where the merger was not found but these towns were never economically dependent on coal mining (or anthracite mining as the article refers to it). Herold has suggested (1997: 179) that,

'[as] the low back merger developed in the mining towns of eastern Pennsylvania sometime between 1890 and 1920, then it is reasonable to look for external triggers of the merger in historical events that were confined to mining towns. These events were almost certainly related to the mining boom of the late 19th and early 20th centuries.

This suggests that the influx of foreign-born immigrants triggered the linguistic changes that took place.

A study which focused on new dialect varieties in mining communities was carried out by Hornsby (2018). This study concerns a former mining village in East Kent where a mix of settlers arrived from around the UK to fill the need for miners. Miners were recruited from other coalfields and came from South Wales, Scotland, north-east England, Somerset, the East Midlands, South Yorkshire and Lancashire to work in new mines (Hornsby 2018: 76), which, due to the lack of housing, led to the creation of a new town. It was an isolated town and speakers were part of dense and multiplex social networks. The linguistic diversity was noted by many of its inhabitants, especially in relation to difficult relations between social groups. However, as sons followed fathers into the mines, groups started to mix more and the new generation came to use a 'new norm' linguistically (Hornsby 2018: 86). The interviews carried out during the study did not consider lexical items, although some came up, and discussed whether the speakers were showing northern or southern features linguistically, due to the contacts with northern and southern speakers.

One study which has looked specifically at the language of coal miners, including the vocabulary used and how this differs in different mining regions, has been carried out by Wright (1972). This study will be discussed fully in section 2.6 which focuses on studies that have concentrated on producing glossaries of miners' lexis. In this work, Wright explains that these terms were discussed during interviews and spontaneous conversation with around fifty miners from around the UK. Wright has commented that as the mining environment changes, so too do its words. He has also related mining to other occupations and says that: 'Coal-miners do not live is [sic] such isolated language communities as remote hill farmers or some inshore fishermen, yet they have always been a race apart; so that, despite movement of labour between coalfields, their language patterns seem much clearer than those of, say, the transport, catering, or construction industries' (Wright 1972: 49). A more recent study which examines language variation and the communicative style of a South Yorkshire coal mining community is Cave (2001). His study focuses on the nicknames, stories and leg-pulling which make up a miner's communicative repertoire. He has noted that 'in a dialect variety such as this, which is dominated by the usage of one occupational group, the boundaries between argot, slang and dialect become even more unclear' (Cave 2001: 89). As well as language being a crucial part of the camaraderie found among these miners, Cave's work also includes some information about the phonological, morphological and lexical features of the language his miners use. Cave considers that the perception of pit closures is seen by local communities as leading to the social degeneration of the community, an emotional loss and a breakdown of social networks, with the addition of the disappearance of the pit as a major topic of conversation, and one of his interviewees notes that this loss will also be reflected in their language as people will no longer understand their terms (Cave 2001: 32, 37).

In another working community, Dyer (2002) has shown that particular linguistic forms can be used by such communities to reflect on particular social characteristics. In her study, short [o] realisations of the GOAT vowel signified Scottish origins for older speakers but indexed a Corby identity (over other local regions) for younger speakers. Generally, occupation is more frequently used as a social variable (see for example Rickford 1986) rather than an examination of the lexical variation found in such groups of workers. Work by Zhang (2005) has examined different linguistic features between Chinese professionals working for foreign companies compared to those working for Chinese companies. This study has found that for those working for foreign companies, their professional identity was very relevant and salient to them (Zhang 2005: 438). Where the state professionals favoured local variants, those working for foreign companies used rhoticity, lenition and full tone to display their working identity (Zhang 2005: 457). There is more literature on style in working language (see for example Cameron 2000 and Coupland 1984) to support the idea that workers can style-shift in different situations.

So, although there is some literature on particular working communities and the language varieties they use, most of these studies rarely focus on the particular lexis associated with specific jobs and instead concentrate on particular ways of using language that may be associated with particular types of speakers – for example, older, more traditional workers. This means that in line with section 1.7, we can see that lexical variation is often neglected in sociolinguistic studies and that work on these varieties is overdue. What is also important to consider alongside particular occupations and how speakers may use language differently, is how many of these disappearing ways of living and working are tied very closely to senses of identity and local heritage. This consideration is the focus of the following section.

1.9 Language and heritage

In the same way that language and identity are closely linked together, so industrial heritage and identity are also deeply interconnected (see for example Berger 2020: 1). A danger facing the preservation of coal mining heritage is that the industrial and recent nature of coal mining means that many people do not consider, never mind value, this heritage. As a result, an important aspect of industrial heritage is at risk of being lost (Ferguson et al. 2010: 287). Furthermore, working-class and labour narratives are frequently not part of official heritage discourse (Berger 2020: 2) and therefore are often neglected. Trinder has stated that industrial monuments in Britain only became the subject of academic attention after the Second World War (Trinder 2000: 65). In addition, little has been written about the demise of coal mining in relation to its cultural heritage or how it was viewed by those inside the industry (Power 2008: 160).

However, in recent years, national bodies such as English Heritage have begun recognising intangible heritage as being equally as worthy of preservation as monuments, buildings and places. Nevertheless, in heritage research priority is still given to the tangible, although there are increased attempts to ensure that the category of heritage is expanded to include different types of objects, practices and traditions (Robinson 2018: 194). When we think of mining heritage, we typically think of tangible artefacts – such as processional banners, mining lamps or tools – relating to the history and memorabilia of mining. However, language is an important marker of community identity and helps people to define themselves in relation to others. The role of language within intangible heritage is complex and problematic, but according to UNESCO, language plays a vital role as a vehicle for our cultural heritage and identity. The language people use contains key information about features important to songs, sayings and legends which can help bind communities together. By focusing on their cultural traditions and language, local people can discover and appreciate the unique and shared values of their heritage and cultural identity. It allows them to explore their own language and culture and compare them with the languages and cultures of other places or regions, empowering communities to take ownership and be proud of their heritage and culture. UNESCO has also recognised that intangible heritage can be endangered due to changing societies and globalisation (see UNESCO 2003).

However, there is currently no systematic approach to preserving intangible heritage and language does not fit neatly into heritage studies. It has been argued (Deumert and Storch 2019) that in order to understand language as heritage we must look at the everyday practices of people. In a similar way to oral tradition, language can be carried anywhere 'but it rarely appears in museums' (Hennessy 2012: 35). This is one of the reasons I became involved in examining the language of miners in the region. I was interested in how these symbols of industrialisation, including language, are in danger of becoming lost and how they should be preserved and passed on to future generations (see also Kearney 2009: 210). There are real benefits of reuniting tangible with intangible, as Douglas has stated: 'Language has the power to connect us with places and history, and with remote or unfamiliar cultural heritage' (Douglas 2017: 131).

Fortunately, there are now growing efforts to add audio material to museums and heritage sites, rather than solely concentrate on the visual as a way of engaging visitors (Beal 2018: 177). This is also a way in which museums and academics can work together, promoting dialect as part of heritage and rising to the impact challenge, which is such an important aspect not only of academic research but also of shared collections. Interviews with workers are important as their narratives are frequently forgotten in history. Karpf has stated that recording aspects of human life had 'fallen outside the purview of classical history' (Karpf 2014: 50), while the working classes often did not leave much documentary evidence. We can therefore use oral histories as well as collected data on working-class communities – and other social groups – and the language they used. We can combine oral histories with tangible objects in museums, which brings collections to life and stops them becoming static (Douglas 2017: 131–132). In a similar way to preserving dying dialects, we can work with community groups and members to ensure that dialect is documented and to raise awareness (Wolfram and Schilling-Estes 1995: 717).

As with any industry, mining has its own distinctive language – pit talk. Despite the importance of this language as part of East Midlands dialect, I have noticed when visiting mining groups that pit talk is taken for granted rather than celebrated. Miners are constantly surprised that their language is actually considered valuable outside of the mining community, seeing it instead as ordinary and every-day. At the same time, these miners increasingly recognise that with the cessation of mining there is no economic need for the language to be carried forward by future generations and therefore it is under threat. Many mining communities want to hold onto the last remaining aspects of their mining heritage, but, as stated above, many have not considered their language and how this may be distinctive. However, 'while words are ephemeral, they become things when transcribed on paper or recorded onto tape [...] words are used to give meaning to objects' (Hennessy 2012: 33). Therefore, I have recorded the language of miners to preserve understanding of this way of life and to allow it to be passed on to future generations. People can use heritage to link to a particular community and place, often in the past, and heritage gives people greater legitimacy in the present (Harrison 2010: 243). Being able to connect to the past allows people to connect to 'cultural capital' (Harrison 2010: 245). Over time, people will know less about objects, and they will no longer have the knowledge connected to these objects, which can serve to disconnect them. Thus, projects to preserve intangible heritage such as language can encourage 'enactive engagement' and 'collective activity' with the past and its associated culture (Douglas 2017: 133).

In her study, Power has noted that participants spoke frequently of intangibles, such as community spirit and their view of heritage, that had to be accessible not only for tourists but also for local people (Power 2008: 167). Heritage was seen as a way of ensuring pride and retaining a sense of identity in the community. It is interesting that these participants did mention the importance of retaining local language related to the coal mining industry and that oral history was an important aspect of this. The study itself, however, does not include any information on such language.

Franks has noted that '[m]ost of the country's pits have vanished, and monuments are gradually appearing across the county. But their significance will soon be lost, because memories are so short-lived that all can be forgotten within the space of one generation. However, through words and pictures, the story can be saved for posterity' (Franks 2001: 4). This is not only symptomatic of the coal industry; the loss of cultural identity and associated language is typical of many post-industrial communities. Being able to develop a sense of pride with these pasts (especially when they are as contested as in the East Midlands coalfield) empowers communities to work with their own identity and heritage. Often oral histories can form a part of developing an alternative narrative (McIvor 2020: 49) and can allow people to raise the issues that were most relevant to them and that form part of collective identities (see Smith 2020: 131; and we will see in Chapter 4 some of the most pertinent issues raised by the coal miners in this project). Not all heritage is worthy of praise but it is an important part of identity (Robinson 2018: 194), and language should not be forgotten.

In this chapter, we have examined the fields of relevance for this study – dialect attrition, lexical variation, industrial languages, language and heritage – and we have introduced the concept of miners having a distinctive language. Chapter 2 provides information about the background of mining history and geography in the UK, with a particular focus on the Derbyshire, Leicestershire and Nottinghamshire coalfields of the East Midlands, before an examination of the specific culture of mining communities and previous research on the language of coal miners.

2 The History and Geography of the East Midlands Coalfield

2.1 Introduction

Coal has been mined in Britain for many centuries, but the most important period has been the last 200 years with the peak reaching 287 tons of coal mined in 1913 (Price 1971: 10). The regional economy in the East Midlands for many years was based on coal mining and there are records of early coal mining in the area as far back as the thirteenth century.

Nationally, both output and employment peaked in the years immediately before the First World War, but whereas in many other regions both indicators fell after 1918, in the East Midlands region numbers and production continued to rise in the 1920s. Productivity, through increased investment, also rose here and employment peaked in the 1950s. In the 1960s the East Midlands region was the most highly mechanised of all the National Coal Board's divisions. It produced 25 per cent of the nation's coal, employed about 85,000 men and women and cut 44.3 million tons of coal in its seventy-six collieries. Productivity in the East Midlands was 40 per cent above the national average and performance was by far the best for the country. Even then, however, mines in the west of the region were closing, and many were already leaving the industry. The emphasis on increased productivity saw the closure of mostly older pits. The final contraction of the industry was rapid and by the 1980s around 70 per cent of mines had closed. When the last mine in the region, Thoresby, closed in July 2015 there had been a heavy impact on these local communities. Today, there are only a few small private coal mines which remain in production in various parts of Britain, along with opencast mining or 'outcropping' as it is known in parts of the East Midlands.

It has been said that: 'The British coal industry was one of the mainsprings of the industrial revolution which, despite its undoubted harmful aspects, raised the standard of living of the British people to the high level we enjoy today' (British Coal 1989: foreword). Coal thus became a crucial aspect of the British economy and was concentrated in several regions of the UK, of which the East Midlands was one. The British coalfield was once the largest and one of the most competitive in the world and produced approximately half of the European Union's coal output, but nowadays it has been reduced to almost nothing (Coates and Barratt Brown 1997: 9). From 1984, about 200,000 jobs were lost in the coal mining industry, of which about 80,000 disappeared between 1990–1994. The coal industry provided about one-quarter of all male jobs located in the coalfield areas. The highest peak of the industry was in 1913 and 1914 when Britain produced a record of 287 million tons, and the Miners' Federation was the biggest trade union in Europe (Lewis 1971: 87; Francis 1979: 19). Freese has written: 'For centuries, Britain led the world in coal production, and largely as a result, it triggered the industrial revolution, became the most powerful force on the planet, and created an industrial society the likes of which the world had never seen' (Freese 2003: 13).

This chapter includes a brief discussion of the coal mining industry in the UK, followed by an examination of the different coalfields in the region, including those in Derbyshire, Leicestershire and Nottinghamshire. It contains information about the history and geography of individual collieries in the region, and it focuses on and examines the movement of miners (see also Amos and Braber 2017). This examination of the British and East Midlands coalfields enables an in-depth description of the coal mining industry in the region and takes more recent developments into account, which have not been covered by many works on mining that were produced several decades ago. This chapter reviews how the region was mined historically and at what stages different mines closed. It does not aim to give a definitive overview of British and East Midlands coal mining history, and references to this can be found throughout the chapter and at the end of the book.

Furthermore, this chapter shows how the mines were a crucial component of the region's community and identity. As mines in other areas of the country closed earlier than those in the East Midlands there was a large influx to the region of miners from Scotland and the north-east, and Chapter 4 will discuss whether these migrants had an influence on local language – a rather under-explored research subject as little or no work has been carried out on this aspect of mining language. Some miners interviewed as part of an earlier study (Braber et al. 2017) reported terms such as *marra* (for 'friend') being typical of north-eastern miners and noted that some of these terms came to be used by miners of the East Midlands as well. A further focus of this chapter is the social aspect of mining communities – including sports, art and culture – which forms an essential feature of a miner's life; reviewing expressions of features such as music and poetry allows for a close examination of the mining communities. Section 2.5 will discuss what was distinctive about mining culture and the way of living for mining communities. Finally, this chapter looks at mining language studies which have investigated the language of miners around the UK and worldwide.

2.2 History and geography of the UK coalfield

The coalmining areas of the United Kingdom were spread out in geographically-specific areas as can be seen in Figure 2.1. As such, the development of mining in these areas shaped not only the local economy and landscape but also settlement patterns as towns and villages grew up around the mines, sometimes in isolated areas (Court 1945: 6). The only new coalfield was Kent, which did not open until 1907 (see also Hornsby 2018), before that the main coalfields that were all mined since the late Middle Ages were: Scotland, Northumberland and Durham, Yorkshire, Derbyshire and Nottinghamshire, Leicestershire and South Derbyshire, Staffordshire, Salop, Worcestershire and Warwickshire, South Wales and Monmouth. There were also smaller coalfields in Cumberland, Westmorland, Gloucester, Somerset, Dorset and Devon (Griffin 1971b: 141). The former coalfields had a combined population of 5.7 million and many of these communities have suffered greatly. This includes both as a consequence of the hard and dangerous work carried out, as well as the effects of the closure of the industry and the run-up to this. Griffin states that 'the history of the miner is a continuous and continuing struggle; and those who forget this do so at their peril' (A. R. Griffin 1981: 1). This section considers the mining industry in Britain more generally, before focusing on the East Midlands specifically.

Britain's Industrial Revolution was made possible from the eighteenth century onwards because plentiful and relatively easily accessible coal was available around the country (C. Robinson 1995:1), but history shows that coal was important long before this time. Most British coal seams were formed during the Carboniferous era, some 300 million years ago (see Francis 1979:1 and British Coal 1989: 8). Coal originates from vegetable matter which accumulates and, when flooded, forms a peat, which is covered over by silt and undergoes compaction under layers of earth. Loss of moisture and complex chemical changes produce coal. As a result of this, and because of changes to the earth's crust, there are different layers or seams of coal at varying depths and of varying quality. Generally, workable coal seams in Britain range from one metre to around seven metres and can be 'clean' (nearly all coal) or 'dirty' (interspersed with other material known as dirt bands). The seams are level or at steep angles and the depth ranges from thirty to 1,350 metres deep as well as rising to the surface, which is called an 'outcrop'.

In early times, coal was mined from surface outcrops or by driving drifts or tunnels into hillsides (Griffin 1971a: 4), and these would be worked until driven out by water, gas or fear of roof falls (Lewis 1971: 6). During the time of the Roman occupation coal was used, but only when it came to the surface (Lewis 1971: 3); traces have been found at various Roman sites in Britain (Freese 2003: 16). Exposure to the elements meant it did not give out much heat and produced noxious fumes. Perhaps as a result of this it was scarcely used for burning

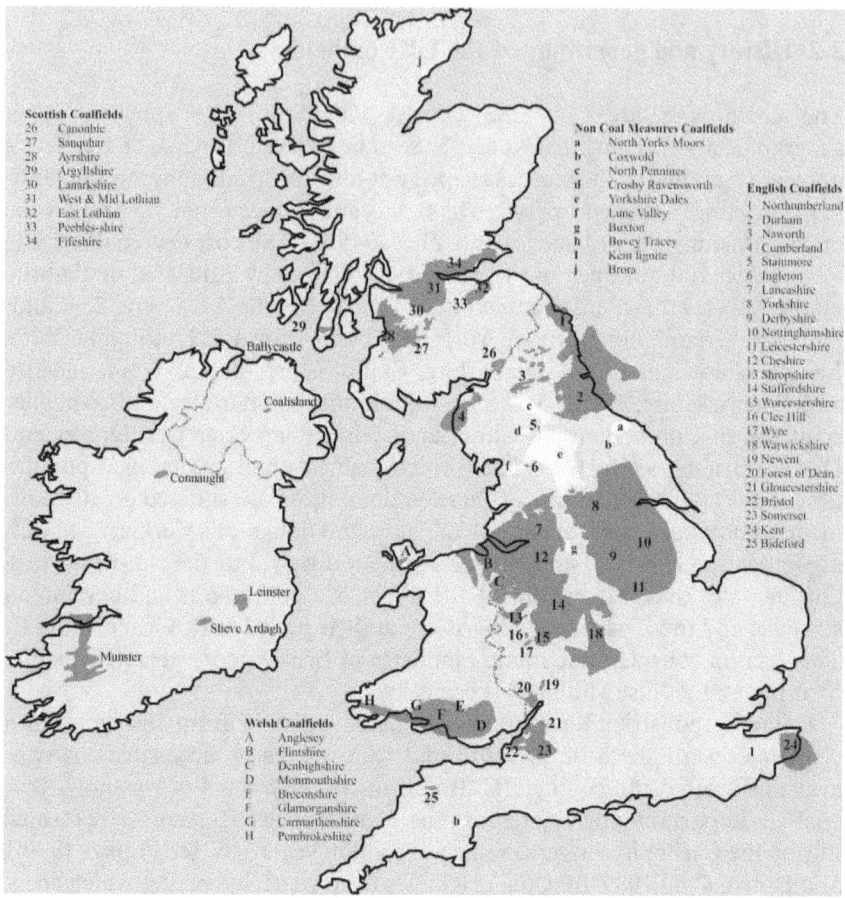

Figure 2.1 Map of the UK coalfields (produced by Northern Mine Research Society: https://www.nmrs.org.uk/assets/mines/coal/index.html)

but was mainly used for other purposes, for example being made into jewellery as it could be easily carved and polished (Freese 2003: 15). After the Roman era, there is limited evidence of coal mining and there is no mention of the activity in the Domesday Survey in 1086 (Lewis 1971: 4), which has led Griffin to suggest that it was of little importance as a potential source of royal revenue (Griffin 1971b: 1). Historians have found references from the late 1100s of coal being used as a fuel (Freese 2003: 21). From these it has been assumed that mining was very localised initially, particularly in the north-east of England. Coal mining slowly emerged in the thirteenth century, with more rapid growth in the fourteenth century (Griffin 1971b: 1). The ravages of the Black Death around this time led to a real shortage in labour and coal miners were able to demand higher wages than they had been paid previously (Williams 1962: 28).

As well as using exposed coalfields at this time and drift pits on hillsides where miners could dig straight into the seam, bell pits – so named because of the shape of the pits – were formed by sinking shallow shafts to reach seams near the surface. These tended to be on level ground, where miners would make small shafts and extract coal from the pit bottom until the sides were close to collapse and would then be filled in. These pits could go as deep as 50 feet (Dury 1963: 141). Coal was initially extracted around the shaft until the roof could no longer be supported and then another bell pit would be sunk. The high cost of transporting coal restricted distribution, and coal did not become really important until the sixteenth century, when the price of timber grew so high as to make coal a more cost-effective fuel (Griffin 1971b: 2). Before the sixteenth century, there were few miners who worked full time as miners, with many also tilling the land (Griffin 1977: 72).

When demand for coal increased, and the bell pits could not produce enough to meet the rising need, the next stage of coal mining was developed: with a downward shaft and side headings built out from this main shaft, and the 'bord and pillar' or 'stall and pillar' system where pillars were left to hold up the roof. This method was known as 'post and stall' in Wales, 'sloop and room' in Scotland and 'pillar and bord' in Tyneside (Lewis 1971: 42). It was very wasteful of coal as much was left below ground to hold up the ceilings. Coal was won by driving roadways through a coal seam (Griffin 1977: 99). Initially, these workings tended to be shallow and did not extend more than forty metres from the shaft and were less than sixty metres deep. But by joining two shafts together, a flow of air was produced which allowed for longer and deeper shafts (A. R. Griffin 1981: picture 9). Difficulties with drainage, ventilation and haulage limited what could be produced, and many of these pits closed in a relatively short time, either as they were worked out or because of technical problems which meant the pit had to be abandoned (Wain 2014: 117). Deeper mines brought new problems, such as gas and water which could no longer be removed easily. This system was replaced by the longwall system in the 1880s, although it was not immediately applied in all areas (see Lewis 1971: 42–43) which explains why, when this method was first introduced in Yorkshire, managers had to be brought in from Nottinghamshire to work the new practice. With this method, all coal was extracted along the coalface and the ceiling was supported by wood (and later metal and hydraulic) supports. The workings continued in a straight line which could be hundreds of metres long (British Coal 1989: 15, see this publication for detailed information on all of these methods) and all coal was taken out, ensuring less wastage. With the advent of the Industrial Revolution, ever more coal was needed and deeper shafts were sunk. It was also a time of important innovations, with the introduction of the steam engine to pump out water, winding in collieries which used baskets and cages to move material and men up and down the shaft, and the use of explosives for undermining the coal (C. P. Griffin 1981: 42).

The greater need for coal also affected population numbers as during this time there was significant population growth in these industrial and mining areas (Kerswill 2018: 23), with more workers needed to keep up with demand. This meant that workers had to be encouraged and mining drew labour away from the agricultural as well as the knitting and weaving industries. However, working conditions in the mines were far from ideal. Coal mining could be intolerably hot or cold, depending on the airflow, and different poisonous gases were always a danger (see also Williams 1962: 26). Freese has noted that 'Coal mining was one of the few occupations in which a person faced a very real risk of death by all four classical elements – earth, air, fire and water. It was probably the most dangerous profession of a dangerous time' (Freese 2003: 47). In Chapter 4, we will see that these different dangerous working conditions were given names by the miners and referred to the different types of gas that were found below ground, such as carbon monoxide and methane. These problems became bigger issues as mines grew deeper (Lewis 1971: 10). Nevertheless, although working conditions were dangerous, mining provided quite a good standard of living in some regions (C. P. Griffin 1981: 84; Lewis 1971: 28). In many areas coal mining was a family occupation in which even young children were employed, and many boys simply followed their fathers down the mines (Power 2008: 161). Griffin has written that 'my dad worked in the pit, you've got to go in the pit', which illustrates this attitude (Griffin 1988: 20).

By 1700, Britain was probably mining five times more coal than the rest of the world combined and in Britain the industry was ten times greater than it had been in 1550. Coal became not only an important domestic fuel but it was also used by industries that switched to using coal from timber (Lewis 1971: 9; Thesing 2000: xi). Coal was also needed as wood had become relatively scarce due to extensive deforestation (Griffin 1971b: 2; Lewis 1971: 8). As a result, until the latter years of the nineteenth century, and the increased use of electricity and oil, coal enjoyed a monopoly as the source of fuel and power (Court 1945: 4). This also led to a larger increase in employment – from around 15,000 miners in 1700 to about 730,000 by the early nineteenth century – and an output in the 1850s of around 70 million tons (Court 1945: 3). The rising demand necessitated technological improvements within the mines and improved means of transportation from the mines (C. P. Griffin 1981: 39–40). In the nineteenth century, the introduction of canals and railways allowed coal to be transported more easily and cheaply and this changed the coal market greatly (Griffin 1971b: 1). Coal could now be transported overland and no longer relied on sea shipping, reducing the Tyneside monopoly (Lewis 1971: 25). Furthermore, improved mining techniques meant that collieries expanded, and those employing 500 or more workers became more common (Griffin 1977: 72). This long period of growth lasted until about 1920 (Griffin 1971b: 2). Lewis has noted that by inclination miners were conservative and 'only erupted into action when essential standards were threatened'

(Lewis 1971: 66). However, this changed over the years and in the 1840s more militant trade unionism came to the coalfields, leading to the formation of the National Miners' Association of Great Britain and Northern Ireland (Lewis 1971: 69). In the years following 1900 there was increasing industrial unrest as wages failed to keep up with rising prices. There was also some disillusionment with the Labour Party (Williams 1962: 393).

In the years before the First World War, productive capacity in the industry increased by 60 per cent and the number employed underground increased by more than 90 per cent and those on the surface by 185 per cent. The coal industry was important. In the elections of 1909, eighteen miners were among the forty-two elected Labour MPs, (Lewis 1971: 87). The growth of the industry was largely due to the application of steam power (Critcher et al. 1995: 8) and much of this increased production was sold on the domestic market (Williams 1962: 173). During the war, there was a very high demand for coal. However, a large number of miners enlisted in the armed forces (Griffin 1988: 125), and while this was not initially seen as problematic (Williams 1962: 518), problems with planned expansion and mechanisation resulted in a shortage of coal (Kirby 1977: 30) and prices soared (Court 1945: 7). Immediately after the war, miners demanded public ownership of the mines and this resulted in the Sankey Commission in 1919 which supported this suggestion (Williams 1962: 554). The Commission also reported that miners' houses were 'a reproach to our civilization' (Jencks 1967: 302). Miners' earnings peaked in 1920 but after this time they slipped and stayed low for several decades (Griffin 1988: 52).

During the inter-war years, decline began as the costs of deep mining increased (Williams 1962: 174). Williams has stated that 'the First World War was an interlude between a golden age and a time of troubles' (Williams 1962: 548). Adverse effects from alternative sources of energy and more competition from abroad (particularly Germany and the United States) all affected the industry (Kirby 1977: 70). Many countries no longer needed British coal (Lewis 1971: 88). Miners were more affected by market depression than any other industry (Williams 1962: 772). As well as unemployment and poverty, housing remained an issue for mining and conditions were improving only very slowly (Williams 1962: 781).

The year 1926 turned out to be a major watershed for the mining industry. In the General Strike miners were joined by nearly 4 million workers from the railways and other industries who downed their tools, but their competitive position worsened (Kirby 1977: 106). The Coal Mines Act of 1926 suspended the seven-hour day and was a symbol of defeat for the trade unions. Miners were demanding a reduction in working time and stable wages, but the number of unemployed miners increased substantially (Kirby 1977: 124), which continued during the remaining inter-war years (Griffin 1988: 23, 1993: 322). In the 1930s the coal industry imposed a quota system, with mines only allowed to remain open for shorter times each week to avoid closures (Franks 2001: 38).

During the Second World War, mining was a reserved occupation, so relatively few miners joined the armed forces. This followed the experience of the difficulties of maintaining a supply of coal during the First World War when many miners did enlist (Power 2008: 162). One of the problems then was that the government had encouraged unemployed miners to enlist so when increased labour was needed to keep up with demand, not enough skilled labour was available (Kirby 1971: 171; Paterson 2014: 33). To solve the problem, around 10 per cent of enlisted men were sent to work in the coal industry and became known as 'Bevin Boys', named after the government Minister for Labour and National Service, Ernest Bevin (Power 2008: 162). Although this help was much needed, many miners considered these men to be not cut out for pit work 'as you were bred into that' (Griffin 1988: 28) and around 90 per cent of the Bevin Boys returned to their original jobs when they were released. It was thought by some that Bevin Boys were conscientious objectors, but only around forty were, out of a possible 47,000 (Franks 2001: 42). Despite government attempts to control prices, in the Second World War the industry was also disturbed by rising costs and shortages of equipment and supplies (Williams 1962: 517; see also Kirby 1977), and the demands of this war could not be met by the industry (Williams 1962: 842). During the war, the industry only produced coal for home consumption (Robinson and Marshall 1985: 12–13).

In 1944, the National Union of Mineworkers was established (out of the Miners' Federation of Great Britain). This union wished to bring about the nationalisation of the mines (Robinson and Marshall 1985: 50) and remove the mines from private landowners. The end of the war saw the election of a Labour government (Williams 1962: 879) and it was realised that heavy demands would have to be made of the mining industry. As a result, in 1947 one of the first acts of the new government was to nationalise mining in Britain, a move that was generally welcomed by miners (Power 2008: 162), and the National Coal Board (NCB) took over the running of the mines. At the time of nationalisation of the coal industry in 1947, there were 958 pits in the United Kingdom, and 700,000 men worked 'down the pit' across the country. For a number of years coal had already been struggling to compete with oil, demand for coal decreased sharply and the numbers of unemployed miners rose drastically. The National Coal Mining Museum for England has a timeline of important events in the nationalisation of the UK mining industry – full details will not be given here, but some of the important events which led to nationalisation were the national strikes, including those of 1912, 1921 and 1926. Frequently, the strike of 1984–1985 overshadows all other strikes, yet these others too were important as miners were striking against poor working conditions and pay. In particular, the General Strike of 1926 was one of the most important and divisive industrial conflicts (Freese 2003: 234). At that time, mines were still in private ownership and miners wanted to ensure that their working hours were not cut and that their working conditions were improved. Jencks has suggested that following nationalisation there was much improvement in working conditions, benefits, management relations, housing, recreational facilities and educational opportunities, and his work contains interviews with miners who echo these sentiments (Jencks 1967). Other benefits included additional provision of welfare, the provision of pithead showers as the norm and the development of more powerful unions (Power 2008: 162). On Vesting Day in 1947, the NCB gained control of 958 mines and 700,000 miners and was responsible for an annual turnover of 400 million tons of coal, but throughout the 1950s and 1960s coal increasingly struggled to compete with other fuels and production costs had to be cut to save money.

In the decade following the Second World War, coal consumption increased in Britain to reach a post-war peak of 217 million tons in 1956. After this time, coal consumption started falling as the prices of oil products fell (Robinson and Marshall 1985: 24). In particular, the conversion of British Rail to diesel and electric power and the discovery of North Sea natural gas decreased the demand for coal, although coal was still used for electricity generation (Robinson and Marshall 1985: 25). Furthermore, the increase of machinery which cut jobs affected employment figures, and many unprofitable mines were closed (Critcher et al. 1995: 9; Griffin 1989: 187). Although recurring world oil crises encouraged a greater reliance on coal – and the NCB planned to improve output by 42 million tons a year (Critcher et al. 1995: 10) – the next twenty years, up to 1970, saw the closure of many pits, and significantly more pits were shut under Harold Wilson's Labour government than under Margaret Thatcher during her time as Prime Minister: 290 pits compared to 160 (Paterson 2014: 39).

Coal was also losing its biggest customers due to severe cutbacks in the iron and steel industry (Franks 2001: 66). Thatcher believed that the coal industry should be self-supporting and not nationalised (Griffin 1989: 188–189), and in 1981 it was announced that fifty pits and 30,000 jobs would disappear in order to meet government targets. In 1984, Thatcher announced the privatisation of the mining industry and even more closures of mines; she stated that 'the coal industry had come to symbolize everything that was wrong with Britain' (Freese 2003: 240). The large number of job losses and the fact that many collieries were operating at a loss gave the mining unions a growing sense of worse to come (Freese 2003: 241) and they decided to take action. This resulted in a year-long strike in 1984–1985, which was very contentious in the East Midlands, where certain groups of miners did not follow the national strike because Arthur Scargill (leader of the National Union of Mineworkers (NUM)) had called for the action without a nationwide ballot – and these miners did not think it was constitutional to be called out to strike (Griffin 1989: 201). Their refusal to join the strike and the establishment of a new union, the UDM (Union of Democratic Mineworkers) weakened the position of the NUM (Critcher et al. 1995: 13). That strike continues 'to haunt the present' and the communities involved in many ways: economically, socially and emotionally (Simpson and Simmons 2019: 8). The Coal Industry Act of 1987 signalled the end of the NCB, which by this time had changed its name to the British Coal Corporation (BCC). The 1994 Coal Act privatised the remaining sixteen mines and set up the Coal Authority to dissolve the BCC. By 1990, coal production was only 93 million tons, compared with 219 million tons in 1950 (Robinson 1995: 4). The Coal Industry Act of 1994 grouped all mines into five regions (Robinson 1995: 10). RJB Mining (named after owner Richard J. Budge) ran most of the newly privatised industry from 1995 until 2002, at which point UK Coal took over and oversaw the deep mining of coal in Britain until its final demise in December 2015, when Kellingley Colliery, near Knottingley in Yorkshire, closed. It was the last large deep coal mine in Britain to close. The physical presence of the industry disappeared rapidly in many areas as pithead buildings were demolished and many sites were left derelict or forested (Power 2008: 164).

Unemployment figures rocketed (for full details see Coates and Barratt Brown 1997: 8 and 20). In the decade from 1984, 200,000 mining jobs were lost in the UK, of which 80,000 were lost in the four years from 1990–1994 (Coates and Barratt Brown 1997: 9). Most of these job losses were in a handful of areas with a total population of about 5 million people, so the impact of such losses was enormous. The main problem for many miners was that the jobs they had been doing were very specialised and many of their skills could not be applied elsewhere. Employment rates in mining areas remained below the national average for many years and the coalfields had a job density far behind the rest of the UK (for full information see Beatty et al. 2019: 21–23). An important issue is that many young people moved away for further and higher education and did not return for employment, stripping the coalfields of highly qualified workers and creating an ageing population. As well as unemployment benefits, many former miners relied on incapacity benefits. As Beatty et al. (2019: 44) have argued,

> if the coalfields had been a 'region' in their own right, all clustered together in one corner of the country, the statistics would probably show the former coalfields to be the most deprived region in the UK. That disadvantage in the former coalfields is dispersed across several regions and nations does not in any way lessen its severity.

This raises the question of whether the history of the UK coalfield is representative of what happened in the East Midlands.

2.3 History and geography of the East Midlands coalfield

From 1550 to 1950 the extent of coal extraction and the number of those employed in this industry expanded at a colossal rate. In 1550 approximately 15,000 tons of coal were mined; by 1950 this had expanded to about 21,600,000 tons. Those employed in the industry increased from a few hundred to more than 1 million people in around 4,000 mines by the First World War (Keyworth and District Local History Meeting Report 2003). The importance of coal led to its name 'King Coal' during its heyday (Waddington et al. 2001: 9) and the East Midlands coalfield was one of the most productive fields in the country (Griffin 1977: 72), and without which the British manufacturing industry would have been severely curtailed (Griffin 1977: 107).

The East Midlands was part of the huge Derbyshire, Nottinghamshire and Yorkshire coalfield, which forms a single geological unit (Price 1971: 10). In the East Midlands, coal mining was concentrated in three different regions: the Leicestershire and South Derbyshire coalfield; the North Derbyshire coalfield; and the Nottinghamshire coalfield along the western fringe of the county, stretching from Nottingham to Worksop in the north of the county. The Top Hard and Deep Hard seams in Derbyshire and Nottinghamshire provided high-grade steam coal, while the Waterloo, Deep Soft and Low Main (Tupton) seams provided domestic coal. The Leicestershire field produced general-purpose coal as the quality is lower (Dury 1963: 175). There will be additional information about the names of these seams in section 4.2.5.

It is of course impossible to give a full history of coal mining in the East Midlands within the scope of this chapter (for that history see for example A. R. Griffin 1971a, 1971b, 1977, 1981; Waller 1983; Williams 1962), but it is important to understand the significance of mining in this area to realise the significance of pit talk to the miners and the region. Coal mining historically formed the bedrock of the East Midlands regional economy, and mining activity can be dated back to the people of the Roman era, who mined lead in Derbyshire (Mapping UK Mining Heritage; Tonge 1907: 3). There are records of small-scale coal mining in medieval Derbyshire, Leicestershire and Nottinghamshire, and some of the earliest written evidence dates back to the late Middle Ages (Griffin 1971a: 3). In Nottinghamshire, Norman overlord Roger de Busli gave the monks of Kirkstead Abbey the right to mine coal from his land (Wain 2014: 11). Coal was not often burned in the homes of Nottinghamshire as the smell of it burning was very unpopular given that coal found close to the surface was generally very smoky (Freese 2003: 24–25). Many of the early mines in Nottinghamshire around Wollaton and Strelley had the advantage of being close to the River Trent (allowing for the transport of coal to a wider area), which was the only navigable waterway in the county until canals were cut in the late eighteenth century (Griffin 1971a: 62). From the middle of the sixteenth century the demand for coal rose rapidly, mainly due to the growing scarcity of wood. The Trent Valley was one of the busiest inland coalfields and employed between 500–1,000 miners by the beginning of the seventeenth century (Griffin 1977: 72). In 1800 coal mining in Derbyshire was confined to the exposed fields (Dury 1963: 140) and Dury has noted that at this time there were likely around eighty-six active mines in the Derbyshire and Nottinghamshire coalfield and around thirteen mines in Leicestershire.

Even though the East Midlands coal mines were technologically backward in the 1840s (Griffin 1971a: 15), later years saw rapid changes. Turnpikes helped (Griffin 1977: 130), and the East Midlands led the way in the coal industry in terms of innovation and technological advances, for example through the use of railways for transporting coal. A traditional problem of the East Midlands coalfields was that they could only supply local markets and found it difficult to compete with the sea-transported coal of the north-east. Road transport was impractical for bulk loads, and rivers and canals could not provide a complete solution. A dramatic yet cost-effective infrastructure change had to be made, and in this way railways came into being to move coal from colliery to user. Canal, tramway and train rail links helped the East Midlands to supply more distant areas (such as London), and many new mining and transport settlements were developed to meet the rising demand (Griffin 1977: 137). Coal was the bedrock on which two of the largest and most profitable British railway companies – the Midland Railway and the North Eastern Railway – built their businesses (Griffin 1971a). In the second half of the nineteenth century the coal companies reached Nottinghamshire's Leen Valley where more seams were found at an even deeper level, so heavy investment was needed to access this (Waller 1983).

The subsequent quickening of demand stimulated further technological developments and the pits in the East Midlands counties developed in a major way in the nineteenth and twentieth centuries, with collieries increasing in size as deeper pits were sunk in more concealed coalfields rather than in the earlier exposed, shallower seams. Many of the East Midlands mines were leading coalfields in terms of technology. Thoresby was the earliest mine in the county to be completely powered by electricity, and it was the pioneering colliery in terms of mechanised production. It was also the first pit to turn over a million tons of coal per year, and by the late 1980s Thoresby was producing over 2 million tons of coal annually.

The East Midlands coal output is thought to have peaked just before the First World War, similar to the rest of the UK. Some studies have suggested that the situation in the East Midlands was better between the world wars than in other regions (Court 1945: 1; Griffin 1993: 323). This was linked to the expansion in the 'Dukeries' coalfield in Nottinghamshire, where new coal seams were exploited for the first time (Waller 1983: 2). Other areas in the region did not prosper as much as mines were already closing (Dury 1963: 174). One of the main problems with the East Midlands coalfield at this time was related to the seasonal demand – as East Midlands coal was heavily dependent on the domestic market, the need for coal was much lower in the summer months (Griffin 1993: 324). After the Second World War more than 45,000 people were employed in the industry, and it is thought that there were around 120 mines in the East Midlands. In Nottinghamshire alone in 1945 there were forty-four mines employing 45,587 men, of whom 34,439 worked underground (Franks 2001: 45). The increase of output from the collieries and technological advances linked to the increase in the workforce had huge effects on surrounding villages as many miners moved to the East Midlands, especially as other regions' mines were starting to close down. Mining villages all around the East Midlands witnessed population explosions and shifts as miners were frequently moved around the country. Jock Purdon, who was a miner, poet and singer from County Durham, wrote a song when he and the other miners were being transferred to the Nottinghamshire coalfield when their mine closed in 1963. It contains the words 'Leave your picks behind ye, ye'll no need them agen. And off you go to Nottingham, join Robin's merry men. Leave your cares behind ye, your future has been planned. And off ye go tae Nottingham, tae Roben's promised land' (cited by Bell 2008: 10; see also Lewis 1971: 102). This movement of men and their families, according to Dury (1963: 176), resulted in different types of housing around the mines, including both the extension of already existing settlements and the creation of colliery villages, some in relatively isolated surroundings. In many cases the coal owners were offering all employment and housing in some of these villages, giving them huge control over the population in a way that was no longer common in twentieth-century Britain (Waller 1983: 7). Between 1890 and 1960 the East Midlands coalfields more than doubled their proportional share of the national output (Dury 1963: 175). This was despite the stringent quotas imposed, where the allowed output of the inland districts was well below their productive capacity, resulting in a reduction of working hours for many miners.

The NCB initially took over the running of 120 deep coal mines in the East Midlands region, one of its nine regional divisions (Williams 1962: 879), and the region was split into eight areas in North Nottinghamshire, South Nottinghamshire, North Derbyshire, South Derbyshire and Leicestershire. Each of these units was made up of different geographical areas which included specific collieries. As well as taking over the 120 pits, the NCB also had to take on all other works and buildings associated with the industry, including five major coking and by-product plants, twelve brick works, two pipe works, six water works, 18,350 houses, 112 farms and more than 14,300 acres of land, which had all been previously owned by the private colliery companies (Williams 1962: 880). During the 1950s, well over 100 pits in the country were closed but there was little opposition as there were plenty of jobs elsewhere (Franks 2001: 52). As well as plentiful jobs and great strides in mechanisation, there was also a considerable decrease in accident rates (Williams 1962: 886). New investment in modernisation and expansion was mainly taking place in a very concentrated number of coalfields, of which the central coalfields of the East Midlands formed one and Yorkshire was the other (Hudson and Sadler 1990: 439; Power 2008: 161), as it was felt that a better return of investment would be made. However, even these regions were not exempt from closures and six Nottinghamshire collieries closed in the 1950s, followed by a further nine in the 1960s. Already at this time miners' pay was slipping below the average wage in other heavy industries (Franks 2001: 54). By 1970, of the 958 mines which had been nationalised only 300 remained in operation (Franks 2001: 63–65). Between 1984 and 1989 mining jobs declined nationally from 181,000 to 66,000, and by 1992 a further 27,000 jobs had been lost. By 1980, forty-nine of the East Midlands collieries were still in production and more coal was being produced in Nottinghamshire than in the north-east of England and South Wales put together, so it was a very important coal area (Waller 1983: 4). It was thought by many that the East Midlands miners were very sheltered in the 1980s, but this was not necessarily the case (Griffin 1993: 342); even though mass unemployment was absent, there was still mass underemployment in the region.

The Nottinghamshire coalfield was of strategic importance to the NUM and to Margaret Thatcher during the 1984–1985 strike (Paterson 2014: 11) and the battle raged fiercely here. Less than 2,000 men finished the year on strike from a total workforce of nearly 32,000. The region had a history of strike-breaking company unionism from 1926, which had seen the emergence of the 'Nottingham Miners Industrial Union', commonly known as the Spencer Union after its leader, George Alfred Spencer (1872–1957). It believed in arbitration to solve disputes and had no strike clauses. Following the 1984–1985 strike, another breakaway union, the Union of Democratic Mineworkers (UDM), was formed of miners who did not support strike action and this weakened the situation in the region for the NUM. With an initial membership of 37,000 who had left the NUM (Franks 2001: 75), the conflict caused deep rifts within mining communities and families. Relations with friends and family members were severed (Emery 2020: 11), some right up until the present day, as many striking miners refused and still refuse to associate with 'scabs', those who worked throughout the strike.

At the time of the re-privatisation of the coal industry in 1995 only seven East Midlands collieries, all in Nottinghamshire, were in production. It was therefore decided to place an emphasis on the last collieries which operated in the various geographical regions of the East Midlands, mainly into the 1990s. The average age of a UK miner was thirty-four, so early retirement was not an option (Franks 2001: 83). By 1995 all remaining mines had been returned to private ownership. The last mine in Derbyshire – Markham Colliery – closed in 1994. In Leicestershire the last mine closed in 1991 (Bagworth). In Nottinghamshire the last mine was Thoresby; it closed in 2015 (for more details see Bell 2006, 2007, 2008). As a result of the closures, many areas of the East Midlands have suffered economically, simply because some of the largest and most important employers in the region disappeared. In the following sections, we will look at the individual coalfields of Leicestershire, Derbyshire and Nottinghamshire.

2.3.1 Coal mining in the Leicestershire and South Derbyshire coalfields

These two regions are frequently considered together because of their geographical proximity and the fact that the coal seams cross the county lines. Generally, the main coalfield was found in a ten-mile radius centred around Ashby-de-la-Zouch, in the counties of Leicestershire and the extreme south of Derbyshire. The coalfield was split into two distinct areas separated by a geological fault called the Boothorpe Fault. This resulted in mines such as Donisthorpe, Moira and Measham geographically belonging to Leicestershire but regarded as belonging to the South Derbyshire coalfield as this border followed the fault, rather than the county lines. The Leicestershire coalfield was mainly in the eastern basin with the South Derbyshire coalfield being in the western basin. In Leicestershire, the pits fell into two geographical groups, the mines based around Coalville (such as Whitwick, Snibston, South Leicester and New Lount) and those clustered around Bagworth (see Figures 2.2 and 2.3).

The origin of mining in this region is uncertain and there is archaeological evidence that suggests it was mined in Roman times. However, the first references to be found are in a charter of 1204 which describes coal that existed at Swannington and a lawsuit of 1293 which mentions the operation of a coal mine in this region (C. P. Griffin 1981: 1). There were mines

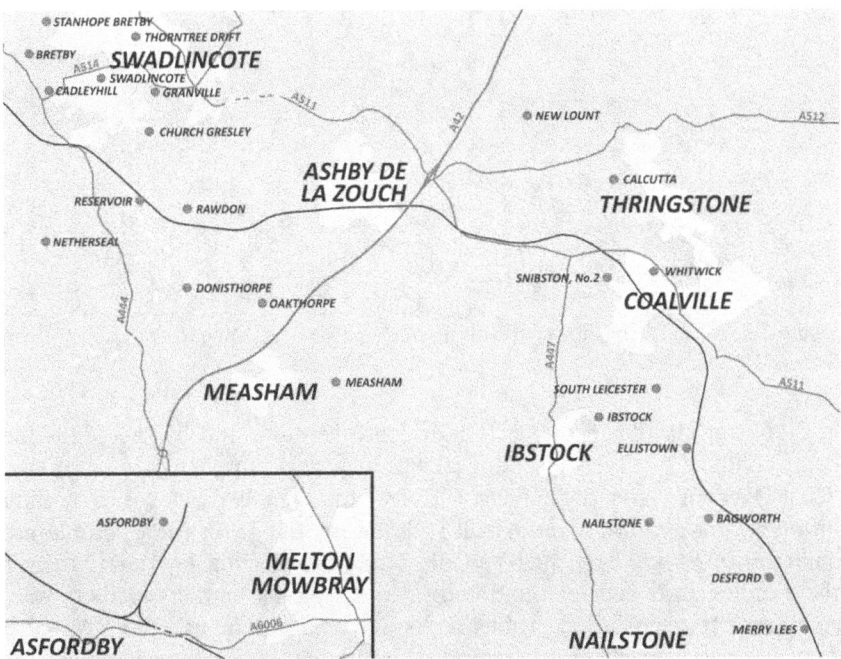

Figure 2.2 Leicestershire coalfield (map from Northern Mine Research Society)

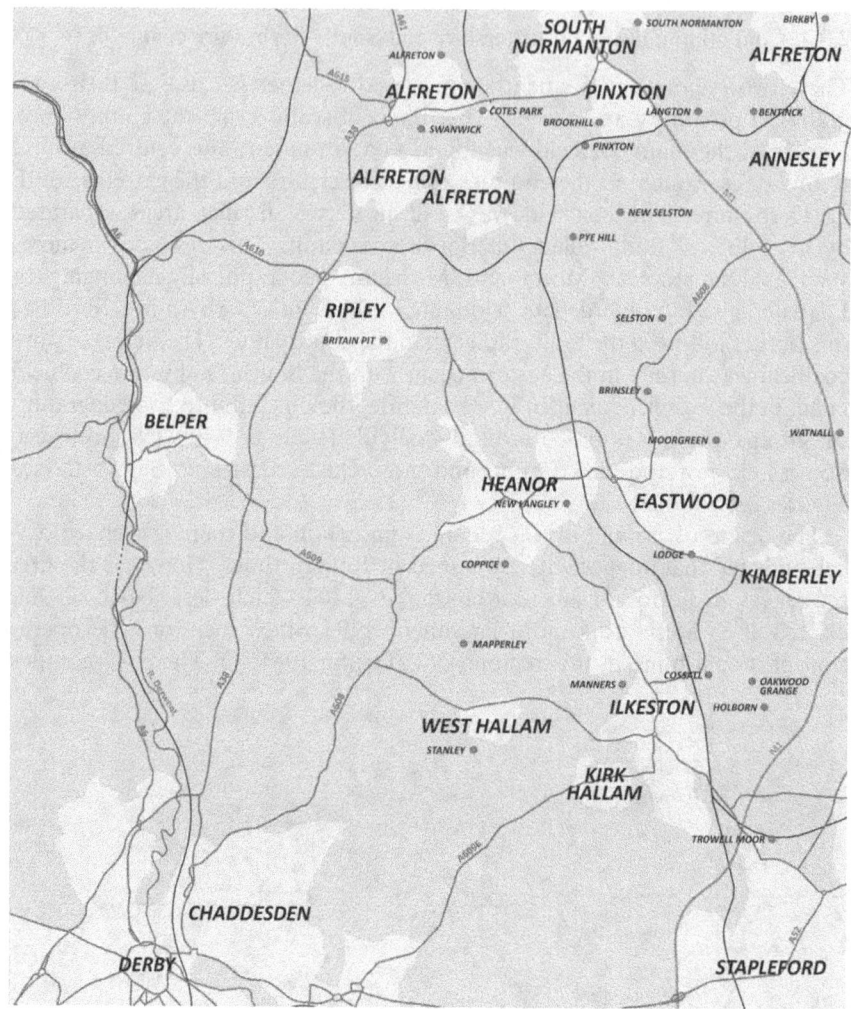

Figure 2.3 South Derbyshire coalfield (map from Northern Mine Research Society)

at Staunton Harold in the early fourteenth century, and by the 1420s the nearby village of Overton Saucy was known as a supplier of coal named 'Coal Overton', later shortened to 'Coleorton'. The early stages of mining in the region were on a very small scale but by the 1570s there were larger collieries operating here, such as Coleorton (C. P. Griffin 1981: 4). Most of these mines produced for the domestic and regional markets as there were significant transportation problems. As well as domestic use, there was also some usage for steam raising, as well as for fired earthenware production, the textile trade and brewing. Documentary evidence of coal mining from the

Swannington area of Leicestershire dates from the thirteenth century. Coal mining on the western side of the coalfield, in the Swadlincote area, dates from the late thirteenth century, with coal mining activity being established by the mid-fifteenth century around Newhall. Through the seventeenth and eighteenth centuries mines were gradually developed to greater depths in the Swannington-Coleorton and Oakthorpe-Donisthorpe-Measham areas. Snibston was bought by George Stephenson (of the railways) in 1831 and he began the sinking of the first shaft at that time which culminated in the opening of the Leicester to Swannington railway in 1832, serving the needs of the coalfields (C. P. Griffin 1981: 57). The Leicestershire coalfield was at the forefront of British railway development as coal owners decided it was of paramount importance to find a way of transporting coal efficiently cross-country. These railways resulted in other regions having to reduce their prices in order to be able to compete (Williams 1962: 41). During the nineteenth and twentieth centuries most collieries set up an adjacent brick and tile works, and a network of railways evolved to link them to the national railway system.

The number of collieries was relatively stable between 1840 and 1914; there were between 17 and 21 operating in the 1840s and between 21 and 24 from the 1860s onwards. In the early nineteenth century the Earl of Moira developed mines, an ironworks and a new settlement called Moira on the southern part of Ashby Wolds, served by the Ashby Canal. Between the 1820s and the end of the century, deeper mines were gradually sunk to concealed reserves south of the eastern basin, as far as Desford. The largest collieries were situated at Snibston and Whitwick in Leicestershire and Moira and Church Gresley in South Derbyshire. In the 1870s major collieries opened at Ellistown and Nailstone in Leicestershire, and Bretby, Cadley Hill, Coton Park, Netherseal and Donisthorpe in South Derbyshire. These were followed at the turn of the century by Desford and Measham (C. P. Griffin 1981: 15). In the Leicestershire coalfield there were about 1,400 people employed in 1841 and this had doubled by 1871. Inspectorate figures from 1874 show a rapid increase to about 10,000 workers over the next forty years (C. P. Griffin 1981: 72). Migration into the region created a large source of labour and in 1851 56 per cent of miners in the region had not been born in Derbyshire or Leicestershire but had come from the Nottinghamshire coalfield, as well as from the north-east (C. P. Griffin 1981: 74). However, this region was still one of the smaller coalfields in Britain and at times attempts were made to amalgamate the mines into a single enterprise but this was stonewalled by the owners (Griffin 1988: 5). The region's mining was particularly dangerous in comparison with other Midlands coalfields and the death rate was higher than surrounding areas. Most of these casualties resulted from roof falls or miners being crushed by tubs or horses. Only from the 1870s onwards was the accident record improved to bring it into line with the rest of the country (C. P. Griffin 1981: 93, 1988: 85). From the 1820s until 1900, deeper sinkings were made in the concealed part of the coalfield, to the south of the eastern basin as far as Desford.

The relatively small size of the coalfield ensured a close sense of belonging in the region. For example, in Moira in the early nineteenth century work spreading was preferred to unemployment (Griffin 1993: 328). This region also saw demonstrations of patriotic fervour as almost 9 per cent of Leicestershire miners had joined the armed forces by May 1915 (Griffin 1988: 21). Miners were in high demand initially because of their tunnelling experience, but this did lead to a shortfall of miners at home to keep up with the wartime demand of coal, and more miners had to be employed both during the First and Second World Wars. In fact, increased demand resulted in increased employment despite improved productivity, and when national decline set in from the 1950s onwards, it was much slower to take hold in Leicestershire than in the rest of the country. Before 1842 Leicestershire miners had no formal union, but the National Miners' Association of Great Britain (NMA), formed in 1841 to encourage local activity, and the Leicestershire Miners' Association (LMA) and South Derbyshire Amalgamated Miners' Association (SDAMA) were formed in 1887 and they became forerunners of NUM constituent areas. Particularly in the run-up to the First World War membership was very high and there were funds to support action (C. P. Griffin 1981: 114, 149).

During the twentieth century, especially from the 1960s onwards, there were many mergers of collieries, which involved linking collieries underground and improving coal transport and handling facilities, both underground and on the surface. Most of the nineteenth-century mines survived into the 1960s, before the rapid abandonment of deep mines in the region in the 1970s and 1980s. During nationalisation in 1947 there were twenty-one collieries operational in the Leicestershire and South Derbyshire coalfields, situated in the NCB East Midlands Division Numbers 7 and 8 Areas, which by 1948 amalgamated to form one No. 7 Area, with area headquarters at Coleorton. In the reorganisation of 1967, all the region's collieries went into the NCB South Midlands Area. The closure of collieries commenced from the 1950s, and by the 1980s many of the regions remaining operating collieries had been in production for around 150 years and were facing exhaustion of viable coal reserves. Snibston and Desford both finished production just prior to the commencement of the 1984–1985 Miners' Strike. The smaller South Derbyshire coalfield did not completely support the strike, and South Derbyshire and Nottinghamshire continued to work through it. This was also the case for a large number of Leicestershire miners, with the exception of the 'The Dirty Thirty' – the thirty miners (out of a workforce of 2,500) who did support the strike. They came to use the title as a badge of honour. It was said that most Leicestershire miners chose not to strike as they had always prided themselves on being independent and moderate and did not want to be told what to do (Griffin 1989: 210–211). Further, in this area most miners lived in communities with close proximity to other types of workers and so were less likely to be influenced solely by other miners. It was said that in Leicestershire there were also other types of job for ex-miners, which was not always the case in the rest of the East Midlands coalfield (Griffin 1989: 211, see also Bell 2007: 29). Furthermore, the belief that the 'super-pit' at Asfordby would provide many jobs for years to come may have resulted in some miners believing they had to safeguard their jobs until it could start to operate. (Asfordby was developed from the early 1980s to the mid-1990s and planned to employ the remainder of the Leicestershire miners, but in August 1997 it closed after producing coal for only two years.) At the time of the strike, unemployment was high in regions such as Coalville (where it stood at 12 per cent), so miners did not want to settle for redundancy as they would be unlikely to get employment outside the mining industry. In South Derbyshire the UDM was voted in by a very narrow margin, so there were two hostile camps. However, violent incidents in this region were rare because heavy picketing was mainly concentrated in Nottinghamshire.

When the Donisthorpe/Rawdon Complex and Bagworth Colliery finished production in 1990 and 1991 respectively, deep coal mining in the Leicestershire and South Derbyshire coalfield ended. The collieries in the region which closed in the 1983–1991 period were perhaps the oldest operating deep coal mines in the whole of Britain, most having been sunk in the 1820s and 1830s. The main centres, which grew during the Industrial Revolution, mainly as a result of coal mining, were Swadlincote, Coalville, Ibstock and Measham. Throughout the nineteenth and the first half of the twentieth centuries, pits in this region were closing when they ran out of coal, and new ones were still being opened (Bell 2006: 10). These collieries were of medium size but with a high level of productivity.

2.3.2 Coal mining in the North Derbyshire coalfield

The main Derbyshire coalfield is a southern extension of the Yorkshire coalfield. In turn, it dips eastwards into Nottinghamshire and north-east Leicestershire (see Figure 2.4 for a map of this coalfield). The North Derbyshire coalfield eventually covered a large area around the town of Chesterfield, with the mining communities of Dronfield, Eckington, Renishaw and Killamarsh to the north and north-east; Staveley, Bolsover, Clowne and Shirebrook to the east; and Clay Cross, Alfreton, Ripley, Heanor and Ilkeston to the south. The majority of the coal seams in the area inclined eastwards into the Nottinghamshire coalfield. Some of the region's large iron companies were amongst the largest colliery owners in the Midlands region, these included the Staveley, Clay Cross, Butterley and Stanton iron companies.

In a similar way to other regions in the UK the incentive for increased coal mining was the huge price rise for timber, and coal needed to act as substitute. We have records of coal mining in Derbyshire in 1256 in the forest of Duffield Frith (Williams 1962: 15), and there are other references to the digging of

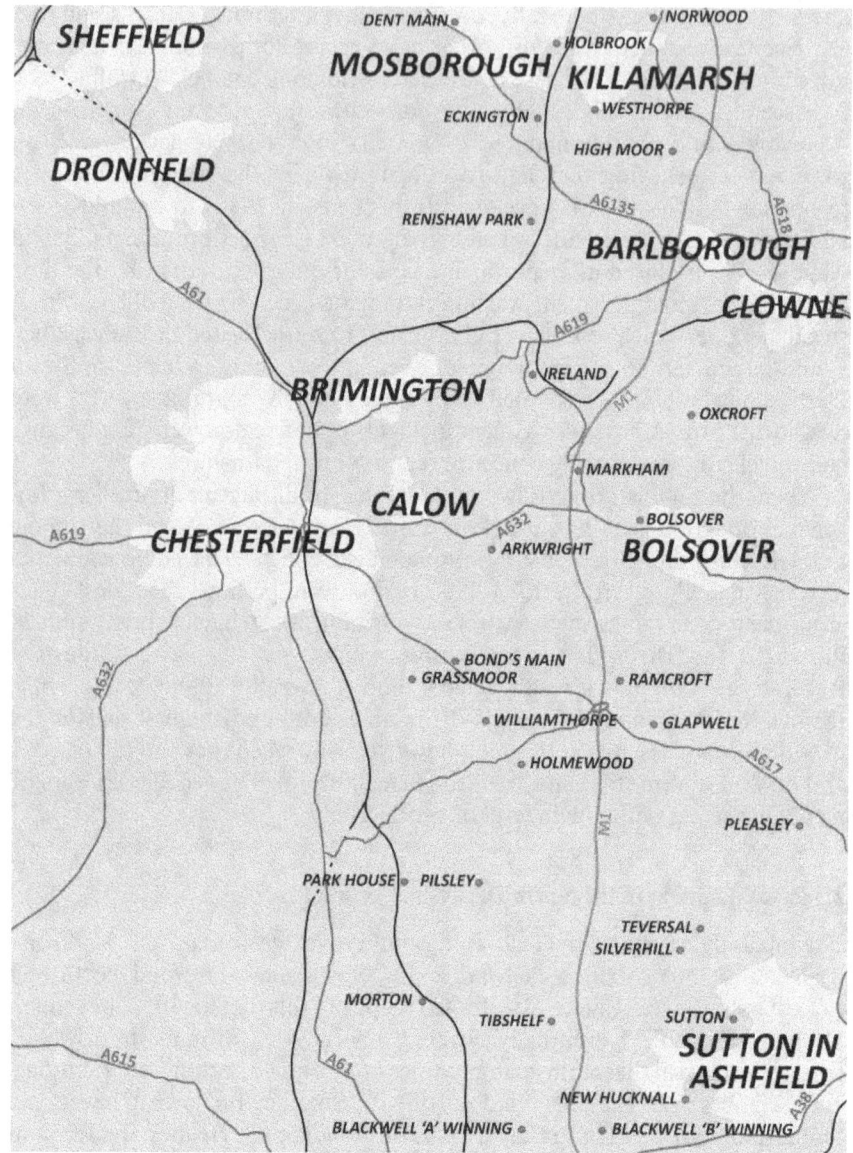

Figure 2.4 North Derbyshire coalfield (map from Northern Mine Research Society)

coal at Denby, Breaston, Wingerworth, Scarsdale and Repton before the end of the thirteenth century. Records show coal mining taking place to the south of Heanor in the thirteenth century and south of Chesterfield in the Wingerworth and Stretton areas in the fourteenth century. By the sixteenth century a number of important developments were taking place, and between 1550 and 1615 references appear to numerous collieries starting work around this time, including in Bolsover, Heanor, Langley, Ripley and others (Williams 1962: 17). The problem for many of these collieries is that they were too far from the River Trent, or even the River Derwent, to allow easy transportation of coal to other areas. A number of Derbyshire mines were very wet and working hours were long, at between 13–16 hours per day. This resulted in a short life expectancy for miners, and although no women or girls were employed in these pits the employment of boys was common (Williams 1962: 64). Many pit villages were relatively isolated and miners were often set apart from other communities and felt looked down upon or stigmatised because of their work (see for example Jencks 1967: 303). Irregular work and low wages meant that some areas of Derbyshire showed very high levels of deprivation (Williams 1962: 452).

During the eighteenth century, Derbyshire began to feel the impact of the Industrial Revolution and coal was needed for a large number of industries. Around this time turnpike roads were made connecting Derby to Sheffield, Manchester and Huddersfield, and then the completion of canals connecting Merseyside and Lancashire increased trade possibilities, for example as the Lancashire mills used Derbyshire coal. Furthermore, the advent of the railways allowed coal to be transported to London and other markets, which resulted in a large increase in production in the region. Despite falling prices, production in Derbyshire increased to 9 million tons between 1880 and 1885. Although early coal mining was limited to the exposed coalfield, coal at greater depths was of a high quality both for industry and domestic usage. As newer and larger collieries with more modern equipment were opening up, many of the older and smaller collieries began to close down, either because they were uneconomic or because they were worked out (Wain 2014: 115). The change in mining, requiring more specialised labour, meant it became harder to find alternative employment in times of poor trade. With the exception of 1929, Derbyshire's coal output declined steadily from 1927 to 1933. The increased demand for coal during the Second World War meant that more men were needed to work in the mines; however, attempts to transfer unemployed miners from other regions were unsuccessful (Williams 1962: 848) and failed to fill in for the 2,323 men who were serving in the forces.

When the coal industry was nationalised in 1947, there were sixty-eight collieries in Derbyshire. One of the most serious disasters of this region occurred at Creswell Colliery when eighty men lost their lives after a conveyor belt caught fire in September 1950. The coalfield suffered significant closures during the period. While Alfred Robens was NCB chairman in the 1960s, many of the region's collieries closed for economic reasons, especially those to the south of Chesterfield. Deep coal mining finished in the Ilkeston region in 1966, around Ripley in 1968, and around Alfreton in 1969, with the last colliery in the Heanor region, Ormonde Colliery, closing in 1970.

Glapwell and Langwith Collieries closed in the 1970s and by the start of the 1980s production was concentrated at eleven collieries in the NCB North Derbyshire Area, at Westhorpe, Renishaw Park, Ireland, Whitwell, Markham, Arkwright, Bolsover, Warsop Main, Shirebrook, Pleasley and Highmoor. Westhorpe and Whitwell were in the process of running down to closure at the start of the 1984–1985 Miners' Strike in March 1984. The NUM in North Derbyshire was fully behind the strike, although not all miners followed strike action and many in the smaller South Derbyshire coalfield did not strike either (Bell 2006: 102). It was thought by some that Markham was Europe's largest mine (Bell 2006: 11); it had more than 3,000 employees in 1950 and had ten working faces. By the start of the 1990s, production was concentrated in just three North Derbyshire collieries. All three collieries finished production in the late spring and early summer of 1993; Bolsover through exhaustion of reserves and Shirebrook and Markham through the effects of the coal crisis of 1992–1994 when significant markets for power station coal were lost. It was indeed the end of an era for the county of Derbyshire; a far cry from the 176 collieries that were operating in the county in 1906. The last five pits to close were Renishaw Park (1989), Creswell (1991), Bolsover (1993), Markham (1993) and Shirebrook (1993). Today the coal mining heritage of the region is kept alive by a group of volunteers who run the Pleasley Pit site. The colliery headstocks, winding engines and associated engine houses survive in preservation and the Pleasley Pit Trust oversees the running of the site for heritage, leisure and educational purposes.

2.3.3 Coal mining in the Nottinghamshire coalfield

The Nottinghamshire coalfield is part of an extensive coalfield which stretches from the west from Derbyshire and north into Yorkshire. The Nottinghamshire coalfield is often split into the north and south coalfields. Moore has said that in this region 'coal was king or very close to it' (Moore 1995: 30). The pits found in each of these regions can be seen in Figures 2.5 and 2.6. The earliest evidence of mining in this region is from the later Middle Ages and these early mines were on the outcrop between Wollaton in the south and Teversal in the north (Griffin 1971a: 3). The oldest workings in the southern part of the county of Nottinghamshire were situated on the exposed coalfield, sometimes referred to as 'the Outcrop', generally to the west of a line between Nottingham and Chesterfield. The earliest records show coal mining taking place at Cossall in 1306, and a significant coal industry, for its time, existed around Wollaton and Strelley in the Tudor period. Early mining was by means of bell pits and in some cases small drift or adit mines.

The numbers employed in the Nottinghamshire region were quite small before the eighteenth century, with the most important of the Trent Valley collieries (particularly Wollaton and Strelley) employing between 150–330

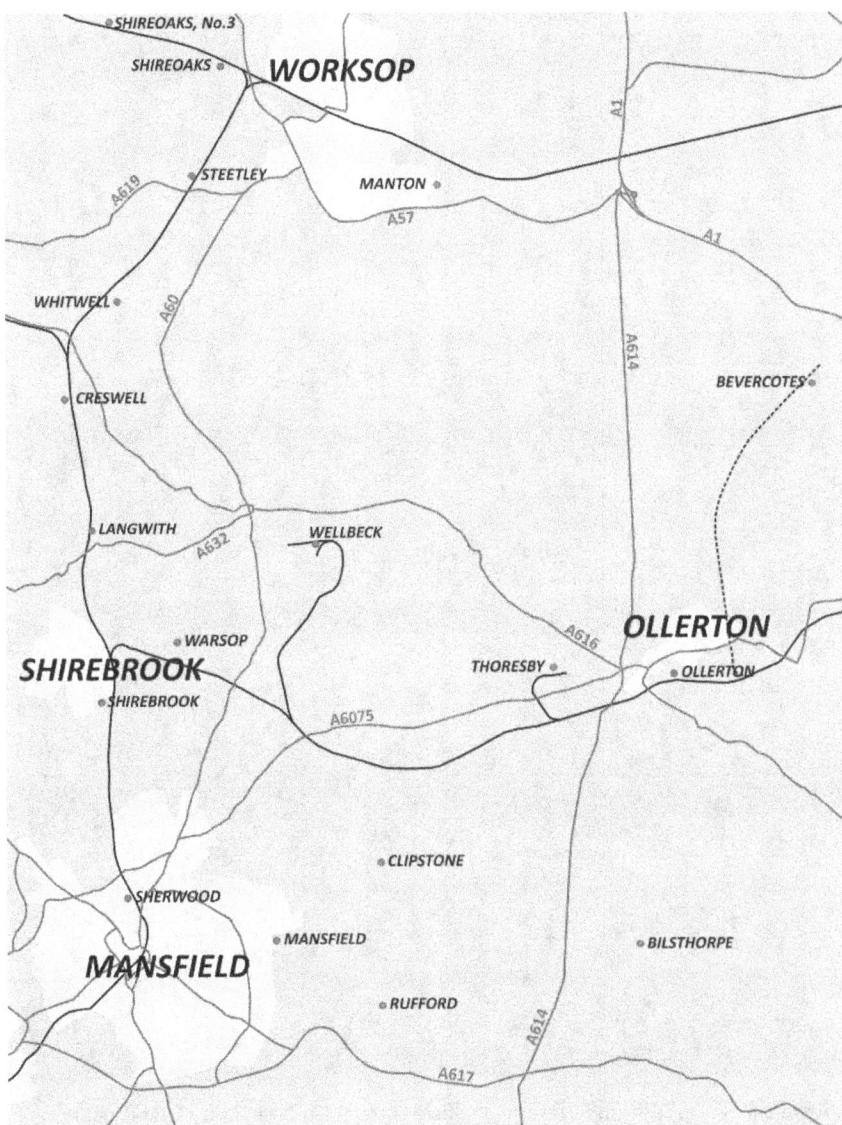

Figure 2.5 North Nottinghamshire coalfield (map from Northern Mine Research Society)

men at the beginning of the seventeenth century and about 500–1,000 men in the eighteenth century (Griffin 1971a: 35). The first significant move towards what could be considered the foundation of modern deep coal mining occurred when Thomas North developed a series of collieries around Cinderhill in the 1840s and 1850s. The Cinderhill pits were also known as

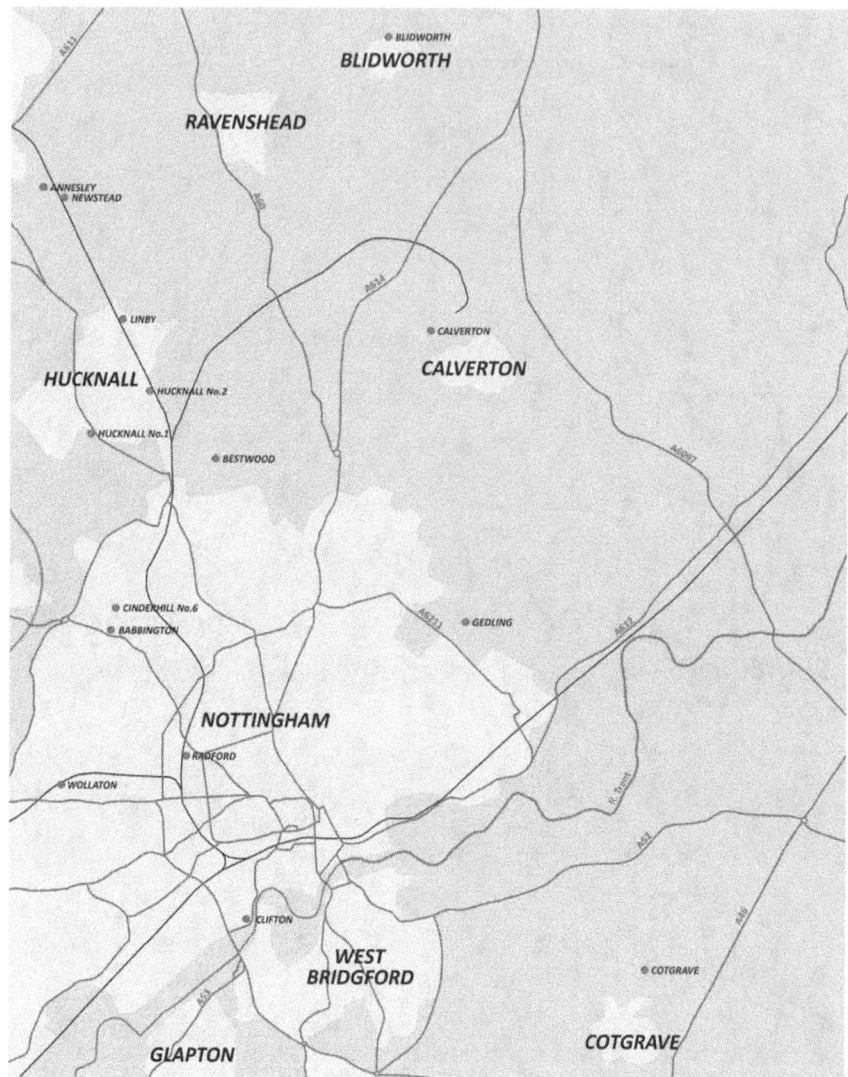

Figure 2.6 South Nottinghamshire coalfield (map from Northern Mine Research Society)

'Babbington' after the nearby village of the same name near Awsworth, where North first started in coal mining. When Babbington Colliery closed in 1986 it was the longest producing Nottinghamshire colliery, having produced coal for 144 years.

The Leen Valley saw a significant number of sinkings of new collieries in the 1860s to 1870s, at Annesley (1865), Newstead (1874), Linby (1873), Hucknall No. 1 (Top Pit) (1861), Hucknall No. 2 (Bottom Pit) (1865),

Bestwood (1872), and a later sinking at Wollaton (1875) and at nearby Radford (1899). It became one of the most productive coal producing regions in Britain during the period between 1880 to the 1920s. Here the coal seams were situated much deeper than on the Outcrop. Sinkings also occurred in a similar period around Sutton-in-Ashfield, with the Stanton Ironworks Company developing collieries at Teversal, known locally as 'Butcherwood' (as the pit was sunk on the site of a small coppice called Butcherwood), in 1868 and Silverhill Colliery in 1875. Nearby Sutton Colliery was sunk in 1873; locally this was referred to as 'Brierley' as some of the initial workers came from Brierley Hill in Staffordshire. Other developments saw the Butterley Company develop Kirkby (Summit) Colliery in the 1890s and the New Hucknall Company open Bentinck Colliery at the same time. The Digby Company, from Giltbrook, sank Gedling Colliery, east of Nottingham, between 1900 and 1902.

There are two main developments of coal excavation in this region. The 'older' coalfield centred around the Leen Valley was developed between 1860 and 1880, and the 'newer', deeper coalfield which was centred around Mansfield, further east, was developed between 1890 and 1930 (Griffin 1977: 164). The North Nottinghamshire Coalfield, in and around and to the northeast of the town of Mansfield, was developed mainly in the early decades of the twentieth century. The Bolsover Colliery Company was instrumental in the development of the coalfield, eventually establishing collieries and coal mining communities at Forest Town, Rainworth, Clipstone and Edwinstowe. Other significant companies such as the Butterley and Stanton Iron Companies also influenced the development of the coalfield at Ollerton and Bilsthorpe respectively. The coalfield became known as 'the Dukeries Coalfield' because of the influence of the aristocratic landowners in the region: Lord Saville at Rufford Abbey, the Duke of Portland at Welbeck Abbey, the Duke of Newcastle at Clumber, and Earl Manvers at Thoresby Hall.

Between 1874 and 1920 the number of men employed underground in Nottinghamshire increased from around 9,000 to just over 41,000 and overall numbers increased from 12,000 to almost 53,000 (Griffin 1971a: 112, see also Griffin 1962). Many sons followed their fathers into the mines, which were the main local employers. The gradual development of the pits meant that in the early days few miners worked full time in the mines; instead digging coal alongside agricultural work (Griffin 1977: 156). It was only later that mining became less seasonal and miners became more specialised and increased numbers were needed to keep up with demand. The Nottinghamshire mines benefited greatly not just from the canals but also from the railway, resulting in a smaller number of much larger pits rather than a larger number of smaller pits. The improvement in transport led to a marked expansion of production, more than doubling between 1874 and 1890 and then rising by a further 67 per cent by 1914 (Moore 1995: 11). The region became less supportive of strike action and in 1926 the Nottinghamshire Miners'

Non-Political Industrial Union was formed, led by George Spencer (Griffin 1988: 206), which had implications for later strike actions as this union 'vowed to work closely with the mine owners, never to strike, and to stay out of politics' (Bell 2008: 12). This union was known as a 'gaffer's union' or 'scab union', and its policy of non-action or strikebreaking was, and still is today, seen by many as the ultimate crime (Griffin 1990: 13).

In 1944 there were forty-two mines in Nottinghamshire, which employed around 45,000 men. At this time the standard of living was relatively high for mining families because of full-time employment during the war (Franks 2001: 45). When the coal industry was nationalised in 1947, there were forty collieries in Nottinghamshire. The only significant sinking in the North Nottinghamshire coalfield following the Second World War was the development of the high-tech Bevercotes Colliery, near Retford, which started production in 1968. Further developments in the South Nottinghamshire coalfield took place with the opening of Calverton Colliery in 1952 and Cotgrave, south-east of Nottingham, in 1964. Both of these were NCB pits: Calverton initially started as an airshaft for the Top Hard workings at Bestwood Colliery in 1937 but Cotgrave as a brand-new colliery. Both pits saw significant migration in the 1960s, especially from Northumberland and Durham, and became known locally for the large influx of miners from the north-east. Eighteen collieries formed the new NCB South Nottinghamshire Area in 1967. During the 1950s, six pits in Nottinghamshire closed, followed by a further nine in 1968 (Franks 2001: 52). At this time there was relatively little opposition as there were still plenty of jobs available in other collieries.

When the NCB North Nottinghamshire Area was created in the reorganisation of 1967 the coalfield boasted fourteen collieries in total, which included some of the East Midlands' highest production collieries, known as 'big hitters', and which were mainly in the Dukeries region. The NCB North Nottinghamshire Area was often referred to as the 'jewel in the NCB's crown' and for many years it was the most profitable NCB region in the whole of Britain. Thoresby was the first mine in the country to be completely powered by electricity and it pioneered mechanised production. It was also the first pit to turn over a million tons of coal per year, and in the late 1980s it was producing over two tons of coal per year (Bell 2008: 9). Around 70 per cent of Nottinghamshire coal was burned in power stations (Nottinghamshire County Council 1986: 2).

In March 1980 almost 43,000 men worked for the NCB in Nottinghamshire, which made up around 16 per cent of all male jobs in the county, but by March 1985 the number had fallen to 34,000 (Nottinghamshire County Council 1986: 1). Before the 1984–1985 strike the Nottinghamshire coalfield produced more than 20 million tons of coal – 20 per cent of national deep-mined production. It was protected from national decline as a result of the low price of coal (Collins 1975: 1) and mining remained one of the main employers in the region (second only to Yorkshire for the highest proportion of miners compared to the general population, see Paterson 2014: 45).

Severe cutbacks in the iron and steel industries meant that coal was losing very important customers and, in this region, Teversal Colliery closed in 1980. The miners in Nottingham who supported the 1984–1985 strike formed a minority, and many did not support Arthur Scargill and the NUM. One miner noted that:

> If Scargill had gone round it the right way in the beginning he would have got every miner in the country to come out on strike. But because he was dictating to the miners that they would go on strike, without a democratic vote basically, I think he got a lot of the Nottinghamshire miners' backs up as well as a lot of the other miners. And as we said at the end of the day we're entitled to a vote and he was trying to put the miners on strike without voting. (Franks 2001: 74)

According to Moore, the Nottinghamshire miners had long been known for their moderation and lack of militancy (Moore 1995: 14–15), while others have said that Nottinghamshire miners were reluctant to join the strike because of the relative wealth and harmony of their region (Waller 1983: 109). Bell has also discussed the situation at Teversal in 1980, which as some have suggested influenced the Nottinghamshire miners in 1984. In 1980 Teversal was set to close and miners asked the NUM for help – but this did not materialise. These circumstances led to real long-term problems during and after the 1984–1985 strike, including teams splitting up, equipment being sabotaged, and miners refusing to speak or work together (Bell 2008: 111).

By 1992, twelve pits in Nottinghamshire had been closed and 27,000 jobs had been lost. The average age of a miner was thirty-four, so early retirement was not an option. By the start of the twenty-first century just four of the area's collieries remained in production – at Clipstone, Haworth, Welbeck and Thoresby – with Bilsthorpe Colliery closing in 1997. The last pits to close were Calverton (1999), Annesley (2000), Clipstone (2003), Harworth (2006), Welbeck (2010) and Thoresby (2015).

The sections above have given a history of the East Midlands mines. In this history, migration played an important role; many miners moved around in search of work, and particularly when mines were closed in Scotland and the north-east there was a significant movement to the East Midlands where jobs could still be found. An interesting feature of this movement is the possible effect that this might have had on the language miners used in their daily working life, as it was different around the country. Before we look at studies which examine different mining languages in section 2.6, it is worth considering further the movement of miners (in section 2.4) and the culture that makes up mining life (in section 2.5).

2.4 Mining migration

Due to mine closures around the country at different times, large-scale migration took place when miners and their families had to move for work (Waller 1983: 25). Some of this movement was to new colliery villages, other movement was to already existing cities, towns and villages. Some miners were probably attracted by family and friends who had already moved and word spread about where jobs could be found (Waller 1983: 36).

There was a large movement of miners from County Durham to Leicestershire in the 1830s (Bell 2007: 9). These miners and their families were first housed in tenements and then cottages in what later grew into the town of Coalville. This movement was followed in the 1960s by the miners from Scotland who came to settle in Leicestershire. Many of them settled in Thringstone, where you can still find the 'Rangers Supporters Club', named after the Glasgow football team.

In the early 1920s there was a large movement of miners from South Wales to Kirkby in Nottinghamshire (Griffin 1971a: 168). This was probably due to the new colliery villages being built east of Mansfield and the mines there needing more manpower. As well as this movement, there was also migration from the west side to the east side of the Nottinghamshire-Derbyshire coalfield; records show that migrants could both be from both short or long distances (Waller 1983: 38). For example, in Ollerton in North Nottinghamshire, about 75 per cent of migrant miners were from the close coalfields in West Nottinghamshire and over the county boundary in Derbyshire, whereas the remaining 25 per cent came from more distant coalfields. The newer collieries were further away from existing cities, towns and villages, and many houses had to be built for these workers and their families, resulting in new areas of residence built around the pit. A local pamphlet from Clipstone, a colliery village in North Nottinghamshire, suggested that while it may have been a Nottinghamshire mining village, miners also came from Derbyshire, Yorkshire, Northamptonshire, Suffolk, Gloucestershire, Cumberland and Staffordshire (Fareham, date unknown: 1). Not all of these new communities conformed immediately to the classic mining communities' stereotype of neighbourliness, and initial segregation could be found (Waller 1983: 50).

Waller has noted that miners could be distinguished by the way they dressed, their attitudes towards work, how they carried their water bottles or food, and by the way they spoke. He added:

> local isolation dies hard, the men bring with them their old customs and their old local outlook. To the Durham man and the South Wales man the Dukeries is still a passing haven. The melting pot is working slowly; no unity of feeling has yet been created. There is a Dukeries coalfield; there is as yet no Dukeries miner. (Waller 1983: 46)

Regardless of these differences, it seems that this strong sense of belonging and of being a miner runs through many narratives. However, the job of mining itself was only a part of what it meant to be a miner, and there were many other aspects of life.

2.5 Mining culture

As Louis Fenn commented in the journal *The Miner* around 1926:

> the typical mining village is grouped around the pit-head and has no reason for its existence except the requirements of the pit. It is inhabited almost entirely by miners and other grades of mineworkers ... the miners have for years been segregated from contact with other trades, and have become a specialised and peculiar folk, living their own lives and thinking their own thoughts ... the homogeneity of the mining village makes for an extraordinary cohesion. (Cited in Griffin 1990: 7)

Although obviously not all mining communities were homogeneous, this concept of a closely-knit community where much of life revolved around mining is something which is frequently reflected in the literature, and also in the interviews that we carried out as part of this pit talk project. Rita Sharpe, Coalfield Development Officer in Nottinghamshire Rural Community Council, commented: 'Coal is not just a commodity, it is a culture' (quoted by Franks 2001: 83). Power has stated that these tight-knit communities were often mobile as miners needed to move to retain their jobs. Mining was seen as a job for life but not necessarily in the same place (Power 2008: 162). In many communities, miners who may have come from different regions still had more in common with each other than they did with the communities that were already established there. Furthermore, miners were often seen by outsiders as 'a peculiar race' (Colls 1977: 54).

One of the most important features of a mining community was the Miners' Welfare Institute, which was involved in much of the community activities. It ran bowls, football, tennis, cricket and other games teams as well as brass bands and youth clubs (see also Simpson and Simmons 2019: 9). It often organised day trips and holidays and was a meeting point for miners and their families (see Figure 2.7). Griffin has noted that particularly in more isolated communities 'the welfare is central to the life of the community and is an indispensable institution' (Griffin 1977: 167). Lewis also believes that this sense of isolation shaped both personal attitudes and community development. For example, traditional music and folklore formed an important part of mining culture (see also Colls 1977: 53; Wales 2006: 127). Lewis has compared miners to sailors, soldiers and farmers. There are mythologies, superstitions and other traditional features which supported survival

Figure 2.7 Thoresby trip to Skegness (photo credit: Mansfield and Ashfield Chad)

and helped the miners through their difficult and dangerous everyday lives. The sense of camaraderie (which will be further discussed in Chapter 4) was crucial and miners had a very strong sense of solidarity, sometimes compared to soldiers in wartime (Freese 2003: 45). Mining education also formed an important part of this culture, both in formal and informal learning (see also Power 2008: 163). Day-release classes and other evening classes organised by the Miners' Welfare Joint Adult Education Committee were available to many (Griffin 1971a: 170). Historically, readings and religious activity had been part of some collieries' influences and were seen as ways in which miners could be educated (see Williams 1962: 81). Other aspects of life which latterly influenced mining culture, mainly after the First World War, included housing, as some of the houses built for miners in pit villages in the East Midlands had hot and cold running water and large gardens and were regarded as some of the best examples of mining housing in the UK (Franks 2001: 20). Williams has also noted that these houses 'may seem ugly now but at the time they were much better than the older back-to-back housing supplied to miners' (Williams 1962: 443) and they very different to 'the hovels' referred to in the Children's Employment Commission in 1942 (A. R. Griffin 1981: picture 65).

The restructuring and final end of the coal industry cast a dark shadow over the future of mining communities and for many 'the coal mining regions and localities were seen as amongst the last remaining bastions of support for labourism and the collectivist values of social democracy' (Hudson and

Sadler 1990: 635). High unemployment has led to areas of high deprivation; a report has shown that Ashfield and Mansfield are joint 413th out of a possible 438 for average household income (Beatty et al. 2019). This had a particularly high impact on mining as 'no industry centres itself in the middle of a community like mining' (Power 2008: 160). The disappearance of this industry raises huge questions about the well-being of the communities that depended on it, financially and otherwise (Beatty et al. 2019: 8). One of the slogans during the 1984–1985 strike was 'Close a Pit: Close a Community' (Shaw 2012: 49). These feelings continue, as the mine was 'believed to be a living, breathing force of life' (Shaw 2012: 118), and it was felt that communities would cease to exist, either with miners having to move or to remain jobless in the former industrial hubs, as the locations of pit villages affect where former miners can work (Lewis 1971: 29; Coates and Barratt Brown 1997: 29).

So it is clear that mining communities have or had a culture of their own and that is something that is reflected in language. Moreover, a specialised job requires its own specialised language and the next section considers some of the research which has been carried out on different mining languages, both throughout the UK and worldwide.

2.6 Mining language

As stated above, for many years coal mining formed a crucial part of local economies and employment, and the pit talk used by miners was an important aspect of local cultural identity and community cohesion. Despite research on the life and language of miners in other regions (Douglass 1973; Forster 1969; Griffiths 2007), the mining language used by miners in the East Midlands has not received any academic attention.

Dent has noted that the coal mining industry is 'the only non-agricultural and urban industry to have been studied dialectologically' (Dent 2013: 118) and has referred to the work that Wright (1972) carried out in this field, which is very valuable and gives us much information, but more work is needed to examine in more detail the variation found around the different coal mining regions. Lewis has said that, 'Immediately one starts to study coal-mining history it is not only apparent that a glossary of terms is needed but also that regional differences make generalisations extremely dangerous' (Lewis 1971: ix), and Wright has added that a 'bewildering variety of answers' can be elicited when discussing regional variation (1972: 43).

Much research into mining in the East Midlands has reviewed specific events or memories but it has not focused on language usage (Bell 2008). There are examples of individuals who have been collecting mining vocabulary in the region (such as the research carried out by Bob Bradley, a member of the Bilsthorpe Mining Heritage Group), but as yet there has been no research published on pit talk in this area. The work on pit talk which has been undertaken was frequently not carried out by linguists and my research is the first detailed linguistic study of this variation. Further, while much linguistic work on language variation focuses on social categories such as age, gender, sexuality and ethnicity, my work also concentrates on the link between language and the workplace.

The coal mining regions around the UK tend to show some similar patterns of development. Paterson has noted that:

> Mining communities were close-knit environments breeding a distinctive tribal culture. Along with the job of mining itself, often passing down the generations from grandfather to son and from son to grandson, so too was handed down the collective history and folk-tales: of tragedies and triumphs, betrayals and loyalties, victories and defeats, socially, industrially and politically. (Paterson 2014: 17)

Some mining districts were real strongholds for traditional dialect features (Beal 1993: 189) and some of these features show patterns of non-standard variation that are not likely to be found in nearby cities. Miners often belonged to more established networks, and such networks may not have been easily penetrated by innovative language forms (Ju. Robinson 2012: 50). However, many miners had to move for their work (for more detail see section 2.4) and this could also have affected their language, as they may have used different terms for the same objects, processes or job descriptions (Wright 1972: 49).

There is a history of the 'difference' of coal miners and their language. In his travels around Britain in the early eighteenth century, the English writer Daniel Defoe described a miner he spoke to in Derbyshire:

> First, the man was a most uncouth spectacle; he was cloathed all in leather, had a cap of the same without brims, some tools in a little basket which he drew up with him, not one of the names of which we could understand but by the help of an interpreter. Nor indeed could we understand any of the man's discourse so as to make out a whole sentence; and yet the man was pretty free of his tongue too. (Defoe, Letter 8, from the Peak District, for details see https://www.visionofbritain.org.uk/travellers/Defoe/30)

Wright has also said that miners are 'rather a race apart' (Wright 1972: 49) and Wales has stated that the language of miners from the north-east was 'almost unintelligible to outsiders' (Wales 2006: 124). These descriptions suggest that this local dialect is different to other local varieties and Wales has added that this is the perfect 'breeding ground' for an 'anti-language' (Wales 2006: 125).

As coal mining changed over the years and became more mechanised, the language used by miners changed too, but this change was influenced by local factors, resulting in the usage of different terms in different areas (see also Wright 1972: 48). Despite the National Coal Board's attempt to standardise terms in 1947, much variation continued to exist, although a lot of it is now under threat. Writing about north-east coalfields, Bill Griffiths (2007) has said that it is with urgency that we must collect all data held about pit language from the individuals who still have memories of it, as the time of the coalfields is over and the data will soon be lost to us forever. So, mining has created a unique and now endangered lexicon, which differs from region to region, and from village to village, with the same word meaning different things to different people (see for example Douglass 1973; Forster 1969; Griffiths 2007). The use of a different language – pit talk – emphasised and strengthened the comradeship (which many miners during the interviews refer to as *camaraderie* and a *brotherhood*) which existed amongst mining people. This pit talk is now in danger of disappearing. However, language is an important aspect of who we are, where we come from and what we value (Douglas 2017: 136). Wright noted in 1972 that at that time mining language was still vigorous and closely attached to particular areas, but that 'the writing is on the wall, and so, in this rapidly changing world, it would well repay the linguist to study coal-mining language while he may still do so' (Wright 1972: 49). In fact, as Wales has stated, this kind of work is needed now as much as agricultural varieties need to be examined in the nineteenth century (Wales 2006: 126–127).

2.6.1 Studies which refer to mining language in the East Midlands

What studies exist which examine mining language in the East Midlands? Some of the language covered in these works will be discussed in Chapter 4 alongside the data from my miners as well as in the final chapter. Bell, in his books on the memories of the Derbyshire, Leicestershire and Nottinghamshire coalfields (2006, 2007, 2008 respectively), has included a glossary in each of the books explaining particular mining terminology. As one of the miners interviewed by Bell has said, 'There was a lot of different names at the pit, and also for the tools that we used. And each pit had its own vocabulary' (Bell 2006: 110). The guide *British Coalmining* produced by British Coal (1989) also contains a glossary at the end to explain the terms used throughout. Carr's *Tales from the Mines* (1990) and Carswell and Robert's (1992) *Getting the Coal* also include glossaries to describe the words used in the stories, while books such as *Nottinghamshire Miners' Tales* (Franks 2001) and *A Nottinghamshire Pitman's Story* (Coleman 2017) contain much local mining vocabulary but no glossary. There also exist locally produced pamphlets and projects which include oral histories of local miners, and through these language usage can be examined. For example, the Friends of Thringstone group has two publications which centre around the collection of oral history interviews in the region, *Scottish in Thringstone* (2013) and *Memories of Durham Miners* (2014). These projects were carried out in conjunction with the East Midlands Oral History Archive (which had received funding to carry out work on 'migration stories') entitled 'Moving South', and which aimed to document the moving miners and collect their stories for their families and future generations.

There are dialect literature books from the East Midlands which refer to miners, their culture and their language. Dialect literature refers to texts, usually short guides, which may include discussions of local language and have considerable portions written in the local dialect, and these are often aimed at a local audience (see Honeybone and Watson 2013: 312). They can preserve and record specific dialects (Beal 2009: 140) and, as such, they contain much metalinguistic commentary. Dialect literature is seen as an acceptable source of data to examine language variation (see Honeybone and Watson 2013: 315; Miethaner 2000: 534). These works often have a humorous focus and their aim is to entertain, although considerable linguistic analysis can be carried out using such texts. In the East Midlands, both *The Notts Natter* (1979) and *The Derbyshire Drawl* (1975) refer to local coal miners and their language. These little handbooks were both written by Peter Wright, who was one of the *SED* fieldworkers and an academic linguist, so although dialect literature is usually targeted at a popular audience it still can be informed by credible linguistic research. *The Notts Natter* includes a section on 'wok language' (work language) which includes a section on coal mining (Wright 1979: 13). A small amount of vocabulary is given to describe some common words around the work processes involved in the job. *The Derbyshire Drawl* contains different vocabulary on useful phrases to be used in the coal mining industry (Wright 1975: 13–15) and also notes that, 'Students of grammar and phonetics will observe from this glossary that mining (like farming) clings very much to older ways of speech' (Wright 1975: 14). A further publication by Wright will be discussed in section 2.6.2.

Another dialect literature publication which touches on the local mining industry is *Ey Up Mi Duck!* which covers the dialect of Derbyshire and the East Midlands (Scollins and Titford 2000). This publication looks in some detail at phonetic features of East Midlands pronunciation but also touches on local traditions and practices. One such section (Scollins and Titford 2000: 50) is entitled 'A Trip Dairn T'Pit' and includes a description of a typical coal shift, written in local dialect, as well as the changing appearance of local colliers in 1877, 1900, 1930 and 1977, describing typical clothing worn by these miners. There are also examples of local poetry which deal with the lives of local miners. In addition to these examples of dialect literature, some research which examines the coal mining industry includes local words (see for example Griffin 1971b, for instance: 28, 51, 63; A. R. Griffin 1981) as well as glossaries (Griffin 1977). There are also examples of websites such as Healey Hero (http://www.healeyhero.co.uk/rescue/menu.htm) which include historical information about the mines of the East Midlands and the vocabulary used by these former miners. Another place where mining vocabulary can be found is in fictional works, for example by authors such as D. H. Lawrence whose books and poems frequently include pit talk given that his works are centred around mining communities in the Derbyshire/Nottinghamshire region.

2.6.2 Studies which refer to mining language around the UK

In a similar vein to the East Midlands work covered in section 2.6.1, there are books which contain mining stories and tales and which contain glossaries to assist readers in understanding language they may not have come across before, such as Hollows's (2010) *Voices in the Dark: Pony Talk and Mining Tales* which tells of miners' lives. There are a small number of miners' dictionaries (Hooson, originally 1747, republished in 1979) which explain mining terms without a particular regional focus. However, the majority of publications focus on a particular mining region and discuss language used by the miners in that area. Forster (1969) has produced a survey of terms used by miners in the South Midlands, although no further details are given about which mining areas are included in this region. This book contains a general introduction to variation in mining language and mainly consists of dictionary-style entries on mining terms. These contain examples of regions which use specific terms, such as Coventry or South Derbyshire. Forster has explained that 'their language will reflect their identity and their way of life' (Forster 1969: 1). He has also referred to the fact that miners are men apart and that they have developed their own language. The meanings of the words in Foster's book were discussed by the miners, who sometimes commented that meanings could be vague and that they were not always sure what certain words meant. The book also notes the extensive movement of miners throughout the years and states that miners could either continue using their own language or adapt to a new variety. Forster also discusses the effects of mechanisation and standardisation on miners' language and argues that miners were reluctant to 'relinquish' their own words (Forster 1969: 6).

One publication by Wright (1972) is a more academic publication than that considered in section 2.6.1 and it considers coal mining language in the UK more widely. For this study, Wright has applied a dialect questionnaire to gather information about the different vocabulary used by miners around the country and has discussed the findings of these questionnaires, examining variation between regions. Wright has noted that many have warned of the difficulties of tracing mining dialect patterns because of the 'frequent and large-scale exchange of miners and mining words between coalfields' (Wright 1972: 32–34). Wright also notes that the NCB's attempted standardisation was not successful and miners continued using their own lexical varieties (Wright 1972: 44). He has added that linguistic problems began when miners moved to different coalfields and used different terms, but he does also say that these words were very important to miners and helped shape their identity, particularly in relation to those not in mining.

An article by Hornsby (2018) has examined new dialects in mining villages in East Kent. The majority of this article focuses on the new contact variety which has arisen as a result of miners coming from across the country to work in this relatively new coalfield. It investigates use of the BATH/TRAP and FOOT/STRUT vowels, as well as the vowels in NURSE, SQUARE and GOAT. As many of the miners had come from Northern England and the Midlands, the study examines to what extent these northern varieties have survived in this new environment. There are a very small number of dialectal words given by the miners and these tended not to occur during spontaneous speech, but as examples of local speech. The main two were *snap* (food) and *jitty* (alleyway), both of which have an East Midlands origin. It is interesting that Wright has stated earlier (1972: 34) that an official who had worked in Kent's mines for sixteen years commented that there was no such thing as Kent dialect while at the same time the Kent Area of the NUM brought out its own glossary of pit terms in 1965.

The largest amount of work on this subject seems to have been carried out on the language of the north-eastern miners. Both Douglass (1973) and Griffiths (2007) have examined what Griffiths has referred to as 'pitmatic'. Wales (2006) has also commented on pitmatic in her work on northern English. She has written, 'What has been traditionally known in the Northeast as *pitmatic* (first noted by Heslop, 1892, as a jocular term) and used until the decline of the coal industry from the 1980s, is in general terms a broad local Durham or Northumberland vernacular' (Wales 2006: 124). She has added that it is conservative in phonology, conservative in the preservation of old Scandinavian words and 'is overlaid with distinctive occupation terms' (Wales 2006: 124). She has also noted that relatively little work has been carried out on this variety. Some examples are given of this 'anti-language' (Wales 2006: 125) and the explanation that it is almost unintelligible to outsiders. Pearce has also alluded to pitmatic in his perceptual dialectological research on the north-east of England, and although no vocabulary is discussed he has noted that this name was coined in the nineteenth century to describe the craft and technicalities of coal mining and was therefore used also to describe the specialist vocabulary and speech of colliery workers (Pearce 2009: 177), with several participants in the study commenting on the distinctive language of miners. Devlin (2014), who was mentioned in section 1.8, has also commented on the term pitmatic and some of its traditional features, including intonation and lexis.

Douglass (1973) has structured his work on County Durham in a similar way to Forster's study of the South Midlands. This work starts with a detailed introduction to the culture and lifestyle of miners, including song and dress, as well as the movement of miners and the effect this had on the language. According to Douglass, 'It is totally artificial to try and separate dialect, life and humour one from another; they are all directly linked and part of a group feeling, a communal bond which loses much of it's [sic] effect away from work, hence the difficulty in trying to explain it here' (1973: 7). The second half of the book is a glossary which gives very detailed descriptions, with examples, of words used in the pits. Short extracts of songs are sometimes supplied to further describe this vocabulary. More recent work on the variety has been carried out by Griffiths (2007), which includes chapters on the features of mines above and below ground, the different people who worked there, the work practices, and a chapter on everyday terms. All chapters include sections of glossaries to explain the words that were relevant to the workers. Griffiths has noted that little work has been done on this dialect (and this also applies to other regions) despite the fact that there is a wealth of data available through word lists and poems as well as public and private collections. Griffiths has argued that this language needs to be collected before those who use it have gone and we have no way of going back.

Some work has also been undertaken on Yorkshire varieties of pit talk. Dennis et al. (1969) carried out an analysis of a Yorkshire mining community and in this they describe particular occupations underground using mining terminology. In addition, Redmonds (2016) has carried out a study of the vocabulary of coal mining in Yorkshire between 1250 and 1850. Redmonds notes that there are records of mining language over the years but that it can be very hard to examine words used in earlier periods as 'generations of miners worked in close-knit communities and left few written records' (Redmonds 2016: 5). After a short introduction about early coal mining in Yorkshire, the majority of this publication is a glossary which gives very detailed explanations of words, adding the primary sources and attestations of such usage as well as some images to accompany the words. Finally, Cave (2001) has carried out research with a South Yorkshire mining community and although much of the focus is around nicknames, teasing and the telling of stories, there is also extensive information about the phonology, morphology and lexis of his mining community and how this language is very closely tied to a sense of local belonging and identity.

2.6.3 Studies which refer to mining language around the world

The main source of studies which have examined mining languages around the world comes in a special issue of *International Journal of the Sociology of Language* in 2019, entitled 'Language in the Mines' and edited by Leonie Cornips and Pieter Muysken. In the introduction, we read that 'All over the world the language practices surrounding mining activities pose a particular challenge for sociolinguistics, since mining activities create a number of very specific social ecological circumstances' (Cornips and Muysken 2019: 1). The migration of miners is treated as a particular concept of importance as new language varieties coming together for a particular purpose can affect language usage. The articles in this volume frequently focus on code-mixing, code-switching, linguistic borrowing, having to speak the language of other speakers, and considering language choices. This can result in linguistic innovations which change language usage. This particular special issue focuses on mining locations in Africa, Northern Europe and South America. Mesthrie (2019) has focused on the language of Fanakola in South Africa, which is a special register of technical terms used in the mining industry with sources in Zulu, English and Afrikaans and which has been in use since 1867. This pidgin is seen as a way of allowing work to be performed but also as 'a tool of domination and a ceiling for upward mobility' (Mesthrie 2019: 16), although more recently it was used by miners as their language of preference by strikers. Some lexical characteristics are described as are examples of Fanakola being used in official written mining communications.

In the second article, Cornips and de Rooij have compared the effects of language contact processes in two mining areas, the African Katanga region (now the Democratic Republic of Congo) and Heerlen in the south-east of the Netherlands. Both areas had to recruit miners from outside to cope with demand. The article examines the effect of these multilingual speakers on the mining languages used for work, and it focuses on the regularisation of grammatical properties and the expansion of aspect marking. New linguistic varieties 'took on strong indexical values of professional pride and solidary, as well as local price and community belonging' (Cornips and de Rooij 2019: 65).

A variety used in a geographically close place to the Heerlen communities has been examined by Pecht, who focuses on a linguistic variety called 'Cité Duits' spoken by coal miners in Belgian Limburg, many of whom came from Eastern Europe. Features of this variety are a fusion of southern Dutch, German and the Maaslands dialect spoken in the area. Pecht's findings show that the features found in this variety can be encountered in the contact languages, but it also contains structures that are entirely new and others that are hybrid or mixed (Pecht 2019: 72). Pecht has stated that this code (which locals would not be able to understand) strengthened a feeling of belonging, and the disappearance of the mining industry meant a loss of mining culture and mining life.

In another Belgian study, Marzo (2019) has examined the effects of language issues Italian mine workers encountered when they arrived in Flanders. Marzo's study does not simply focus on the original miners who arrived in the region in the 1960s but also on how their linguistic practices were used by second- and third-generation miners' children to link them to the city of Genk. Language was used as a sense of belonging, not just as miners, but as inhabitants of an area.

Moving on to South America, Muysken (2019) has studied the multilingual setting of the silver mines in Bolivia and the relations between Spanish, Quechua and Aymara. In this region, a separate code with specialised vocabulary developed in the mines which resulted in a language of the mines being written in 1610 to cope with the different native languages of the miners working there. Muysken has stated that with such a diverse background, 'innovation is even more important to provide a shared vocabulary' (Muysken 2019: 129). This article examines language mixing, for example, the use of nominalising suffixes across different languages.

The final article stays in South America. Álvarez López (2019) has analysed specific vocabulary to investigate the existence of a mining language spoken by descendants of Africans in Brazil by examining lexical items in specific semantic domains that could be related to mining activities. She has examined the possible etymology of these words, considering that this was a mining region where miners of various origins came to work. In a final contribution, Pietikäinen has noted how all of these studies show how frequently multilingualism had to be managed in the mines and how language could be used to express a sense of belonging (Pietikäinen 2019: 171–172).

These studies have all shown that language does make up an important part of what it meant to be a miner, and this has also been found by Power, who has written in her study that 'Language emerged as a key area of heritage that needed to be identified and preserved' (Power 2008: 174). Furthermore, physical spaces are important to people and their language, as suggested by Britain (2000, 2013) who notes that physical spaces are socially constructed and experienced thereby given meaning as places by speakers which can affect linguistic behaviour. This is important when people come together from a wide variety of places. 'When miners from different areas meet, using different terms for the same idea, there is usually no language barrier because the idea is common to their occupations, and each miner retains his own terms. However, when they move permanently to other coalfields, confusion over technical terms can sometimes cause accidents' (Wright 1972: 48–49).

This means that a coal miner can use language to adopt a stance belonging to such a specific group or community. This has also been discussed by Devlin et al. (2019) who have shown that when speakers discuss particular topics, such as coal mining, their linguistic forms can change, resulting in these forms reflecting a specific local identity; not just the place, but also the fact that they are miners. My own research project specifically examines the words used by coal miners as part of their daily lives and reviews whether these vary throughout the East Midlands. The examination of which words were used, how they changed and whether local miners perceived differences with miners who came into the region will be discussed in Chapter 4. Before that, Chapter 3 describes in detail the methodology used in this project for data collection and analysis.

3 Methodology

3.1 Introduction

The information in this book builds on the research conducted as part of my pit talk projects, which will be described in detail in this chapter. These were funded by Nottingham Trent University and also by the British Academy. I have carried out other work with coal miners and the arts as well as work on community engagement but these will not be discussed here. This chapter discusses the methodology used in the projects which have allowed for the data collection that forms the basis of this book.

As part of my research on general language variation in the East Midlands, I have interviewed local people to collect conversational data which allow me to examine different linguistic features. As the East Midlands falls between the salient 'north' vs. 'south' distinction in England, I was curious whether such speakers used particular vowel sounds associated with either region or that were part of a transition zone, for example, producing intermediate or fudged varieties of the FOOT/STRUT and BATH/TRAP vowels. Furthermore, I also investigated features such as yod-dropping, velar nasal plus, as well as the happY and lettER vowels. This research has suggested that the East Midlands does have distinctive linguistic features which make it a recognisable dialect area, such as continued yod-dropping following several phones such as /t/, /d/, /st/ and /n/. Some of these features are distinctly northern, such as the short BATH vowel. There are linguistic features which appear to be changing due to novel forms occurring in the region and we can see new linguistic forms, such as /ɛ/ in happY words being increasingly used by younger speakers (for more details see Braber and Flynn 2015; Braber and Robinson 2018). Furthermore, when examined in more detail, it seems that other features are also in a process of change. Regarding the FOOT/STRUT vowels, we have established that the changes do not concern the increasing distance between FOOT and STRUT as expected, but mainly FOOT-fronting in Leicestershire and Nottinghamshire and STRUT-retraction in Derbyshire, which seems to be leading to an increase in overlap between FOOT and STRUT in all three counties (for more details see Jansen and Braber 2020).

Methodology

At the same time, I was interested in comparing the linguistic features described in dialect literature of the East Midlands and comparing this to literary dialect set in the region to see whether these descriptions matched (for more details see Braber 2020). This work also included an examination of lexical items which were used to symbolise the East Midlands and this work resulted in a non-academic publication on Nottinghamshire dialect (Braber 2015).

During the interviews, there were several references to coal mining in the region: how miners were an important part of the region's population and that their language was distinctive. One interviewee said that her grandfather had been a coal miner and had 'his own language'. I found this idea of a coal mining language intriguing and decided to carry out further research into the issue. Through internet searching, I noted that there were websites and books examining the life and language of miners in the north-east of England, North and South Wales, Scotland, Staffordshire and other countries such as Canada – and that these were referred to as being a 'unique and bewildering terminology' (Fox 2012: 92). But there was no published research on the East Midlands and only a small number of web resources linked to this topic. As discussed in Chapter 2, coal mining was an important aspect of the local economy and employed many workers, so I thought this would be an interesting avenue for further investigation. This initial work was funded internally by Nottingham Trent University as part of a funding programme to encourage undergraduate students to work as part of research projects. This started in the summer of 2014 with Alice Cope and Christopher Dann who were second-year undergraduate linguistics students, and we began by looking for miners to interview. Alice was the daughter of a former miner who was very keen to talk about his life in the mine and more than happy to suggest former colleagues, which gave us wider access to local miners to start the project.

The interest expressed in the project was immediately overwhelming. From 'story of the week' on the Nottingham Trent University web page, within two weeks the project was mentioned on ITV news, BBC local radio, BBC news online, teletext and local newspapers and leaflets. As a result, we were inundated with miners who wanted to take part and organisations who were interested in mining and preserving mining memorabilia but had not considered language. This also led to the initial contact with mining heritage groups around the region who were to be of invaluable help in recruiting miners and providing places to record interviews, as miners frequently met there for social events.

This preliminary work on the project found that the language used by miners differed in the East Midlands (within the region and compared to other coal communities). However, this highlighted the need for further research in order to identify, classify and record the words used and to critically examine their contribution to identity. Further funding followed from the British Academy Small Grant programme. The project's aims were widened to bring together the words spoken by miners of the East Midlands in order to preserve a dying dialect. The funding allowed us to employ two research assistants (Claire Ashmore and Suzy Harrison, both PhD students at the time at Sheffield Hallam University and Nottingham Trent University respectively). They conducted additional interviews and we extended our range of interviews, particularly in the Derbyshire and Leicestershire regions. This accommodated an examination into how the mining vocabulary had related to the wider language of the region and had been incorporated in a literature of story and song. The interviews are discussed in more detail in section 3.4.

The project resulted in a non-academic publication (Braber et al. 2017) and much outreach work with heritage groups and coal mining heritage groups, including a celebration event held at Nottingham Trent University and attended by many of the miners who had taken part in our interviews. Following this project more interviews were carried out (which will also be discussed in section 3.4). In the additional interviews the focus was on the most experienced miners, those who had worked for a particularly long time within the coal mining industry. The extra interviews were all carried out with two or three miners together to encourage discussion and debate. They were also conducted by a former miner, Dr David Amos, which had its advantages and disadvantages (see section 3.6.1). A final round of additional interviews was curtailed by the COVID-19 pandemic. Instead, postal questionnaires were mailed out to a final group of miners to complete data collection (these will be discussed in section 3.5).

As a result, this study applied three main methods to collecting the data: first, interviews conducted by linguists and heritage specialists with individual formers coal miners around the East Midlands, which discussed mining terminology; second, interviews by a former miner with small groups of former miners; and, third, a written questionnaire sent to former coal miners around the East Midlands. This methodology was used to determine the levels of knowledge of particular lexical items of the coal mining industry. Finally, we compared and analysed the collected data to data from other available sources – including other mining research, both in and outwith the region. Both interviews and questionnaires are part of many dialectological and sociolinguistic variationist studies. The first set of interviews also used an additional resource to add to the lexical data collection through the use of Sense Relation Networks (SRNs) (i.e. Llamas 1999). All of these methods together have allowed for the fullest amount of data collection which can also be used by future studies. Many of these miners are now elderly and this knowledge, which has now been recorded, can be used to document this disappearing lexicon.

Some of the earliest work I did was to put together some of these initial words so that they could be accessed by a wider audience, for example in the already mentioned book (Braber et al. 2017), but also through a website

Methodology

(https://coalanddialect.wixsite.com/coaldialect) which included the 'word of the week' feature that focused on words used in the interviews as well as extracts of interviews. This stage of the project was funded by the British Academy. As well as a short dictionary-style list of words used by coal miners, the second half of the book contained extracts of interviews about some of the most prominent subjects of the interviews, such as the life of miners, mining camaraderie, danger and working conditions and tools and equipment. These descriptions allowed us to present the words in actual context and show how they were used by the miners. As Adams has discussed, dictionary entries can allow for analysis of particular words in a sociolinguistics style (Adams 2014: 171). For example, the headword can be followed by information about variant forms, etymology, lexical category information, restrictive labels, definitions and sense analysis in cases of polysemy – all very relevant information for a sociolinguistic study.

As Upton has noted (2013: 180), words are not easy to collect and codify once collected; however, there are ways of ensuring spontaneous usage can be captured. For instance, by avoiding formal interviews and collecting in 'informally-delivered language' (Upton 2013: 181), words can be collected if the interview is structured sufficiently to allow particular words to be discussed – which is harder than for phonetic or morpho-syntactic patterns that can be collected relatively easily. Using the SRNs (discussed in section 3.4.1) allows for words to be collected specifically but in an informal way, which may be less problematic than the more formal SED-style questionnaire that took a long time to collect data. In fact, in the *Voices* project it was found that participants were very enthusiastic in producing many informal words following prompts (Upton 2013: 182).

For many years, sociolinguists have been using the interview as an effective tool of collecting data on different linguistic features (starting with Labov's work on New York and Martha's Vineyard in the 1960s). Being able to control the topic is crucial. If a topic does not come up during the interview, then the words associated with a particular semantic domain will not be used. Additionally, style-shifting due to the perceived formality of an interview can also affect the language collected (see Pearce 2020: 490). Pearce has added to this that corpora tend not to be good places to collect dialect data as they appear very infrequently, regardless of the frequency and traditional dialect corpora are not readily available. Pearce has used the internet and in particular web forums as an arena to collect dialect words, for example the web forum 'Ready To Go', for fans of Sunderland AFC to examine disappearing dialect lexis. He has shown that the dialect word 'plodge', which does not figure in large corpora of English nor even in specialised English dialect corpora, appears widely in this forum (Pearce 2020). This tells us that words which may look as if they are no longer in use can be found if we mine suitable resources. Unfortunately, such fora are not available for coal mining vocabulary. Therefore, other printed sources have to be used for comparison.

As well as discussing in detail the interviews and questionnaires in sections 3.4 and 3.5, this chapter also explains the sub-divisions within the lexis which will be used in Chapter 4. This includes words used for specific tools, job descriptions, equipment, dangers within the mine, names for different shafts in and out of the mine, and names that miners used to refer to each other (see section 3.5).

3.2 Sources

There have been other collections of pit talk in the UK. For the north-east see Douglass (1973) and Griffiths (2007). Yorkshire mining language is covered by Redmonds (2016). Forster (1969) is concerned with the South Midlands (see section 2.6 for a discussion of these books). The use of these collections allows comparisons between different varieties of pit talk to investigate the particular language used in the East Midlands. After nationalisation in 1947, the National Coal Board attempted to standardise mining terminology across the country, but anecdotal evidence shows that miners avoided this standard, with many miners preferring to continue using local terms. Where possible, comparison with other linguistic mining communities (for example the north-east and Yorkshire) is made to examine to what extent lexical items were transferred by the movement of miners in these regions.

I also draw on other sources which have collected mining vocabulary from the region. Most of these sources are not specifically about East Midlands mining language. The National Coal Mining Museum has a very short introduction to mining words, which states that mining terminology varies around the country, but only a handful of examples are given. Another short introduction is included on Wikipedia, but this does not focus on regional terms or outline where terms may be used. A useful website, Healey Hero, contains information about mining fatalities and history. This very detailed work on mining history has been produced by Dr Robert Bradley, a retired mining surveyor and mining historian (the details of the full nine-volume history produced by Bob can be found on this website and is also held by the British Library. Bob received an honorary doctorate from the University of Nottingham for this work in 2019). It contains a glossary of useful words and the website references other mining language resources which are not limited to the East Midlands (links to all of these resources can be found in the web resources section which appears after the references at the end of this book).

Other sources which can be accessed include online glossaries, many of which come from Northern America, such as the Anglo-American list of terminology and a Canadian version produced by the Canadian government. There is also an online list of Scots mining terms, which have been taken from work from 1886. Additional sites include references to terms used in Welsh mining and the Forest of Dean as well as Geordie terms. Finally, some books on mining heritage contain short glossaries (these are discussed in section 2.6).

One of the sources I used was the work carried out by Peter Wright in mining communities during the 1950s. When Wright started work as a supply teacher in a mining region, he noticed that the people who lived in such regions were using linguistic forms that were very different from Standard English. He decided 'that there was a great knowledge of mining terms and interest in them waiting to be tapped' (Wright 1972: 32). Wright has also mentioned that many thought that the frequent movements of coal miners would make such a study impossible, and he has noted that linguistic problems would start when miners from different coalfields communicated. Wright devised a questionnaire and collected data in the 1960s from fifteen different sections in the English, Scottish and Welsh coalfields. He tried only to collect data from elderly or middle-aged men, but a small number of younger men were interviewed. The questionnaire was devised on the lines of the *SED* and data was collected from direct conversations and fieldwork in different locations, such as miners' homes, down the pit, in a village hall and in a miners' hospital. Over time, some of the questionnaire items were dropped as they did not produce any interesting results. However, all questions can be found in Wright (1972: 35–38). I used a number of these items at the end of my questionnaire to allow for comparative work and these will be discussed in the final chapter.

3.3 Participants

Interviews with a variety of miners from the different mining communities around the East Midlands were needed to examine to what extent there were local differences between Nottinghamshire, Derbyshire and Leicestershire, as well as to investigate the differences between language used in the East Midlands and other mining regions in the UK. This involved different methods of contacting potential participants. As outlined in section 3.1, already at the very beginning of the project we were gaining much public interest through local media and word of mouth. That gave us many initial contacts which, combined with the fact that many of these mining regions had long been very close-knit communities, helped us greatly. Also, through contacts at four main coal mining heritage groups (Bilsthorpe Heritage Museum and Bestwood Winding Engine House in Nottinghamshire, Pleasley Pit Trust for North Derbyshire, South Derbyshire Mining Preservation Groups for South Derbyshire, and Leicestershire and Coalville Heritage Society for Leicestershire) we were able to make good use of their extended networks to get in touch with miners and invite them to take part in this project. Applying the method of 'snowball sampling' (see for example Milroy 1987) allowed the miners we recruited to suggest others to take part in the study.

The people we spoke to were all active or former miners. When the study started, the last remaining mine in the region was still working in Thoresby and we visited it for a day. However, most of those interviewed were no longer working as miners and there was much variation among the miners regarding where they had worked, how long they had worked in the mines, how long ago they had worked in the mines and how much contact they still had with former colleagues. We also attempted to ask women to take part in the study, but they were very reluctant as they felt 'they had nothing to say and that this had been the men's work'. We did manage to include two women who were willing to take part. One of them had worked in the mining canteen and the other was the wife of a miner and agreed to be interviewed alongside her husband. Full details of all the interviews are given in section 3.4 below.

3.4 Interviews

The interviews were set out in such a way that similar data could be collected, while keeping the situation more like an informal chat than a formal interview.

The information provided here is based on a qualitative linguistic and content analysis of interviews and questionnaires. The interviews consisted of sociolinguistic interviews recorded with individual miners (mainly Nottinghamshire and some Leicestershire), the participation of one mining heritage group (Derbyshire) and one visit to miners working in Thoresby. This stage of the project formed a pilot study that confirmed that there was indeed a distinct mining lexicon and that this varied from pit to pit. In the second stage of the project, we interviewed more miners, spread among the three counties (see Table 3.1 for the overall numbers for both projects). For the final set, we interviewed an additional twenty-two miners for more in-depth interviews to follow up on some of the initial findings (see Table 3.1 for the overall numbers for the interviews, with the pilot numbers included with the interviews conducted as part of the British Academy funding).

Table 3.1 shows that throughout all stages of the project there have been more interviews with miners from Nottinghamshire than Derbyshire and Leicestershire. Although we had links with miners throughout the East Midlands, the majority are based in Nottinghamshire. This could be a result of the fact that the mines in Nottinghamshire were open longer than in Derbyshire and Leicestershire and so there were more miners based in that region. In the interviews, we did ask miners about terms used in other mines in the East Midlands to find out if they were aware of local differences (this will be discussed in detail in Chapter 4).

The interviews were conducted in the location of the miner's choice – either at home, at their current place of work, at a mining heritage centre or at the university. In all of these locations, the interviews were carried out in a private and quiet area, where interruptions or distractions were less likely. With all of

Table 3.1 Number of miners involved with both projects

	Pilot project/British Academy funded project	Additional interviews
Nottinghamshire	26 (including one group interview at Thoresby)	12
Derbyshire	13 (including one group interview with a mining heritage group)	7
Leicestershire	9	3

the interviewees, we talked about their experiences of being a miner as well as 'pit talk'. The first set of interviews was carried out either by me or by the research assistants (Alice Cope and Christopher Dann in the early stages, and Claire Ashmore and Suzy Harrison in the later stages). The second set was carried out by David Amos. The first set of interviews were carried out with only one miner, others with two, depending on the preference of the miners (and there were also two sets of group interviews). The second set of interviews were all carried out with two or three miners. All interviews followed a general outline of topics, but miners were able to lead the conversation.

This type of interview is a standard aspect of many sociolinguistic studies (see for example Milroy and Gordon 2003). In our project, we asked all miners similar questions but were also led by the miners themselves as some had more information about certain aspects, due to their experience or memories. While encouraging a free flow of conversation, we also made use of predetermined questions as reference points (for example, by using Sense Relation Networks (SRNs), originally used by Llamas 1999; however, these were tailored to pit talk, see Figures 3.1 and 3.2 below). We also used specific word lists to allow consistency of data capture across the geographic area, so that valid comparisons could be drawn (see also Adams 2014: 168). As these miners were of different ages and worked in a range of pits, our data allowed us to look at language variation over time in a specific community. Asking for descriptions helped us to clarify the meanings of words and give context to the lexical items. Chapter 4 gives supporting quotes around these words, as these can convey cultural as well as semantic information (Adams 2014: 169).

Miners were given an SRN in advance of the interview (see below, section 3.4.1) to give them time to consider terms they may not have used for a number of years. Interviews were very informal and started with some general background information about the former miner, where he had worked and what he had done in the mines. This scenario ensured that all interviews took place in a casual and friendly atmosphere and allowed a relaxed conversation to take place. All informants were given some background information about the project and signed a consent form giving permission for their data and recordings to be used as part of future work. Interviews were recorded on a

Sony 4GB PX Series MP3 IC Digital Voice Recorder ICD-PX333 and lasted between thirty minutes and two hours, with the majority of interviews being just over an hour long.

This general background information about the (former) miner, where he had worked and what he had done in the mines, was necessary to find out where the miners were from and where they had worked but it also helped the miners to settle into the interview and overcome any initial nerves. They were asked their names, when and where they had been born, when they had started mining, what jobs they had done in the mine, whether any of their family had also been miners and information about their first job. They were then asked about any other jobs they had had while working for the colliery, and about their experiences of working as a miner. Next, we talked about the life of a miner, which included what their typical working day would be like, the high and low points of working as a miner and what they did in their spare time. After that came the main section of the interview, asking about 'pit talk'. We asked them whether there were terms which they thought were specific to mining. While talking about different words, the interviewers could bring up different areas of the SRNs to discuss different names for job descriptions, tools, processes, equipment, pieces of coal and coal layers, to name but a few. As mentioned above, although we used the SRNs, we were very mindful to follow the miners' lead in the conversation. As they had had such different experiences, with different jobs and varying amounts of time worked in the mines, one size of interview could not fit all. When they were discussing particular lexical items, we sometimes also asked whether they recognised particular words (which other miners may have used), as well as discussing whether the mine(s) they had worked at had seen much domestic or international migration and whether this had affected the words used by incoming miners as well as the miners from the region. We asked them whether they were aware of terms which were different depending on whether miners came from other mines, both inside and outside of the East Midlands. We asked them whether there were terms which were only used in specific mines. As many different terms were given, we sometimes asked for assistance in how a word would be spelled or pronounced, although we tried to avoid this where possible as many miners may not have needed to write down such words. In addition, many had mentioned leaving school at an early age without many qualifications and we did not want to make them feel uncomfortable. We also discussed whether any of these terms would be used outside the mines and whether there were other local words that would be used by miners in their everyday lives. We tried to interject as little as possible in order to allow the miners to tell their stories.

Many miners spoke of the mining strikes, particularly the strike of 1984–1985 and the situation at the time and following it. They were also asked about activities outside of the mine, of life as a miner, whether they had seen any ghosts or heard ghost stories (as this was a theme that was discussed in

Methodology

some of the earliest interviews). Miners were also given the opportunity to add details which they thought were important to the life and work of a miner. Many miners chose to comment on the close relationships they felt they had with their fellow miners (this will be discussed in more detail in Chapter 4) and they referred to the 'camaraderie' or 'brotherhood' of the miners as well as the social activities that formed an important part of life for many.

After recording, the interviews were transcribed orthographically. Each interview was analysed for the discussion of particular words. Extractions of the data, such as particular lexical items of interest, were stored on an Excel spreadsheet, noting the region the miners came from and any additional discussion around the vocabulary to allow comparison between interviews and regions. Much of the discussion was also about their way of living and working (this will also form part of the analysis in Chapter 4). Some of the men were able to remember in much more detail the different terms which were used but some, particularly those who had only worked as a miner for a short period of time, found it difficult to recall some terms.

Because of differences in the words used by these miners, it was decided to follow up these interviews with more interviews, focusing on a wide geographical area from around the East Midlands with men who were closely involved in the mining heritage, many of whom formed part of different labour and heritage groups. These additional interviews were mainly carried out in twos to help spark ideas, and they were also carried out by a former miner, who was able to focus on the differences between the regions. This also provided an opportunity to discuss particular words and issues raised in the first set of interviews. There are strengths and weaknesses in using dyads for interviewing (Devlin 2014: 91). Although many respondents are likely to be more relaxed when interviewed with a friend and may produce more natural language, some interviewees may be quieter in groups. By adopting a friendly and informal stance and engaging with the interviewees throughout, all speakers were encouraged to participate. The men in the dyads also all knew each other which was helpful and ensured a relaxed atmosphere. Many said that they really enjoyed the interviews and having the opportunity to talk about their former experiences. As Kerswill et al. (1999: 261) have discussed, a way had to be found to ensure the collection of informal conversational data but in a way that allowed it to be analysed linguistically, in this case to examine lexical variation. It had to be less like an interview and more like a conversation. Furthermore, 'simply *talking* about lexical variation does not yield comparable or quantifiable lexical data' (Kerswill et al. 1999: 262). As a result, a different way had to be found to be able to do so. This method will now be discussed.

3.4.1 Sense Relation Networks

Beal and Burbano-Elizondo have noted that the prevalent variationist methods of the semi-structured interview – reading passages and word lists – were mainly designed to elicit phonetic variation (Beal and Burbano-Elizondo 2012: 12), and other methods were needed to investigate lexical variation. Such studies used tools designed for the Survey of Regional English (also known as SuRE) methodology which were designed by Carmen Llamas (1999) to provide lexical information for researchers and were used in Middlesborough (Llamas 2001). This method was designed to explore social variation in different locations in order to provide uniform and consistent data collection in studies of language variation and change across the UK (Llamas 2001: 66). One of the ways of carrying out such a methodology is by using a Sense Relation Network (SRN). These have also been referred to as 'spidergrams' (see Jo. Robinson 2012: 24) and are visual prompt sheets. They contain visual representations of words (see Figures 3.1 and 3.2) linked to particular semantic fields. This method has been inspired by the concept that a 'web of words' exists and that these networks define linguistic expressions in the mind (see Kerswill et al. 1999: 262). It allows the interviews to follow a particular line of questioning, related to particular topics or domains of interest, in a similar way to the *Survey of English Dialects*, but it allows participants to give more than one word. Researchers such as Wales (2006: 196) have commented that some questionnaires may skew results towards passive use and may not fully illustrate 'real' language usage. SRNs are a way of combating such issues by allowing participants to discuss different words and the contexts in which they can be used.

Devlin et al. have said that 'a Sense-Relation Network data elicitation task evaluates respondents' awareness and usage of dialect-specific synonyms for standard notion words in terms of distribution and social meaning locally' (Devlin et al. 2019: 309). Giving standard words as pointers to start discussion is more effective as indirect elicitation techniques can be much more time-consuming than direct techniques (Kerswill et al. 1999: 262). Beal notes that SRNs have many positives (for full details see Beal 2006: 62) and these include: that the participants can initially complete these in their own time, i.e. the empowerment of the informants; that the follow-up interviews can reveal differences in uses for the same concept; that they can elicit both active and passive vocabulary; and that informants can explain their insights of usage by different individuals if that applies. Also, by giving standard words as a basis to work from, participants are not prompted by a particular dialect word but can come up with their own suggestions.

Interviewers can use these prompts to initiate discussion about alternative words and expressions used by individuals or groups to explore any contexts associated with such variants. These methods were also adapted by the BBC Voices project (see Jo. Robinson 2012). They were also used by Esther Asprey (2007) in the West Midlands, Kate Wallace (2007) in Southampton, Lourdes Burbano-Elizondo (2008) in Sunderland and Peter Lee (forthcoming) with East Midlands Gypsy, Romani and Traveller English speakers.

The SRNs were adapted by us to fit with the lexicon of coal mining (see Figures 3.1 and 3.2). These word prompts helped the participants think of

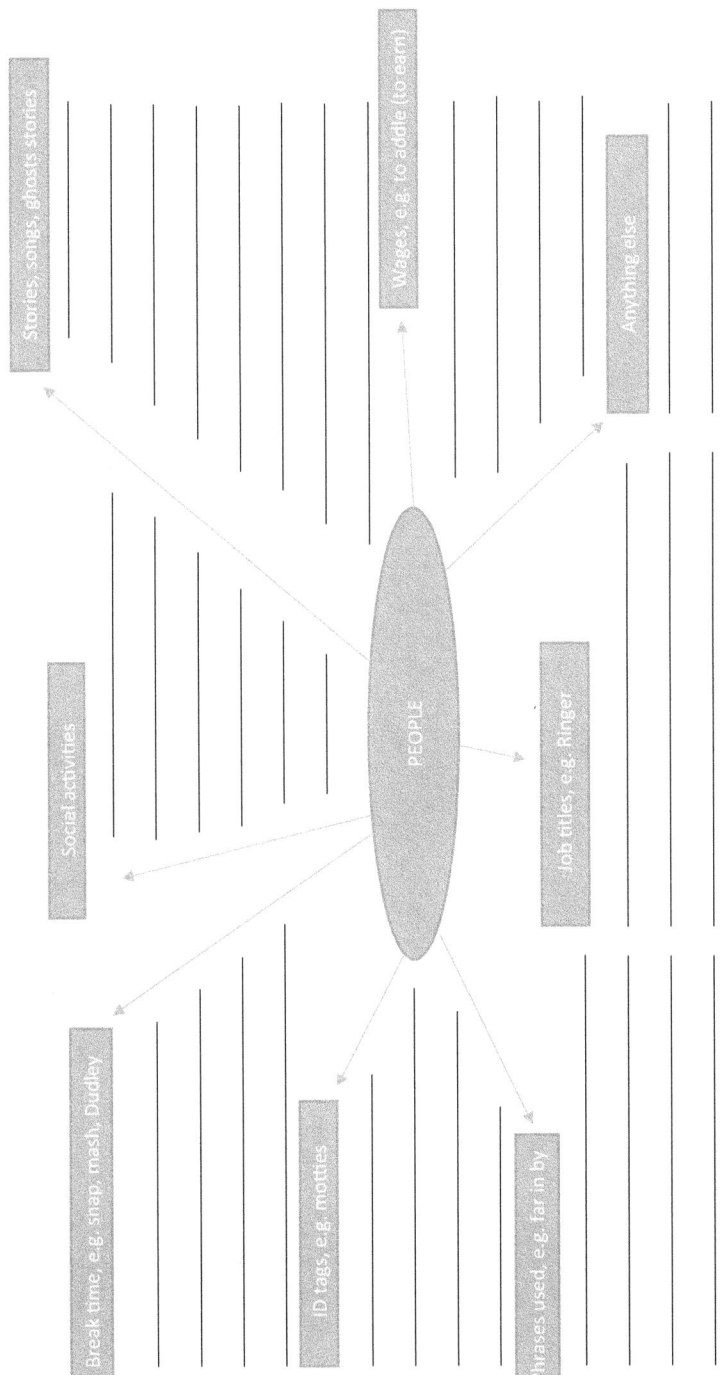

Figure 3.1 Sense Relation Network 1 (created by Claire Ashmore)

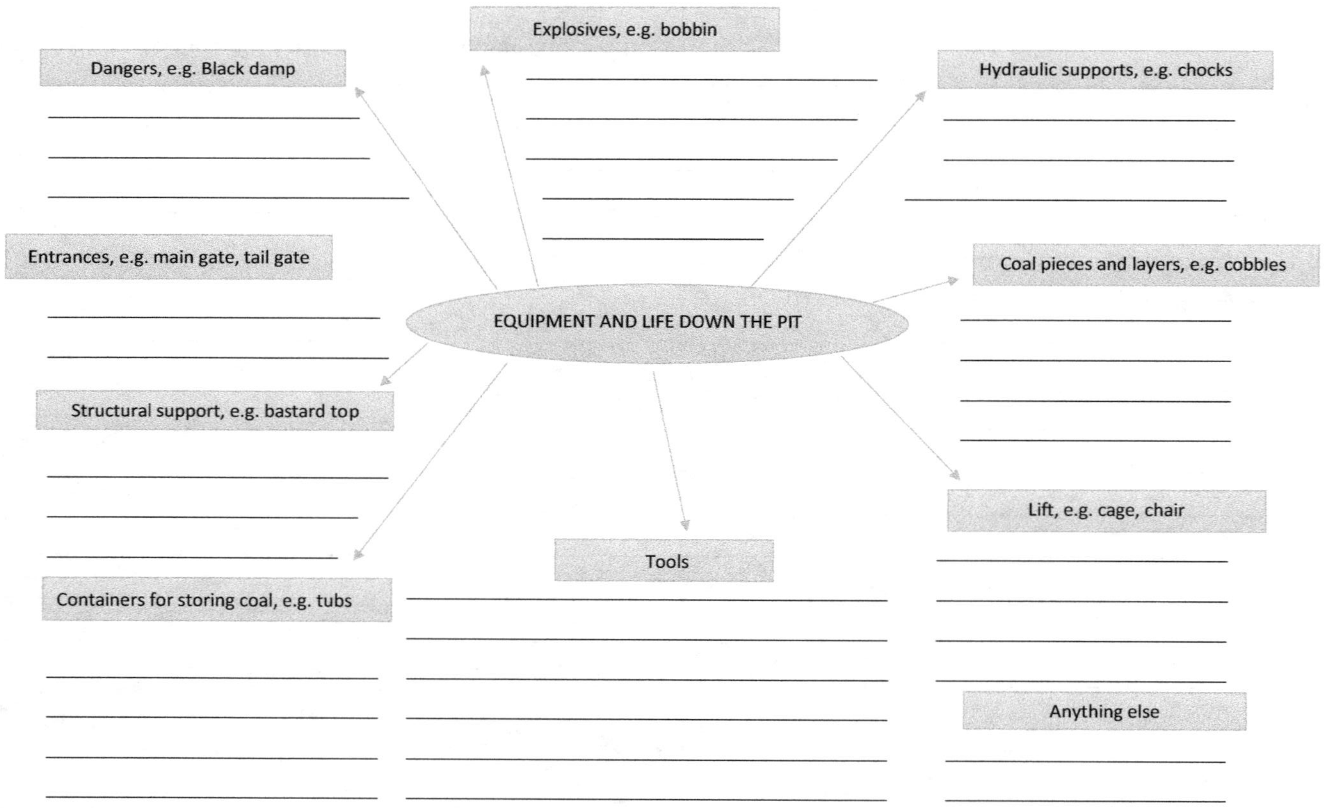

EQUIPMENT AND LIFE DOWN THE PIT

- Hydraulic supports, e.g. chocks
- Coal pieces and layers, e.g. cobbles
- Lift, e.g. cage, chair
- Anything else
- Explosives, e.g. bobbin
- Tools
- Dangers, e.g. Black damp
- Entrances, e.g. main gate, tail gate
- Structural support, e.g. bastard top
- Containers for storing coal, e.g. tubs

Figure 3.2 Sense Relation Network 2 (created by Claire Ashmore)

particular concepts and words that they may have for particular objects, practices or roles. While going through the interview, respondents and interviewer discussed particular words on the SRN and any local terms, or terms that were used in their mine, for these standard words. This also encouraged participants to use non-standard or dialectal words. Furthermore, this type of elicitation seems less like a test than some indirect methods and can put the interviewee at ease as well as producing the most relevant data. By giving the miners the SRNs in advance, it also allows the participants some time to think about words before the meeting and stops the mind from going blank. So, where possible, SRNs were distributed a number of days beforehand (although it wasn't possible in all cases). The interviewees were asked to consider which items of the SRN they knew or other terminology they were familiar with and whether they were aware of differences in different mines in the region, or whether miners from outside the region used other words. By discussing the SRNs during the interview, the participants could avoid any possible ambiguity and define and delimit individual words in detail (see also Beal and Burbano-Elizondo 2012: 16).

The semantic fields employed in the SRN used as a focus the work carried out on the mining language of the north-east and the South Midlands, where particular lexical items were raised as local, and this allowed us to compare the usage of such terms with miners from the East Midlands. By recording the discussion of the SRNs we ensured that all responses could be retained and listened to again later, particularly following discussions by other miners. Furthermore, by using SRNs, miners could also give variants which they assumed were 'general', even if they were actually regional (see also discussion by Beal 2006: 62). This gave us a considerable amount of lexical data, which could then also be used for phonological and grammatical data analysis if needed.

3.5 Questionnaires

Questionnaires have long been used to collect lexical data. Millar et al. have said that 'questionnaires have stood the test of time as an element of dialectological (and to a lesser extent sociolinguistic) practice' (Millar et al. 2014: 45). Boberg (2005: 24) has mentioned several studies which were carried out in Canada and North America using questionnaires that participants completed themselves and which involved thirty lexical variables. In these questionnaires, participants were given definitions of the variable, followed by a list of the most common variants known. Participants were then asked to circle the variant they used themselves or write down the word they would use if it did not appear in the list. Boberg has discussed the strengths of this method in that it avoided having illegible entries and variant spellings. However, it might encourage participants to circle different lexical items without thinking through carefully which one they would use themselves, and of course participants may not be aware of which forms they actually use. It might also discourage participants from writing down additional words which did not appear in the list. In the analysis of these questionnaires, Boberg used 'net variation' (Boberg 2005: 32), which examines the frequencies of terms given to work out absolute differences between regional frequencies of each variant and adds these up to get an accurate measure of the total amount of regional difference. Boberg has also used major isoglosses to examine variation in his responses. Quantitative analysis of this kind was not possible for our coal mining study with a relatively small number of participants as they do not all include all the same terms.

Pearce (2020: 489) has discussed the difficulties associated with using questionnaires; they can be associated with more formal data and this data has to be actively elicited from the speaker. He also noted that there can be the feeling too that questionnaires can lead to a skewing towards passive knowledge, rather than just identifying a speaker's active vocabulary. He has added: 'In order to counter such problems, what is needed is naturally occurring, contextually embedded instances of dialect lexis rather than elicited instances which are largely meta-linguistic in function' (Pearce 2020: 489). Of course, this was not possible with our questionnaires. However, much of the data was collected through informal interviews which allowed exactly for this kind of discussion, and these questionnaires serve as further evidence of the usage of such terms. Millar et al. have also suggested (2014: 45) that questionnaires suffer from a degree of formality that interviews do not. Using the SRNs in an informal discussion was our preferred method of data collection, but for the final participants this was not possible due to the COVID-19 pandemic which started in 2020. Therefore, it was decided to finalise data collection using adapted questionnaires. All of the participants had volunteered to take part and were aware of the project, so most of those taking part would know that it was not a 'test' as such, with 'right' and 'wrong' answers, but a way for someone who is interested in the coal mining industry to take part in an ongoing research project. One of the strengths of questionnaires is that they allow for direct comparison between participants. Our return rate of questionnaires was around 50 per cent, which is relatively high, and several participants added additional information in the form of vocabulary lists.

The questionnaire included the questions from the interviews to ensure consistency. The questions were drawn from lexical items of interest raised in Forster (1969), Douglass (1973) and Griffiths (2007). The questionnaire also contained definition questions which were influenced by Wright's work (1972). Wright's study used eighty-one questions which ask the participant to give particular definitions, for example, question 42 asked for 'the empty space where the coal has been taken out' which aimed to gather the response 'waste space' or other variants. In conjunction with the interviews, this questionnaire data add a valuable amount of information to the project which

Methodology 77

can be fully analysed and compared alongside each other. In the final stages, a total of twenty-three questionnaires were submitted by miners, sixteen from former Nottinghamshire miners, two from Leicestershire miners and five from Derbyshire miners. All participants were male and had worked in one or more East Midlands pits during their mining career. The age range of the miners who took part in the questionnaire ranged from 50–89, with the majority at the older end of the scale. Of the group, three men were in their fifties, three were in their sixties, nine were in their seventies and eight were in their eighties.

All participants received an information sheet about the project and also signed a consent form giving permission for their data and information to be used in the research. The first section of the questionnaire collected metadata about the participants. They were asked for their name, age and current place of residence. This was followed by questions about their mining work – they were asked which pits they had worked in, when and for how long, what job(s) they did in the mines and also whether their mine employed a lot of miners from other regions. They were also asked whether anyone else in their family had worked as a miner.

In the next section they were asked about mining vocabulary. This section included a short introduction to explain that the questionnaire was particularly interested in local words for such items and whether they may differ from terms that may have been suggested by the NCB for national use. It also explained that knowing where the respondents worked and where other miners in their pit were from would help the researchers work out whether terms differed throughout the region. The introduction also ensured that miners would feel free to put down more than one term if they felt this was appropriate, and also that this was not a 'test' as such, but that they were being asked for their opinions on particular lexical items. Some of the miners may not have used the terms for some time and we wanted to make certain that they did not feel anxious about not knowing the words (one of the respondents did in fact include an additional written comment that they found it hard to remember all of these words after so long out of the mines, and this was also the reason for carrying out interviews in dyads where possible in the second stage of data collection that preceded these final questionnaires).

The next section focused on specific aspects of mining life: wages and shifts (asking for different terms for overtime, bonuses, shift patterns, etc); terms for friends and co-workers; clothes worn in the mine; job titles; management levels; dangerous conditions in the mine (including terms for different types of gas, warnings shouted and injuries); different types of containers for storing coal (including general containers, flat cars and trolleys); safety devices on these containers as well as on the tracks; names for different types of tools (including hammers, spanners, drills, shovels, crowbars, picks, axes, (pneumatic) drills); names for the different strata of coal in particular mines, and different sizes of coal pieces; names for water or reservoirs in mines; side channels or roadways coming off the main roadway; names for hard or lazy workers; names given to the floor lift and ways of lowering it; names for food and drink (also including names for food and drink containers and break times); names for waste material and where this was placed behind the coalface; names for the coalface; names for the shafts and roads both entering and leaving the mineshaft (or towards and away from the coalface); names for the different shafts used for bringing men and materials in/out of the mine; names for different types of support for the ceiling; names for coal cutting machines and coal conveyors; for unworked areas of coal; for lamps, headstocks, lifts, identity tags, underground trains for transporting men, explosives, the coal preparation plant, spoil heaps, and union officials. The participants were also given space to include any other words they thought had been missed out but were important to the miners.

In the next section, the miners were asked specifically if they were aware of language differences between such terms in different mines (both in the East Midlands and outside the region) and if they knew of any terms that were brought in by miners from other regions. The last question in this section was whether they were aware of any changes that had taken place in the language over the years that they had worked in the collieries.

Finally, the last section of the questionnaire contained some of the individual expressions which were posed by Wright in his mining questionnaire. There were too many to include all of them but, based on all the previous interviews carried out with East Midlands miners, certain words were selected as they had generated the most interesting discussion in the interviews. Some of these words also appeared in the main body of the questionnaire and could be used to cross-reference and also to compare to the results found by Wright, which are also discussed regionally.

Questionnaires can introduce a tendency for people to submit singular answers, rather than to give a list of possible variants (see also discussion by Millar et al. 2014: 49). This was the case for some participants, but others did give multiple items. In particular, the section which asked for other terms and asked for the miners' thoughts about language movement allowed some miners to write in some detail about their experiences, which were very interesting to include in the analysis.

Many words which have been discussed in other coal mining literature (such as Forster 1969 and Douglass 1973) were outdated, and these were avoided during the questionnaire. We tried to focus on more contemporary job descriptions and machinery to get the most detailed information from our participants. We had noticed during the interviews that many miners had been through different stages of mining and although some were able to remember historical items as well as more recent ones, we did not want to risk extending the questionnaire and confusing the participants by asking for changing practices over time. Although there are disadvantages of using questionnaires – there was no one with the participants if they had any

Methodology

questions when they were completing them and there were some issues with difficulty reading handwriting – on the whole, the questionnaires provided very rich material. During the interviews, although we were able to ask questions, the conversations were mainly led by the miners which meant that they did not always cover every term. With the questionnaires, most of the miners did fill in most of the boxes; there were of course some blank boxes but, on the whole, the questionnaires allowed for a very clear comparison between the different men and the process was also much less time-consuming than carrying out and transcribing interviews. It was very rewarding to see the number of miners commenting positively on the interviews and questionnaires that they had really enjoyed the experience and the opportunity to talk about their mining lives.

3.6 Working with communities

Although we realised that the data collected and analysed as part of this project would be presented to academic audiences, an important focus of the project was to ensure accessibility for and engagement with a non-academic audience. Our final celebration event of the British Academy-funded part of the project used posters and information sheets to inform those who took part in the project about our initial findings. It included a photographic exhibition of coal mining photos and live music with coal mining themed songs. Further, this work was published in the form of a book, *Pit Talk in the East Midlands* (Braber et al. 2017), which is suitable for non-academic readers and forms a legacy of the early stages of the project, thus ensuring that the project has longevity.

We also used social media (blogging and a Facebook page) to involve the communities engaging with the project and to keep them updated with its progress. This aspect of the project also created a further legacy, meaning that other individuals and groups can continue to engage with the work carried out on the project once it has ended. As many of the miners we contacted were part of mining heritage groups, they were interested to know what the other groups in the region were doing and whether they were facing the same difficulties. With some representatives of these groups, we set up the East Midlands Coal Mining Heritage Forum, which meets twice a year and allows the different groups to come together to share ideas and good practice. We have also held different training workshops to show them how to use social media, conduct oral history interviews and apply for external funding, and we have hosted conferences and workshops with external speakers. Prolonged contact with the mining heritage groups involved in the project has resulted in continued collaboration on other projects and further partnerships look likely. There is a real desire to take part in future projects and raise the profile of mining heritage in the region.

Furthermore, we are looking into the possibility of making the recordings and related transcripts available online through the East Midlands Oral History Archive (EMOHA) website, which is a well-established digital resource in the area and could potentially be shared with the British Library. Due to the sensitive nature of some of the recordings, we are still in consultation about how best to achieve this.

Our project also engaged with young people and adults who do not have a mining background. We also worked with artists and arts organisations, including the creation and performance of music, songs, creative writing and art and soundscapes. An important concern for the miners we spoke to was that people would soon forget about the former importance of mining in the region, and they wanted others to understand what that way of life had been like.

Involving the communities which helped with the data collection in the project remains important. Ewa Czaykowska-Higgins (2009: 34) stated: 'Linguistic research is [...] at the very least a social act and not simply an isolated intellectual act.' Throughout this project the research has taken place in the community, and it would have been impossible without the collaboration of the miners. Many of them are concerned that very soon younger people will not have any memories of the mining industry and they want to ensure that it remains in the public memory. Therefore, the collaboration with communities – which was an integral part of the project – continues to the present day.

3.6.1 Positionality

As was explained in section 2.3, the coal mining industry in the East Midlands has remained fractured since the 1984–1985 Miners' Strike. There are many groups and individuals who still will not communicate with each other. This was an important issue we had to bear in mind for the project interviews. The majority of the interviews were carried out by myself and Claire Ashmore and Suzy Harrison, which provided a real advantage. None of us has ever been miners, we are all female, and Suzy and I do not originate from the East Midlands. This meant that we did not pose a threat to either side in the strike dispute as we had not been part of the industrial action nor had parents or grandparents who had been part of it. This ties in with Cave's comments (2001: 76) that local researchers are active co-participants in the data rather than neutral observers, but because of our distance we were accepted by both sides. During one pre-interview meeting, a former miner, who had played a very active role in the National Union of Mineworkers (NUM, which did strike), said that I was the closest to neutral that could be found in such a difficult situation. Due to such sensitivities, we did not ask miners whether they went out on strike or not, but most miners talked voluntarily about the strike and its after-effects on the community. While all the miners spoke about the

Methodology 81

camaraderie in the mines, the strike was a topic raised frequently during the interviews, with very different views from different individuals.

The final interviews were carried out by a former miner known for his membership of the Union of Democratic Mineworkers (UDM), which did not strike in the 1980s. Therefore, there were some implications we had to bear in mind and there were certain groups we were unable to approach for these final interviews. However, we have ensured a wide spread of locations and standpoints due to the different interviewers taking part in the project. For the first set of interviews and with the questionnaires we were able to work with both sides, which meant that we secured good coverage across both sides of the divide.

The aspect of relationships, particularly with the mining heritage groups, was a crucial part of our project. Building relations took time and years of collaboration. Solid relationships are based on mutual trust, which researchers have to earn. For projects that deal with sensitive issues, a high level of trust is crucial to the integrity of the project and its results. Although this can be a problem for short-term funded projects, which are time-limited, for this project I have been working with many of the individuals and groups for a number of years and I have taken part in other activities and events. One of the outcomes is that with three other founder members we were able set up the East Midlands Coal Mining Heritage Forum, which allows different mining groups to come together and share knowledge, information and methods of best practice (see details in previous section). We also organise talks and training sessions to help the groups learn more and to collaborate further.

Working with such groups has also allowed me to engage them in the importance of preserving their language; of course, more work is still needed to enable them to work more closely on preservation in their own collections and archives. One of the biggest problems for these groups is their ageing membership; very few young people join the groups. By working with local museums as well the National Coal Mining Museum for England and the Coal Authority we are trying to find additional ways to ensure that such information is retained to engage more young people (for more details on working with communities, see Braber (forthcoming)).

3.7 Conclusion

Adams has referred to 'identity lexicography' and the fact that many glossaries and vocabulary research are motivated by curiosity, stimulated by hearing someone use language in a particular way (Adams 2014: 166). He has also said that this can result in researchers setting out to capture the localism of a particular area or group of people. This kind of participatory research can be a very effective way to examine language variation. As I found with my participants, you do not have to be part of the group to be able to engage, and we had many fruitful conversations about the usage of particular words by certain speakers.

The particular lexical fields of public interest covered by the data collection included: job titles and descriptions of such jobs; tools used in the coal mining industry; processes of extracting and processing coal and the associated equipment needed; names and descriptions of dangers found within the industry; names for pieces of coal and various coal strata found in the different regions; underground transport of men and coal; and descriptions of everyday life.

Collecting data from interviews and questionnaires and comparing this with available sources allows the examination of the lexical variation of a particular community, in this case the coal miners of the East Midlands. As we will see in the following chapter, in our examination there are frequent disagreements about certain terms, while other terms are more universal.

4 Analysis

4.1 Introduction

This chapter analyses topics such as identity, culture, language and humour. As discussed earlier, the coal mining industry was of crucial importance for the East Midlands economy. The mining areas were also essential for local identity and were important for a sense of community for many miners and their families. This is not to say that labour relations always ran smoothly or that mining offered an easy way of life. Mining communities have traditionally been isolated and working class. Furthermore, working in mines was dangerous. Serious injury and even death were a constant threat. Therefore, miners tended to develop a very powerful camaraderie and group ethos. Within this, they displayed a sense of humour which is specific to this group (Bell 2008: 30; Cave 2001). It formed part of the mining culture and language. Douglass has written that '[t]he mine necessitates a different attitude of mind, a different temperament to that on the surface; necessarily it gives rise to a culture and language which are peculiar to that environment' (Douglass 1973: 1). The sense of humour formed an important element of many of the interviews conducted in this pit talk project. Many of the participating miners also spoke of their close relationships with their colleagues, saying they all had to look out for each other. Often, the interviewees had worked in the industry for many years, had specialised jobs and had to undertake very specific functions as part of their daily work. This also gave rise to a specialised use of language. But it was more than technical jargon. Simpson and Simmons have noted that 'speaking the same language' is not just about vocabulary but is also about attitude to life, in particular a sense of humour (Simpson and Simmons 2019: 14). This chapter will look at these issues.

A 1969 survey of terms from the South Midlands has explained that miners had their own language and that the basis of this language seemed to be a mixture of local dialect and technical mining terms, but the survey also stated that it is crucial that '[t]he language of the miner has come to express his whole culture' (Forster 1969: 1). A study on pit talk in County Durham by Douglass (1973: 1) has suggested that:

> [t]he miner's 'language', however strange it appears to the outsider, is an inevitable part of him. The language of the miner, regardless of what dialects it embraces, is an intricate and inseparable part of his whole culture. It is directly related to his community, his work and the way he handles it, his trade union struggles and movements, his songs and stories.

Information sheets created by curators at The National Coal Mining Museum for England indicate many words that are unique to the mining industry, especially to coal miners. Not only does mining, like any other industry, have a number of technical words or jargon, but miners working in different regions also had different dialects. For example, a person who hauled the wagons or tubs might be known as a *waggoner* in one part of the country (the information sheets do not state which part this is), a *hurrier* in Yorkshire, a *drawer* in Lancashire, a *putter* in Northumberland or a *haulage-man* in Scotland. There are also cases where the same word means very different things. For instance, in the East Midlands and Yorkshire, *snap* is the food a miner takes with him to eat, but to a Durham miner *snap* is an instrument used on the screens to cut waste material off coal (some of these terms can be controversial; Thomas Devlin (personal communication) notes that the miners he interviewed in the north-east did not recognise this term with this meaning, but this is the meaning given on the National Coalmining Website). The Durham miner calls his lunch *bait*. In Scotland it is a *piece*. Local variations in dialect and use of words can vary even between villages within one area as well as between coalfields. Some mining villages were rather isolated and Freese has noted that this could lead to them developing different habits and speech, in addition to a 'fierce sense of solidarity, similar to that of soldiers in wartime' (Freese 2003: 45); Wright also refers to coal miners as being 'a race apart' (Wright 1972: 49).

More variation can be caused by migration. As discussed in Chapter 2, there was much movement of miners around the country, particularly when mines started closing in Scotland and the north-east of England. There were also miners coming to the UK from abroad, for example from Ireland, Eastern Europe and the Commonwealth. Foster has suggested that if miners arrived in groups, they tended to retain and take pride in their own language, although they could use the 'new' language if needed (Forster 1969: 3). There were also some mines newly opened with men coming from all over the country, and differences in the language used could be immediately apparent. Forster has described a situation where a Scottish miner stated that '100 yards in front of him is an old Staffordshire miner who regards him as "baiting", while behind him is a group of Warwickshire men who regard him as "dinting", and he calls himself the "pavement brusher"' (Forster 1969: 3).

Analysis 85

Many miners have said that regardless of such variation, they continue to think in terms of their own terminology, as in where they first worked (Forster 1969: 3). There are studies of mining language or pit talk, also known as *pitmatic* or *yakka* in the north-east coalfields (see section 2.6.2 for more details), as well as lists of mining terminology (for example on the 'Coalmining History Resource Centre' website), but many of these publications are generic and are not specific to a particular region.

Furthermore, the introduction of new technology and increasing mechanisation in the mining industry meant a change in tools and methods, and we can examine new terms that were used in the industry, as well as cases whereby older terms were still used to refer to new items as well as to old tools and methods (see Forster 1969: 5). Regardless of the 'standardisation of terms' which was the policy of the National Coal Board (NCB) since nationalisation, local terms survived and were used by miners. Wright has suggested (1972: 44) that many miners avoided the use of terms advocated by the National Coal Board and preferred to continue using their own local words. Miners have words which are far more specialised than others outside the field will recognise (Wright 1972: 46) and they make distinctions between different types of tools – for example, hammers, spanners or drills – where others would not do so. Some words may have changed their meanings or disappeared from use over time.

All the miners interviewed for this project said that there were differences in the terms and language used by different miners, and that as a result of these differences the language in one pit was sometimes hard to understand for those who came from other pits. This confirms what other researchers have found earlier. Griffiths has written that a mining dictionary of Derbyshire in 1747 contains only a few words in common with north-east mining vocabulary and much that is 'quite alien' (Griffiths 2007: 13). It is thought that some technical terms may show regional consistency, but many familiar terms also show extensive variation (such as job titles, names for food and drink, and names for tools and equipment). We will also see in this chapter that there is much variation between which terms were used and where they were used. Miners working in similar regions did not always say they use the same words. Some of these words may also be used more generally (for example the terms *gaffer* for a boss or manager and *sparkie* for electrician are found outside of the coal mining industry). For example, it was noted by a reader of a piece I wrote for The Conversation that the term 'powder monkey' for a person holding explosives originated in the navy. However, what I wanted to find out were the words used by these men in their professional, everyday life. What words did they use which they connected to their work as a coal miner? I am also interested to see whether there are influences from other regions. This includes examining whether the extensive movement of miners from around the UK influenced the language of miners in the pits in which they went to work. This study will also allow for the investigation of differences between the East Midlands regions – whether there are differences between Nottinghamshire, Derbyshire and Leicestershire – and also between particular mines. It will also show us that much mining terminology is job dependent and affected by the work undertaken by individual miners.

It is important to state that this analysis is qualitative and not quantitative. Although there are relatively large numbers of interviewees and questionnaires involved in this study, not all respondents included answers for all the terms about which they were asked. However, with the large number of responses and a full discussion around some of these terms, we can certainly distinguish particular tendencies and examine which words show more variation and which words are more stable throughout the region. Many of the miners noted that they found remembering the words to be a challenge; for many, their work was carried out a long time ago. This is discussed as part of the methodology, with many of the interviews taking place with another miner, as well as the provision of the Sense Relation Network, to prompt memories. Many of the miners commented on how much they enjoyed the interviews and tell personal stories about the terms they were asked about. Often, extracts of interviews will be included alongside the analysis to add valuable information and meaning to the vocabulary, and to allow for a deeper understanding of the terms, and to use the miners' own words to represent their life and work.

As there is so much material on many different topics, these will be discussed thematically in the sections below. We will start with words concerned with payment and shift patterns (wages, overtime, sick leave, break times, food and drink terms, shift patterns, shift end, clocking off, bonuses), words used for friends and colleagues when working, words for hard workers and lazy workers, and words for clothing worn in the mine. We will then move on to dangers in the mine (including words for different types of dangers, gases, warnings shouted and injuries). This will be followed by all different terms for tools (including hammers, spanners, drills, pneumatic drills, shovels, crowbars, axes and any others). The different job descriptions and levels of management will be discussed after that. The next section will then include different names for the different coal seams found in different mines and for coal of different sizes. This will be followed by inclusion of the different types of containers used above and below ground as well as the safety devices used with these containers. After this will appear different areas within the mine, and objects and equipment found and used below ground. This will include terms for roadways and shafts (including the shaft entering and leaving the mine, main roads underground and also connecting roads). This is followed by different items of equipment and structure (such as the steel arched supports, the hydraulic support system, coal cutting machines, underground conveyors and transport systems, underground transport, and names for lifts, lamps, electrical systems, identity tags and explosives), and, finally, different

Analysis 87

places in the mine (including water reservoirs, places for waste materials, unworked coal, the coalface, coal preparation plant, spoil heaps and trade union offices). As well as all of these terms for equipment, processes and job types, I will also provide information where relevant about the very important social network, about camaraderie, about the language used by miners from different regions, and about changes which took place. Discussing all of this terminology and comparing variations of terms enable us to gain an extensive understanding of the vocabulary used by coal miners of the East Midlands.

4.2 Analysis

4.2.1 Payment and shift patterns

This section deals with several topics linked to money and the particular shift patterns worked at the pit. It includes terms for: wages, overtime, sick leave, break times and food and drink consumed during these breaks, shift patterns, end of shifts, clocking off, and bonus systems that could lead to additional payment.

The first term the interviewees were asked about was the name given to wages paid to miners. Of the forty-three miners who give a term for this, most use just one term, with common terms including *wages*, *wage packet*, *wage slip*, *pay*, *pay slip*, *pay packet*, *pay check* and *money*. There are also single references to the words *dosh*, *sheckels*, *pennies*, *lolly* and *bread*. There are two references to *collecting your wedge*. Some miners refer to the *butty system*, which was an older method whereby one miner was put in charge of a group of miners, who he himself could choose, and was paid all of the money, which he them distributed among his group members. There are ten references to wages being referred to as *in 't tin* or *money in 't tin* and two different reasons are given for this particular expression, which appears in all three regions (Derbyshire, Leicestershire and Nottinghamshire). DWN who worked at Pye Hill in Derbyshire says this expression came from the way in which miners used to be paid. He explains that before 1952 wages were put in a little round tin and, after a shift, miners would have to go to the office window, say their number and be given a tin which had all of their wages in it. ABS from Gedling in Nottinghamshire thought that the term went back to the days when miners were paid by a *butty* (who would pay the men working for him directly) and that he paid this money from his own tin. Both of these versions show the local feature of definite article reduction and this pronunciation is mentioned by a number of the miners – it is not referred to as *money in the tin*, instead it had to be *in 't tin* (examples of local pronunciation will be raised when relevant in these discussions).

The next term which was asked about was the name given to overtime worked by miners. Of all those questioned, forty-eight miners give at least one term for this and about half of them provide more than one term. Of these, thirteen miners state that the only term used for this was *overtime*. Many of the pronunciations are distinctly local, sounding more like *ovvertime* (we will also see this for a term in the management system in *ovverman* in section 4.2.4). Some other varieties given by only a very small number of miners include *bonus, remaining after shift, golden hour, bull week* (which refers specifically to doing lots of overtime in the week before the annual holiday to earn more money for the holidays), *ding dong, nifs, double shift, double 'un, stopping over* and *pinger*. There are small numbers of references to miners choosing to work overtime as being greedy, where they are referred to as *grabbers, grabbing* and *gobbling*. There are several references (which the miners specifically state as being local to their mines) to *nob, nobs* and *noggin'* where *nobs* is used more by Derbyshire miners and *noggin'* by Nottinghamshire miners. These terms tend to be used to refer to working an additional quarter-hour and one miner also says that overtime can be referred to as *a quarter* or *one 29th* where the overtime worked is an additional 29th payment on the shift. A term which is given by all Leicestershire miners (or by the other two groups who refer to only Leicestershire miners using this) is a *doddy*, which some suggest is an additional hour added to the shift, and some miners also refer to a *double doddy* or to *mekadoddy* (which reflects the local pronunciation of the FACE vowel). RCH adds that at Whitwick, in Leicestershire, the miners 'would start at six and work till quarter past three and you'd get your double doddy'.

Around half of the miners offer a word they would use to describe taking sick leave. There are just one or two occurrences of words related to being sick, including *sick money* and *sicky*, and *throwin' a sickie* and one reference to getting a *sick note*. There is one reference to *skivving, signing off* and *compo* (referring to compensation). A few of the terms refer to the state of the miner, including *bone back* and *glass back* (we will be coming back to *glass back* when we discuss names for idle workers). Other terms which are named just once or twice are *havin' a greenun*, which refers to the green document that needed to be completed for sick leave, being *on the box*, being part of a *sunshine club, easy 3* (meaning unknown) and *DCM/DCF* (which means workers who *don't come Monday/don't come Friday*) and being *badley*. There are also a small number of references to *swinging lead* (which according one of the miners is a naval term, but he gives no further details), having *idlitis* and *having a bevin*. This last term refers to the Bevin Boys, named after Ernst Bevin, a Labour politician who served as Minister of Labour and National Service in the wartime coalition government and who set up a system whereby a proportion of young men conscripted into the army were sent to work in the coal mines between 1943 and 1948 in order to increase the rate of coal production, which had been in decline through the early years of the war. As these young men had not chosen to be miners, they were sometimes looked down upon in the mining industry. Two miners suggest that if a miner was off sick his colleagues would ask him if his wife *was laying on yer shirt tails* which

Analysis

had stopped him getting out of bed. There are also a few references to *being on 't giro* which refers to a financial method of transferring money. The most common term, given by almost thirty miners, is related to *club*, either being *on 't club*, having a *club note* or one reference to *the sunshine club*, but no further details are given about these terms.

Miners were also asked what they called their break times, as well as terms for food and drink that were consumed during the breaks. This section shows some of the highest agreement between all the miners from the East Midlands region, and also the most mentions of variation beyond the East Midlands. Just over sixty of the miners specifically mention that their break time was referred to as *snap* or *snap time*, and see Figure 4.1 for some miners having their snap (although some miners say that they did not have *snap time* at their mine or that they had *paid snap* where they could be paid extra to work during their lunch break). The word *snap* also refers to the food that was eaten during this break and was mentioned by over eighty miners, making it one of the most common terms used by all miners in this region. There are a couple of references to words for break time used in specific mines, three miners refer to the term *grabbit* which was only used at Warsop, one to *scran* and one to the term *bait* being used in Ollerton, Nottinghamshire. The term

Figure 4.1 Miners having snap in Clipstone in the 1960s (photo credit: Coal Authority)

bait is frequently mentioned as a term used by the miners who came down from the north-east (often called Geordieland in the interviews) and it is stated that many of these miners continued to use this term and that, in some instances, local East Midlands miners started using the term in mines that had large numbers of miners from the north-east. One miner, JS, who worked as a miner in Australia for a short time, says that this was called *crib* in Australia. There are also references to *piece* from Scotland, which Scottish miners used. Another interesting aspect of *snap* is that it is a term which is still used widely in the region by people outside the mines. It would be interesting to find out whether this usage is mainly by those from mining families or whether it has now also spread to the wider population in the region, but such a review lies outside the scope of this book.

When talking about *snap time*, the participating miners explain the different types of food they ate and what they drank, which varied. BBY2 says that young miners should never tell their mother if they liked a particular *snap* as they will then get this same lunch for the next three years. Another story was told of two miners who are both fed up of the same lunches and agreed to swap, but when they did so, found they both have the same food. There are extensive references to *snap tins*, *snap bags* and *snap boxes*, and also to words used in modern times when miners started bringing their lunch in Tupperware boxes instead. Snap tins were traditionally metal or aluminium tins which were the shape of a slice of bread and were oval at the top end (see the photograph in Figure 4.2). Many of these were emblazoned with the logo ACME, the company which made these tins, and it is said that this stood for All Colliers Must Eat. (There is one reference where the C does not refer to colliers but to cunts – much mention is made of bad language and swearing which was part and parcel of the everyday life that miners had to be able to cope with.) JS also mentions that new apprentices were often told the story of the French miners who had to have 4-feet snap tins in which to store their baguettes. MH says that the end of snap tins came with the introduction of polythene bags in which bread was later sold, and that miners could hang up their lunch to prevent vermin getting at it and after eating would be able to throw out the bag so that they did not have to carry a snap tin home. In a few of the colder mines, and for those working above ground, tea (and the associated local term *mashing* for brewing tea) was drunk, but most miners had water with them. Only two miners refer to a *flask* to bring in their drinks. This water was either held in a *dudley*, which was a metal drinks container (which in the early days had a cork stopper and can also be seen in Figure 4.2), or later in water bottles. These bottles also reflect local pronunciation, as many miners pronounce (and write on their questionnaires) that these were *watter bottles*, with one miner spelling it as *wetter bottle*. It is felt that the plastic (or glass milk and lemonade bottles which were used by some for carrying water according to DWN) improved the taste of the water, rather than the metal *dudleys*. The term *dudley* is quite divisive – some miners state that this is the

Analysis

Figure 4.2 Snap tin and water dudley

only term that was used, whereas others, even in the same region, say that they have never heard of this term at all. Some miners suggest that *dudley* was the name of the company which produced the bottles. KC says it was the inventor's name but some, such as RCN, believe that this company was based in Dudley and that this is where the name came from. Many of the miners comment that the mines they worked in were so hot that they would bring down frozen water, which ensured they had cold water to drink during their shift. Others also comment that the heat influenced what they included in their lunch, as meat would go rancid and would therefore not be included. Many of the stories about the *snap tins* and *snap boxes* suggest that containers (whether metal or plastic) were needed to keep out vermin (and DA mentions that in Annesley mice were referred to as *moggies*, which normally is used to refer to cats) and also to prevent pit ponies eating the food before it was lunchtime. BK notes that if mice did get at your snap, you still ate most of it and just threw away the bit that had been nibbled. BM, who worked in the canteens, says that miners on the night shift were entitled to a *meal ticket* if they worked an hour's overtime, which would get them a free breakfast. We can see here that a term which affected all, or certainly most, miners – that of having a lunch break – shows a large amount of vocabulary associated with it but also much consistency between the miners, with *snap* being the most overwhelmingly used item throughout all of the interviews and questionnaires. It is also a local term and different to other mining regions of the UK.

The next terms miners were asked to consider were the names of the particular shift patterns. Here there is very little variation, with most men commenting on the three-shift pattern found in most mines which were made up of *days*, *afters* or *afternoons* and *nights*. Some miners also refer to the day shift as *mids* and the *night shift* as *back shift*, *lates* or *twilights*. ABM comments that *twilight* shifts were for the non-drinkers and that anybody who liked to go to the pub for a drink hated working that shift. DH adds that the *twilight shift* filled in between the *afters* and *night* shift, often when repair work was carried out, and JK explains that this shift tended to run from 6.30 pm until 1.15 am. In many of the mines, the day shift was when much of the development work would be done. Much discussion centres around the actual times at which all of these shifts started and whether time was given for getting to the coalface or getting up and down the mine shafts, which varied from mine to mine as some miners had to travel much further underground to get to their place of work. ABS from Gedling also says that if you were on *the last draw*, the last lift full of men out of the pit, then you would be in the pit longer than you were being paid for as it could take a long time to transport all the men back above ground. There are differences among the preferences of miners, some of whom hated working particular shifts, such as the night shift, given that the irregular working patterns could be very hard to fit in with family life. In our coal mining pit anthology, there is reference to the early shift being referred to as *early daze* rather than *early days* (Braber and Amos 2021: 48). There is also significant discussion about the different work carried out during these different shifts, where only some of the shifts resulted in coal cutting and others were aimed at preparing the coalface so that the next shift could start working on it, or repairing particular areas and the machines needed there. BW from Markham in Derbyshire explains that,

Analysis 93

the way our pit worked, it'd have a shift when they undercut coal, with a coal cutting machine, and then all that they cut out they'd have to throw it onto the conveyor and then, the next shift, they used to be timber draws and they'd pull supports out, and then they'd have to, that shift, they'd have to move the conveyor, haul the conveyor forward and then, after it had been undercut, then the next shift would come and fill out coal.

DWN names a term which he says was unique to Newstead where they had a shift that was called the *tissue shift*. This was conducted by the men who brought the flimsy racing pages into their shift to read up on the races for the coming day and the day shift would come up and go straight into the bookies to put money on particular races.

The terms for the end of the shift and clocking off at the end of this shift can be considered together. The terms *knocking off* and *clocking off* are used by just under half of the miners interviewed. Some refer to finishing their work time as *bath time* (whether this had to be done at home or in the pit baths that many collieries installed) or *home time*, also spelled as *'ome time* by some miners. There are also individual references to being *done and dusted* or it being *time to goo* (spelling included by this miner). Some of the terms which are only used occasionally also refer to the processes that took place when leaving the mine, such as *get keys/key out*, *paddy time* (where miners had to get on underground trains to get back to the lift to get out of the mine), *checks in* (where miners' identity tags were handed in when leaving their shift, which will be discussed in more detail in section 4.2.8) or *swiping out* in more modern mines that had a swipe card system rather than identity tags for miners working their shift, as well as one reference to *ragging up* where clothes were changed from work clothes to clothes worn outside the pit (clothes will be dealt with later in this section). Approximately ten miners call the end of the shift *loosall* (which is spelled in different ways by those completing questionnaires), which was said to the miners being released from their work and signalled the end of the working shift. MH from Nottinghamshire comments that the term was originally used to refer to ponies, when they were turned out of the mines at holiday times, and was only later also used for the miners themselves. A term which is only used by miners from Leicestershire, and just by four of them, is *rodding up*. This concerns the fact that in these mines, tools were stored on a bar (which was called the rod) by the coalface; at the end of the shift, the miners would return their tools to the rod before leaving the mine. There are also two references to the end of the shift being called *lillycock* but no further information is given by these miners as to what this term refers to. There is, however, a reference to this term in Lewis (1971: ix) where he states that, 'In the Midlands coalfield in the nineteenth century the signal which ended a shift was the cry "lillycock" but in the North-East the same message was conveyed by the shout "kenner" or "loose all".' As shown in this section, many of the East Midlands miners used the term 'loosall' without any reference to a north-eastern influence.

Miners were also asked about terms for bonuses or money paid for additional work. Here the most common term, given by around fifteen of the miners, is *bonus*. Some of the miners discuss the changing payment system, which moved from such bonuses to payments of a loader agreement with *contract work* where miners worked particular shifts for fixed wages; even so, some miners could be paid additionally for *ad hoc* work and *piecework*, with miners sometimes coming in to do additional shifts, which is also referred to by some interviewees as *sat bonus* (Saturday bonus) or *weekend tickets*. Such references to *piecework* tend to relate to contract work, which was normally carried out at the coalface and could also include development work for opening up new coalfaces or seams. On the other hand, *ad hoc* work related to one-off contracts and DCR adds that these ad hoc contracts led to much hard feelings between miners as certain workers were paid more even though they might be doing the same work as other miners. The contracts were introduced by British Coal in 1988 and remained in the industry until it closed in 2015. Many miners also talk about the *power loader agreement*. This system had been introduced in 1966 to standardise payment at the coalface so that all miners in the same job would be paid the same. It was to end local disputes over *piecework* and resulted in many miners having to take a pay cut, with some arguing that it decreased productivity as there was less incentive to do additional work. Some miners discuss that they were sometimes given particular *incentives* if extra work was needed, and there are also occasional references to *grab money*, *golden hour*, *extras* and *fiddles*. Some interviewees also mention that miners could be paid additional money for working in particularly unpleasant conditions, such as *watter money* for working in mines which either had high standing water or where water was constantly dripping down onto the miners.

During the interviews and questionnaires, the participants were also asked about words that they used for their friends and colleagues and what terms they had for hard or lazy workers. Many of their answers are followed by long and detailed descriptions of nicknames, often with comments that these are not very polite or politically correct, but, as with swearing, this was something that miners had to be able to put up with and to use to be part of this particular community. This is a common theme found in mining communities around the country, see also Cave (2001), and it forms an important part of mining life. One such term, which is given by DCR, is the term *ham sarnies*, which was used for men who were shown round the pit as they were moving from other collieries that were shutting down. These men were given a full tour of the pit (and other facilities such as housing) and then taken to the manager's office for some lunch (with food that was seen as being high quality, such as ham sandwiches) to encourage them to come and work in that particular pit.

Starting with names for friends and colleagues, just over eighty miners give a term they applied to their friends and co-workers, and here most of the

Analysis 95

miners give multiple terms. In this category we also notice terms which are local, some from the East Midlands and some used by miners who came in from outside. Approximately twenty miners refer to the word *marra* as a term used by miners from the north-east and who say that this term often came to be used by other miners in the mines that had high numbers of miners from that area. There is one reference to a *crossmarra*, which is the person who did your job on one of the other shifts, so someone you would not usually work with but who was still seen as an important worker. This worker is also referred to as your *oppo*. There are also many mentions of terms which are used more widely in the UK, such as *bud, mate, chaps, pal, mucker* (also spelled *mucka*), *partner, cocker* and *team*. Terms which are more specific mainly to mining and also more regionally to the East Midlands are the terms *sirree* or *surrey* (which is spelled out and pronounced in many different ways) as well as *mi owd* (reflecting l-vocalisation which is very common in words such as *old* and *cold*) and *butty* (which refers back to the butty system whereby one miner would be put in charge of a group of miners who he would choose and then pay himself out of the money given by the pit manager). There are also references to *youth* (regardless of the age of the speaker) and *duck* and *mi duck*, which is a very common term used throughout the East Midlands for both men and women. There are two references to a term which was thought only to be used at Langwith, which was *shag*. In an environment where working closely together and relying on one another is such a crucial part of working life, it is not surprising to see so many terms for friends and colleagues. Maintaining good working relations was a crucial part of working safely and many of the miners comment that much of their spare time and social life were also spent with other miners, so these words really reflect this close relationship that many had.

Terms for hard and lazy workers are also often followed with stories of specific miners who were either known for their extraordinary work ethic or lack thereof. Over fifty miners give terms in this category and, in a similar vein to the nicknames given to colleagues, many of the terms used for both extremes of workers are accompanied by long and detailed stories of where such names came from and the miners they described. Some of these terms also occur outside the coal mining industry, but the stories that accompany them are a typical feature of the camaraderie and community feelings found among miners. The terms referring to lazy workers include reference to being *bone, bone idle* or *idle* (as in *idle buggers, idleback bastards* and *idlejacks*). There are also references to *dossers, slackers, sherkers, shacklers, dodgers, skivers* and being *workshy*. There are also terms which are mentioned just once or twice such as *bad attender, useless tool, giro wallowers*, being *not worth a light* or *idler than Ludlam's dog* (and it is stated that nobody knows who Ludlam or his dog are) and of these men being *spineless*. One miner also comments that *you wouldn't pay them owt in washers* as they did so little. These men are also referred to as *magicians* (as they always disappeared when work needed to be carried out), *LDVs* (look, duck and vanish) and *NVQs* (not very qualified). In a work environment which was highly unpleasant and dangerous, these types of workers are viewed with disgust and dislike. There are other references to physical attributes such as *ragarms* (not being able to lift arms to work) and having seen *more life in Mick Jagger's vest*. These workers need *nicking under arms* (to be pulled up) and DWN states that 'somebody'd say he's a bit workshy, he's an idle bastard or summat like that, just to say he want some bloody ash plant he does, cause the shaft on a shovel was made of ash and he'd say he wants some bloody ash plant, that will get him bloody going that will'. RG says about lazy workers: 'Another word we used to call people is lagging boards because they used to get like a lagging board what we used to chock mine cars up and they used to lean on them and just sit down and do naff all, all day, if you know what I mean they were lazy gits.' ABS from Gedling explains that if someone was struggling to keep up with their workload, another miner could be told to go and *pap them off* or *give them pap* which meant helping them with their stint, which ABS thinks comes from the expression to give a baby pap, i.e. to help with feeding them. However, that miner would then be docked money for the help he had received, so miners would not want to receive such help.

In the same way that these lazy workers are despised, the hard workers are revered and treated with the highest esteem. They are most frequently referred to as *grafters*, but also as *sloggers* (and an individual as a *slogger piece*), *big hitters*, *workers*, *work 'oss* (local pronunciation for *horse*), *top man*, *king of the day*, *king of the mountain* and someone who *would give it some clog*. At one particular pit, the two hardest workers were known as *the Denby Dynamos*. It is interesting to see that there are fewer terms for hard workers than for lazy ones, and having to deal with men who avoided (hard) work is clearly regarded as a negative aspect of being a miner. Cave did not find the same in his South Yorkshire mining community, where many of the stories centred around disregarding work and trying to do less work (Cave 2001: 289), but these values do not seem to be held in high regard by our interviewees. It is not clear why this should be so different, but it could be linked to the passage of time, where our miners were reflecting back on their years of hard work and graft.

The last category in this section concerns the clothing worn by miners while working. Around half of the miners gave an answer to this question and the responses vary from general terms for clothes to particular examples of items that were needed or worn during their working days. Often the answers include information about the general conditions of the pit (such as how hot or cold it was, or how wet or dry) as this affected the clothing needed. With reference first of all to general terms for clothing worn in the mine, many miners name *overalls*, *workwear*, *pit togs*, *pit cracks*, *pit mucks* or *pit rags* (one miner says that these were also called *glad rags*!) as well as *scruffs*, *keks* and *clobber*. There is also a discussion about when the situation changed from men having to supply their own clothing in the mine (and therefore usually just wearing clothes that were too old and threadbare to wear outside of work) to gear supplied by the mines and the National Coal Board, which were usually the orange overalls and helmets seen in more recent times, as AB explains. DWN says miners had different qualities of clothing: *best clothes* which would be worn to weddings and funerals, *shifting clothes* which would be those worn to and from the pit, and *pit clothes* which were the clothes they worked in. He also adds that most houses would have a *pit corner* next to the fire where wet items would be dried overnight, ready to wear again the following day. When specific items of clothing are mentioned, these were for example *donkey jackets* and *moleskin trousers* (which were needed above ground or in colder areas of the mine; JHN2 notes that these trousers could be stood up after a shift as they were so hard with sweat), as well as *pit knickers*, *vests* (including *sham vest*) and *shorts* (which were more suited to the warmer areas of the mine, where men would often strip as much as possible due to intolerable heat). RG, who worked in Rufford and Gedling, adds that some miners received salt tablets as they lost so much liquid through sweating. There is one reference to a *ganzi* for a coat, which is also a local term often used for a jumper. Such items were needed in some of the colder areas of the mine, and MW, who worked in Cadley, mentions that as it was a drift mine, it could freeze and sometimes icicles had to be broken off the manrider before it could run. PT explains that even in one mine the temperature could vary widely. He describes that for most of his shifts he would just wear shorts and boots, as it was so hot that you would be wet with sweat, but then that face would break down and you were sent to work for one shift on another face closer to the pit bottom, and that was freezing cold and the cold wind froze you in your shorts. In wider literature, Griffin has mentioned the term *shookies* for cloth caps (Griffin 1988: 81) but this is not mentioned by any of the miners in this project, and Cresswell mentions *pit gear* when referring to miners' clothes (Cresswell 2008: 20). BC, who worked in pits around Nottinghamshire, states that miners from Lancashire were nicknamed *cloggy* because they wore clogs down the pit, instead of boots, but that most men soon changed that practice.

In this first section – which has considered issues such as wages, shift patterns, end of shifts, break times and food, hard and lazy workers, and pit clothes – we can already see patterns forming. There are many mining terms which are influenced by local pronunciation, and miners are very aware of this and are keen to point out how such words were pronounced (or written in the questionnaires). We have instances of *ovvertime, watter money* and *in 't tin* which show pronunciations that are typical of the East Midlands. We can see that some terms are used throughout the East Midlands region, such as *snap* (which is very local to the East Midlands, and it may also be the case that some Yorkshire miners also used this term), as well as some generic terms, such as for the shift patterns and wages. Some terms can be linked back to older times, such as the *butty system* and *piecework*, where practices may have changed but many of the words are still retained with slightly changed meanings. We can also see that some terms are local to particular areas within the East Midlands, with terms such as *doddy* and *rodding up* mainly used by Leicestershire miners, who are sometimes discussed as being different to other miners in the way they spoke, and that some terms vary more widely around the region, with terms such as *dudley* and *loossall* being used throughout the region but not by all miners. There is an awareness of terms being different in other parts of the country, particularly with terms such as *bait* being associated with miners from the north-east. We also see in many terms the humour and leg pulling which is such an important aspect of mining life, in terms of how miners refer to each other through nicknames, the stories of hard and lazy workers and the discussions and jokes had during break times. As has been suggested earlier, much of this teasing could be linked to trying to cope with the dangers of working underground, which is discussed in the next section.

4.2.2 Dangerous conditions

As has been mentioned before, coal mines were unpleasant and dangerous and there were many different problems which men had to be prepared for: gas, fire, water, explosions, roof falls and different injuries that could result from their work. This section focuses on the different types of danger, with a focus on particular types of gas and what they were called, as well as warnings shouted to each other, and particular work-related injuries. Some interviewees relate that some miners had something they call *pit sense* (as did some ponies) and would sense and step away from imminent danger. AW adds that those who did not have such a pit sense were very injury prone, sometimes leading to very serious injuries or even death. JK explains: 'If I said it was a young man's game, I mean I've seen some old miners who is retired and they used to say hard work never killed anybody and I said no, but it twists them into some funny shapes.'

When asked about particular dangerous conditions in the mine, over fifty of the miners give examples of issues they had to deal with on a daily basis and some comment that everything was dangerous, as AB says 'everything you could see, touch or smell'; *complacency* was also seen as an important issue by one of the participants. Many do not give particular words for these conditions and describe what would happen, but if particular words are given they will be added here and explained throughout. Many miners also highlight multiple dangerous aspects of the jobs. There are several clear themes: roof falls, gas (which we will come back to in the next paragraph), being trapped or stuck and, more rarely, danger from water. There were multiple references to *roof falls*, which could result in miners being *buried* by a roof fall or by *coal slides*. There are a few references to a *runner*, which is the name given to such

Analysis 99

a roof fall (although we will see that it has an alternative meaning in the next paragraph), as well as to the terms *cave in*, *shed's in* or simply *fall*. In addition to roof falls, pressure from above was also a great danger and is referred to as *weight on*, which meant any sort of pressure coming from above. Sometimes bits of the roof could flutter down, which is referred to as *scabby*, *flaking* or *bitting*, and often a deputy's job was to go around the roadways checking the roof with his *yard stick* to ensure the safety of the roof. RCH comments that miners would warn each other 'don't go up there, it's bitting'. A weak roof is sometimes referred to as *nesh*, which is also a local word used in the East Midlands for something which is weak and delicate, usually a person. PB, who worked in Haworth, also comments on the warning phrase, *it's gonna lob*, which refers to a large piece of coal or rock which could fall from the ceiling.

Another very common danger was being trapped by mine cars or tubs or ponies (we will discuss the terms for different coal containers in section 4.2.6), and usually interviewees refer to this as being *trapped*, *pinched* or *penned* as well as using the term *get fast* (which meant to get stuck). A loose mine car could be called a *mainer* or could be referred to as *runaway tubs* which could break free and potentially cause great danger, extensive injuries and death. DR from Silverhill in Nottinghamshire mentions another term for such runaway tubs, *runners*, and says that if 'people screamed runner, you knew something was running away from you' (in this section we have seen that *runner* can also refer to a roof fall). Another dangerous aspect of work was linked to the conveyor belts which were often used to transport equipment and tools underground. Most of these belts (which will be discussed fully in section 4.2.8) were not manriders, so miners were not permitted to travel on them, although this was done sometimes and could lead to serious injuries, including trapping parts of the body and causing injuries to the head resulting from hitting into objects, and the movement of equipment, as well as faulty equipment in general. ABM from Teversal and Silverhill comments that such illegal manriding was sometimes referred to as *tiddly-dee*, to refer to the noise that the tubs made when riding across the tracks.

Other dangers included *water inrush* which is also referred to as *raining*, when water would suddenly enter the mine (either from other seams or from above; many miners had to permanently pump water out of the mines). SF comments that in Moorgreen the water used to rain in and stain miners' skin brown. Airborne dust was not only a hazard when it came to breathing but could also cause explosions or *combustion* which occurred below ground and could result in the release of gas or fire. Furthermore, tools (which will be discussed in section 4.2.3), machinery and the haulage chain could be faulty or cause sparks, and tools could fall and cause injuries. Bad roadways posed dangers of tripping and falling. Another term which is used almost unanimously was *floor lift* for the sudden raising or breaking up of the roadway; other more unusual terms are *floor heave*, *floor hoove*, *floor blow* or *floor boiled up* which describe the same occurrence. The method for dealing with this problem is either referred to as *dinting* or *denting* (there is discussion in several of the interviews that these were two different words, and that *denting* was mainly used by Leicestershire miners).

As a result of so many dangers which could be present at any time, the miners comment on terms that they used to warn each other of potential danger. Some of these are rather generic and include *look out! hey up! watch out* or *watch your back!* Other terms are *fire load!* when about to set off an explosion (*shot firer* will be discussed in job descriptions), *get yersen shifted*, where we can see reference to the non-standard reflexive pronoun which is common in the East Midlands, and *get your fetlocks out* as well as *board!* or *below!* if a broken floorboard was a danger. Some of the miners say that understanding and being able to read the situation underground was crucial to survival; ABS says that 'your coal would talk to you' and describes how experienced miners could tell by different noises and situations whether something dangerous was likely to occur and therefore would avoid injury, which is linked to the idea of *pit sense* discussed earlier.

The most common warning given by around twenty miners is *hold up!* which is more commonly written and discussed in the interviews as being *owd up!* (showing l-vocalisation typically found in such words and which is specifically mentioned in the spelling by MH from Nottinghamshire), and which meant be careful or look out when walking underground, or even to stop loading coal onto the conveyor if this belt had temporarily stopped – this could also be signalled by shouting *stop the belt!* Some miners also comment that *hold down* and *hold across* were used as warnings that there was a danger from below and from the side, respectively. There were other ways of signalling danger, such as turning the cap lamp on and off (torches and head lamps will be discussed in section 4.2.8), switching lights on and off, banging tubs or sounding an alarm by banging wires, and shouting *pap pap* to warn of impending danger. There were also codes used to warn of managers coming along and these included shouting *tiddly-dee* and *whistling the red flag* which referred to a particular whistle call. DH also mentions the warning *19* which meant 'look busy, manager is coming', explaining that it came from the card game Crib, where 19 is the lowest score you can get. JPE mentions that certain calls could differ depending on the job and that in his case *owd up* was meant to slow the hoist up or down as he would be sitting on top of the lift, examining the shaft sides.

During the interviews and in the questionnaires we also asked the miners to consider some of the most common injuries which resulted from coal mining. These range widely from *black nails* (where hands or fingers had been *trapped* or *pinned*) and *spanner rash* (knocking your finger) to *bosted bones*, which included all sorts of *cuts* and *breaks*, and *loss of limbs*. Wounded men could be referred to as *stumpy*. Serious injuries were referred to as *stretcher cases*. Miners could also experience damage to eyesight known as *nystagmus* due to poor lighting conditions, deafness due to loud working conditions,

Analysis

and *miners' tattoos* (also referred to as *blue marks*) where they experienced blue/black tattoos due to coal dust getting underneath the skin following cuts which then remained under the skin permanently. Some miners suffered from *white finger*, which is a condition to the nerves, joints and blood vessels of the finger and hand due to long-term, excessive exposure to vibrating hand-held power tools. Injuries to backs are sometimes referred to as *glassbacks* or *having your back off of sprocket*; the sprocket was like a piece of machinery in the conveyor belt.

One of the most common dangers referred to is the presence of a number of different gases below ground. Freese (2003: 47–48) has noted that miners faced three deadly gases. These gases are generally referred to as different types of 'damp' (from the German *Dampf* meaning fog or vapour). The three were: 'choke damp' (carbon dioxide, which suffocated miners quickly and occurred when carbon trapped in oxidised coal was exposed to air), which is also sometimes referred to as 'black damp' (see Griffin 1977: 121–122); 'white damp' (carbon monoxide which is a product of incomplete combustion and mainly appeared after a fire or explosion; mice and canaries were brought in as they were more sensitive to this gas than humans and would pass out, warning miners of high gas levels so they could retreat back to safety); and 'fire damp' (methane, also formed by decaying vegetable matter, which could seep from coal seams). Griffin has also commented that black damp is usually heavier than air and is a far greater danger in shallow mines than fire damp. We will refer to our miners' comments in relation to these statements. References to gas being present are *there's gas* or *there's juice*, and one miner states that miners could sometimes say *there's juice in lip* if there was gas near where they were coaling. Most interviewees are aware of different names for gases and more than fifty give different terms, sometimes using the names of the gases, such as *methane, carbon monoxide, carbon dioxide*, with *methane* by far the most frequent, but many also give the terms described by Freese and Griffin above. In addition to the terms *fire damp, black damp* and *choke damp* (the last of which is only mentioned twice), the miners also give the terms *stink damp, after damp* and *marsh gas*. One of the miners says that *stink damp* refers to carbon monoxide, and most seem to be in agreement that *fire damp* refers to methane and *black damp* to carbon dioxide. Two miners state that *black damp* refers to methane but it could be that some of these terms are confusing, with some miners saying that the terms are hard to remember. MH comments that black damp was found mainly in poorly ventilated roadways, and as it was heavier than air it was mainly found closer to the ground and would put out the flame in your lamp, while after damp was found mainly after explosions. It seems important that all miners use universal terms for these gases, because avoiding confusion would be crucial in the life-or-death situations which occurred when gas was found in the mine. There is also discussion about the different methods for measuring dangerous gas levels as well as the fact that mining could be stopped if an area was *gassed out*, when stoppages would occur due to a high level of methane. We see some of these words used in *Jobey*, a fictional story of an East Midlands miner, in the lines, 'He entered the old workings, testing for gas. He kept his lamp held high in front of him, watching the flame all the time for the tell-tale rise, which indicated firedamp. The man behind him kept his lamp low, watching for black-damp' (Williamson 2002: 225). Telling stories about different dangerous situations and accidents which had occurred during their working life was common and served to illustrate how perilous the working life of a miner could be.

In this section we can see again the influence of local language varieties on the pronunciation of certain words, with expressions such as *owd up* and *bosted bones* reflecting local language. This appears to localise many terms for these miners and, as it is something they frequently comment on, it seems to be very important to them. We can also see that some terms appear universal – such as the words used for the different gases – and it seems that to take the example of the dangers of mining it is very wise to have relatively little variation to ensure that miners are immediately aware of the dangers, even if they have come from other regions. We can also see that miners' personal work experiences can also influence the words they use, as particular jobs would have led to certain dangers and warnings being used more often. As we saw in the previous section where hard workers were seen in a very positive light, this is also the case for miners who have a lot of experience and who have what is termed pit sense, an almost innate understanding of how the mines worked. Many of the miners talk of the miners who taught them particular jobs when they were apprentices and how much they learned from these men. Such relationships were very important and made the working environment safe and more bearable. Many miners also commented on learning about the best ways of working with and handling tools, which is the focus of the next section.

4.2.3 Tools

In this section we asked the former miners about the tools they used in their working day and whether there were any local terms for certain types of hammer, spanners, (pneumatic) drills, shovels, crowbars, picks or axes, as well as additional tools they may have used that do not fall into these categories.

Many of the terms given to hammers referred to the weight of the hammers and included *2lb* (also known as a *lump hammer*), *4lb* (also known as a *tuffee hammer*, which is local dialect for 'sweets') *7lb*, *14lb* (also known as a *shifter* or a *blacksmith's hammer*), *28lb* and even a *56lb* hammer (which LM says that only the Lord and gravity could drop). It is also noted that the term *'ommer* was more typical of Leicestershire miners. In addition, the term *hommer* is given. Some of the miners comment that the term *hammer* by itself refers specifically to a *sledgehammer*. For example, RG who worked in Nottinghamshire explains that when he first started work at sixteen and was asked to fetch a hammer, he thought that they meant an ordinary hammer, but it was a sledgehammer. The most common term given for a hammer is the word *noper* (used by around thirty-five miners and variably spelled and pronounced; many of the interviewees discuss how to spell this and include *numper, nooper, nopper, nuper, nouper, nopper nose, nomper, newper, knopper* and *nopee*). Some of the miners suggest that these types of hammer refer to a hammer which also has a short pick at one end, used to remove metal roof supports. Other terms given for different types of hammer are *Monday hammer, road hammer, poker, prodder, knocking stick, roadman's hammer* (a special hammer for the men who laid the tracks on the roadways and needed a special hammer for knocking in *dog nails*), *grandfaither, sledges, claw hammer, groshel, maundrel, tadge, boster* and *electrician's screwdriver*. Also given are the terms *mell* (said to be used by north-eastern miners) and *thammer* (used in Lancashire; however, whether this word is related to the definite article reduction remains unclear as this is also a common feature of East Midlands speakers). The *Monday hammer* is said to have different origins in its meaning, but many interviewees refer to the heavy weight of this hammer, and JS comments that 'you brought it up and the good Lord brought it down'. Some say it was called the *Monday hammer* because it was as popular as a Monday, and another says that if you lifted it on a Monday you couldn't use your arms for the rest of the week as it was so heavy. JK adds that your arms would be too tired to work on a Tuesday after using this hammer. A final suggestion for this name is given by MH, who states that Monday tended to be the day that workers needed to straighten any bent angles that had come over the weekend, and so it would be mainly used then. A final interesting term was given by one miner, BK, who stated that a name for a hammer was a *mortek* and that there may be a connection to Eastern European miners. The Polish word for hammer is 'młotek', so there may have been usage of this word by Polish miners which was then adopted in the mines in which they worked.

Quite a number of terms are given for different types of spanners, with the two most frequent being *rat tail* and *ring spanner*, the first to do with its shape and the second to do with its purpose (adjusting the ring bolts on the arched supports). Other terms given are *bodger* (a flat-ended spanner with a spiky handle; MC adds that you used this 'if something didn't quite fit you'd put the spear end in and you would make it fit'), a *shifter* (a spanner with a long, tapered end on one side which could also be used as a hammer) and an *adjustable*. Less commonly found are *brasskey, ratchet, shifter, chock spanner, popeye, rail spanner* and an *electrician's screwdriver*. Two miners from Leicestershire also refer to spanners as *Whitwick hammers*, but are unsure where this name came from. Others say that some spanners are called *Whitworth's* which is linked to the manufacturer of this particular type of spanner (its name was written on the tool). It is also said that these were *fitter's tools*, meaning they were often used by mechanics when fixing machines. AD, who worked in Clipston, adds that there were *ratchet* and *taut* spanners and that the latter was a spanner that 'once you wind it up to a certain pressure [it] won't go any tighter so it cannot damage the ring bolts'.

During the interviews and questionnaires we also asked for the terms for the drills and pneumatic drills used in the mines. There are quite a number of different responses. One of the most commonly suggested is *borer*, as well as terms which referred to the length of the drills used, such as *3ft*, *6ft* and *yard drill*. One miner says that drills could vary between 4 and 8 feet long and we can see an example of such a drill in Figure 4.3 (in this image we can also see the mining lamp carried by one of the miners, which we will be discussing in section 4.2.8, and also that all miners are carrying a self-rescuer, which would give them air to breathe in case of explosions). One of the most common terms not to do with length is the *jigger* or *jigger pick*, also less commonly known as *windy picks*, which are compressed air drills. Some terms which are less common are *japs* (and it is stated that they were used by miners who worked at Grassmoor mine), *gadjett*, *burnside borer*, *wombat*, *bolt cropper*, *air leg* (which worked off compressed air and was held by hand), *pistol drill*, *aurora*, *titches* and *screamer* (because of the noise the machine made). One miner comments that the *Holmon rock drill* which also used compressed air was particularly noisy and that using these on a regular basis caused deafness and white finger (see injuries in section 4.2.2), which was likely to be the case with many other pneumatic drills too. What is interesting about the names for drills is that a very common term describes what these drills would look like,

Figure 4.3 Drilling at Shirebrook Colliery in the late 1970s (photo credit: Mansfield and Ashfield Chad)

Analysis 105

as they are referred to as *ram's heads*. A number of miners explain that the handles that they held onto were shaped like a ram's horns and that is why this name was used. Less common is the reference to *bull's head* and *pig's head*. Throughout the discussion of mining equipment and terminology, there seem to be many terms which include reference to animal names, which may be linked to what an object looks like or what it is used for. MW comments that such animal words are 'like terms of endearment'. This strong connection to animals is interesting and could have different backgrounds. Cave (2001: 182) has commented that there is a significant influence from agriculture, which is not surprising as many coal miners who began working in the coal industry when it boomed in the latter half of the nineteenth century had come from an agricultural background and so it is not unexpected that some terms could carry this influence. But it has also been suggested that a love of animals and nature could be linked to the long hours worked underground. In the fictional story *The Secret World of Polly Flint*, the father, who is a coal miner, explains his love of pigeons, as well as other birds, and this presumably could be assumed for other animals as being 'when you're down there under the ground, hours without a glimpse of daylight, and working sometimes in tunnels that narrow you can hardly stretch – well, the thought of them birds, winging and flying and making patterns in that great huge sky somewhere up there – well, that's a good thought. One you can hold on to down there' (Cresswell 2008: 9). This love of pigeons is also found in poems produced in our pit anthology (Braber and Amos 2021: 111) where it is explained that the father's love for his pigeons was more than that for his family.

Shovels are the next piece of equipment which our miners give terms for; almost fifty name this tool. Although one miner mentions that shovels were also referred to by numbers, this is far less frequent than it was for hammers or drills, but there is reference to a *number 4*, a *number 6* and also one to a *number 9* (which is also referred to as a *collier's flat*) shovel. It is said that rippers used a number 6 shovel and that this is a flat shovel. Other names given for shovels are as follow, with the first listed as the most common. This is the *elephant's tab*, which is the biggest shovel used, is round and refers to the local dialect word 'tab' for 'ear', which shows another animal reference. BBY3 says that the strongest colliers used this shovel as it allowed most coal to be loaded at one time. This shovel is only used underground for shovelling coal, also known as *coaling*. DR, a miner from Nottinghamshire, adds to this that there were two sizes of *elephant's tab* and that these were known as *African* and *Indian*, where the first is the bigger of the two. Other shovels had different purposes, a *dung* or *dot* shovel was used solely for dirt (reflecting local pronunciation; we will see this later with *dot hills* as well in section 4.2.9) as well as a *stone shovel*, there was also a *ripping shovel* used by rippers which was a bit smaller and was pointed at one end for ripping (which was taking out stone to make a roadway and is once referred to by BBY as *scrufting*) and square at the other end for loading coal onto the conveyor. A shovel used solely for loading onto a conveyor is also known as a *belt shovel*. They also had a *banjo* shovel which was round. We also see reference to the *square shovel*, also named a *bull nose shovel*, and a *blind-nosed shovel* (which was used above ground). A *flat, longpan* or *gumming* shovel was long and pointy and used to clean under conveyors and machinery. JPE from Derbyshire comments that a longpan had a long handle and was therefore also used to refer to tall people, 'he looks like a longpans wi' o'ercoat on!' Other less common terms include a *Durham shovel*, a *spoon, flatee, idiot stick, silly stick, spade, copper shovel, rogger out* (used for undercutting) and a *stone shovel* (used for packing). We can see that many of the terms used to describe shovels revolved around their shapes, which could vary widely depending on their function. These different shapes can be seen in Figure 4.4, which shows the different shapes of the shovel itself, but also the handle which could be long or short, depending on its function, and we can also see a faceworker in action with a shovel cleaning up underground in Figure 4.5.

We find much less variation in the different terminology used for a crowbar as, of the forty-five miners who give another term for this, only one does not use the term *ringer* at all. All other miners solely use this term, and eight use another term alongside it. PT explains that it is called a *ringer* because of the noise it makes when striking rocks. One miner says that the term *ringer* is used by Leicestershire miners, but other results show us that this is not the

Figure 4.4 Different shovel shapes

Analysis 107

Figure 4.5 Faceworker cleaning up with a shovel in Pleasley Colliery in the 1960s (photo credit: Coal Authority)

case and the word is used throughout the East Midlands region. One miner describes it as a round metal bar of approximately 4 feet in length with a flat pointed end. The other terms given are *ring spanner*, *pry bar*, *tommyboy*, *stang* (which is said by this miner to be distinctive to Gedling in Nottinghamshire) and there are also four references to *pinch bar* (with one miner stating that this comes from the north-east). We see a roughly similar pattern with words used for picks. Of the almost forty miners who have a term for a pick, around fourteen state that this is simply called a *pick* (we see one example of *peck*, which seems a similar variation to the *dinting/denting* variation discussed for some Leicestershire miners, and the only miner who gives the variation *peck* is also from a Leicestershire mine). We also see one mention of a *cutter pick* and one of a *mechanic pick*. The most common term given for a pick is a *shaft* and this is used for the entire tool, not just the handle (as is suggested by one miner). There are five references to *tadge*, which is also used by some miners for a hammer, so for some this is a tool which has two sides, where one is used for hammering and the other side used as a pick. There are other names which are only mentioned once, such as *jigger* (which was also used to describe a drill/pneumatic drill), *crow bell*, *pinch bell*, *chipper*, *slotdowns* and a *maundrel* (which we also notice alongside discussion of *tadge* in the hammer category and is stated to be half hammer/half pick).

There are very few terms given for axes, and several interviewees say that axes were rarely used by miners, with only eight miners responding to this question. One response is that axes were only used in very specific jobs – for example the *woodsplitter* which was used in the woodyard. There are singular references to *bullhead* and *chopper*, and the remaining terms are all *tadge* (also spelled *taj* and *tadger*) which is also used for a combined hammer/pick type tool, suggesting this may be a hammer/axe combination. One miner states that in pre-mechanised times an axe blade was sometimes interchanged with a pick when needed. MH comments that a *tadge blade* was a coal pick with a sharpened pick on one end and a type of spade for chopping wooden props out on the other.

Finally, miners were asked whether there were any tools they used in their particular jobs which they felt had not been covered in the interviews or questionnaires. Only sixteen miners added terms at this stage which focused on different work. These could be to do with the conveyor, as there were three references to *belt knife*, which was a knife used for working on the conveyor belt, also a *Stanley knife* and a *rope splicing needle* (which was used when a haulage rope was broken and needed to be spliced together again). There is also reference to a *sylvester* (which helped in pulling lifts as a winching device, although Bob Bradley's terminology on his website states that *sylvester* can also be used to describe the device for pulling props out of the goaf, which will be discussed in section 4.2.9), a *spitchel* (a tool used for taking coal cutting pips out of the coal cutting machine when they were worn away, although DC comments that he has no idea why it is given this name), a *pritchel* (used for rope slicing according to JPE from Derbyshire) and a *steel* (a tool used for cutting metal bolts which had a handle and needed two men to operate it). There are also *blocks* (mechanical lifting gear), *huck bolts* and *huck bolt cutters* which were a particular type of bolt used. The final term given is a *togal bar*, which is a spanner with a point.

Tools are a crucial part of a miner's daily work and depending on their jobs they would use different tools needed to carry out their work. So we can see from this section that there are some tools which are widely used and therefore have different functions (and names), such as hammers and shovels, and other tools which are more specialised and have less variation. Some of these words clearly can be related to the shape of the tools, so many terms refer to the weight of shovels or the lengths of drills, and there are also many terms which reflect the shape of tools, such as the *banjo shovel*, for example. There

Analysis 109

are many references to animals – the close affinity to animals has already been discussed and this seems to occur with tools as well, but there is also the addition that many tools have animals terms which refer to their shape, such as *elephant's tab* or *ram's head*. As with previous sections, we see that the local pronunciation can affect the way certain words are used, such as *'ommer* and *grandfaither* as well as numerous spellings and pronunciations for *noper*. There is some reference to regional differences, with Leicestershire miners being described as, or describing themselves as, using different terminology. We can also see the influence of miners from outside the region, with terms such as *mell* coming from miners from the north-east, and *mortek* showing influence from Eastern European miners who made up significant numbers in certain areas. As would be expected, miners have most knowledge about the tools they had to use most frequently in their daily work and can make most distinctions between tools where they needed to, for example for particular hammers or shovels that had more specific functions. In the next section we will also see that such particular knowledge is reflected in the terms used by miners; they have more knowledge about the particular jobs they did themselves and how they did them as there were so many different jobs that existed.

4.2.4 Job titles and levels of management

When asked to give job titles, most miners say that this would require a book in itself. There are over 400 examples given by the miners in the interviews and questionnaires, some of these cited more frequently and others only given by one or two participants. Many of the miners focus on their own jobs or those they frequently encountered in their daily work. In all, there are around sixty different job titles and types given by the participants. Some common terms deal with job descriptions that are also found outside the mines – there are *sparkies/electricians*, *blacksmiths*, *welders*, *fitters* (*mechanics*) – and these are terms that are frequently named.

Some of the terms given have changed over time, often due to increased mechanisation, which led to different jobs being needed. This can be followed closely, as signing-on books have been discovered for some Nottinghamshire mines which give job descriptions of all the men employed, and the changes can be tracked over the years. For example, terms such as *hostler* or *ostler* referred to the men who worked with the pit ponies (although these could also be referred to as *gangers*, *ponydrivers* and *hosstenders*) and were in charge of taking equipment along the underground roadways (work that had also been carried out by women and children historically). This job became obsolete due to the mechanisation of the mining process. As many mines stopped using ponies, the term *ganger* was used to describe the men moving equipment and coal along the roadways by other means – either on a conveyor or tram or by *tubs*, the name given for coal containers (these terms will all be discussed in later sections). These *gangers* are also referred to as *supply lads*, *haulage lads*, *haulage men* or just *haulage*. NC explains that a *ganger* is 'a bloke who supplies you supports and materials. It's what we used to call a ganger. The modern ones now, they are on rope haulage, or locomotives. We used to have this by horse at one time. That's why they called them gangers, and then it stuck.' Another term which is described by some miners as disappearing due to ponies no longer being used is the word *limmer*, which was used to describe the way ponies were attached to tubs. In his exhibition catalogue, Brian Morley also writes about *pony ganging* in the 1950s and 1960s before the time of mechanisation.

Many other job titles are descriptive in terms of what the workers did: the *sinkers* were in charge of sinking new shafts (the tunnel down from the pit top); *sawyers* worked in the sawmills, cutting timbers; *cablemen* were in charge of the wires and ropes of the lifts; *beltmen* were in charge of the underground conveyors, which were also referred to as *belts*; and *shaftmen* were in charge of shaft maintenance. As Wright has discussed (1972: 44), the term *miner*, which is most frequently used by those not in the industry, tends not to be used as much by these men themselves. The term *miners* in theory applies to all men working in the mining industry, and those who are working on the coalface or getting access to the coalface tend to be referred to as *colliers*, which meant that the men who were driving the new *roadways* (the tunnels underground), and the *facemen* and *faceworkers*, are those who were working on the coalface itself and cutting the coal. This sometimes had to be done with controlled explosions – the man who carried the explosives was called the *powder monkey* and he would assist the *shot firer* with the explosive work. The *titchman* drilled along the face preparing for these explosives. The men working on the actual coalface itself could also be called *hewers*, *ratchers* or *colliers*. The men who carried the drills and drilled holes were called *borers*; the men who moved up the roof supports to advance behind those creating the tunnels were called *chockers*, *chock fitters* or *chockmen*; the men who removed old supports and set new ones as required were called *back rippers* or *rippers*; and those looking after the supports were called *prop bobbies* (we will discuss *chocks* and *props* in section 4.2.8). Those who set the steel arches were referred to as *lippers*. The men who built the *stable holes* which allowed machines to turn and shear more coal were called *stable hole men*. The men who pushed the conveyor further over the coalface were called *snakers*. Floors in the mine could lift up unexpectedly and the men whose job it was to level these back out again were called *dinters* (and *denters* by two participants, see also this variation on *dinting/denting* in section 4.2.2). A more general name for the men responsible for the roadways was the *roadgang* which included terms such as *roadman*, *roadlayer* or *dogger* (this is linked to *doggies*, which are the rails underground, and *dogging* which refers to the job of attaching the *doggy nails* to these rails or coupling tubs together, which ABS said was a very dangerous job). The men who operated the different shearers and coal cutting machines were referred to as *machine drivers*.

Analysis 111

The coal also had to be transported back from the coalface to ground level and this required a number of different workers. The *gate lad* was in charge of opening the safety gates in the tunnels to allow the *tubs* of coal to pass through which would have been filled by the *hand fillers*. These could be transported by horse or on a conveyor belt which was controlled by a *belt driver* who is also sometimes referred to as a *button man* (RG, who worked in Rufford and Gedling, explains that many men's first job was such a *button job*, where they watched the conveyor belt and made sure none of the chutes blocked and ensured that any blockages would be cleared to allow the face to keep turning). The *onsetter* (or *jigger*) loaded onto the lift and the *offsetter* took it off again. The man who worked at the pit top in charge of the lift and safety there could also be called the *banksman*. And the man at the bottom of the lift was also referred to as an *onsetter*. This man also took the identity tags from the men when they exited the lift so it was known how many men were underground if there was an accident (this will be discussed in more detail in section 4.2.8 and can be seen in Figure 4.6) This lift was also controlled by a *bell man*, *bell lad* or *signalman* who would ring a bell when it was safe to haul the coal up (or down). The *winder* or *winding engine man* was in charge of the winding equipment which raised and lowered men and material in and out of the pit, and the *ropemen* were in charge of maintaining the ropes and cables of the lift. The tunnels which were created had to be supported not only by the *chockers* who moved along with roof supports behind the advancing

Figure 4.6 Onsetter taking identity tags from miners arriving underground (photo credit: Mansfield and Ashfield Chad)

conveyor, or *chock fitters* and *chock men* who were in charge of checking and repairing the chocks, but also by creating walls built up with debris to hold up the ceiling, with the men involved known as *packers*. There were also the *loco drivers* who drove the underground trains for larger mines where the coalface could be a few miles away from the bottom of the shaft. RG also describes being on *spare board* – this is when everyone came to pit bottom to be allocated jobs and if all jobs were taken but some miners were left over, you would be last man standing and you could be put to work anywhere at all, which was unpopular.

On ground level there were *surface workers*: the *stackers* were employed to empty the tubs of coal and to grade the coal (not all coal was of similar quality: some would be used for domestic purposes and had to be of a higher quality, and other coal would be used by power plants which could be lower-grade quality), and the *coal prep lads* worked on sorting the coal. The coal was delivered by a *coal bagger*. The *telephone lad* was in charge of phones and the *tea masher* was responsible for making tea for the surface workers. For those pits which had shower facilities, there were *bath attendants*. The tubs which carried the coal could be damaged and the men who would repair these were called *tub thumpers*. Other job titles mentioned were the *surveyors*, who would not only be looking at developing further roadways but were also in charge of ensuring the safety of existing roadways. *Air samplers* and *ventilation officers* looked after and regulated the airflow throughout the pit. All men entered the pit as *apprentices* or *lads* (PT says that these apprentices were sometimes called *daffodils* because of their yellow helmets, rather than the white helmets most other miners would wear, and RG adds to this that there were also red helmets for those with more experience) and had to work above and below ground to gain experience of different jobs. Many of the miners interviewed said that they learnt everything about their jobs from the men who were put in charge of them and there was much respect for these older colliers. We also see references to job descriptions in the wider literature, for example Griffin has commented that a *screen gaffer* would turn tubs over and try to check whether anything bar coal was in the tubs (Griffin 1988: 42), although this term was not used by any of the miners involved in this research.

The miners were also asked about different levels of management, what titles these jobs had and also what the men who carried them out were called, whether they would be known by their first name or as Mr and their surname. As with the terms used for friends and colleagues, many of the miners noted that managers, and particularly senior management, had nicknames (which of course would not be used to their face) but that they would also be referred to as Mr plus surname, whereas those in lower levels of management would be called by their first name. A very large proportion of the miners said that managers were referred to as *gaffer*, which is a term also used widely in other workplaces. There was also a real range of managers, depending on their job roles within the mine. These ranged from the highest positions, those of *area*

Analysis 113

director, *sub-director*, *deputy director*, *general manager* or *undermanager*, to *deputy manager* and *assistant managers*, many of whom worked in all shifts in the mine, some with a particular job responsibility, for example the *night manager*. The *undermanager* would be in charge of underground operations and would have three *assistant undermanagers*, one for each shift – days, afternoons and nights. North and South Nottinghamshire also had *area production managers*. Some of those interviewed said that from undermanager upwards, terms of address would be much more formal, and many of the miners said that they did not often see this level of management while at their daily work. JHK explains the hierarchical system in the following way: undermanagers were responsible for everything, *overmen* were in charge of the men, deputies were responsible for a face or part of a pit, and shot firers were above normal colliers.

Lower-level managers and those who were part of everyday jobs, and who also required a much less formal type of address, included: *deputies* (who were different to *deputy managers*; these men were directly in charge of a group of men working on the coalface and could also be referred to as *face managers*), *overmen*, *colliery overmen*, *senior overmen* and *development overmen* (often referred to as *ovvermen* which reflects local pronunciation), *shot firers* and *chargemen* (in charge of explosives), *surface superintendent* (in charge of the pit top, so on the surface rather than underground), *safety engineer*, *gate end supervisor*, *face overman*, *deputy mechanical engineer*, *product manager*, *command supervisor* as well as *shift chargehand*, and different levels of supervisor roles, including for example *safety officer*, *ventilation officer*, *fire officer*, *dust suppression officer* and *training officer*, as well as different types of engineer, such as *chief engineer*, *electrical engineer* or *mechanical engineer* – these roles also had *assistant* and *deputy engineers* below them.

There are other terms such as *coddy* and *corporal* (who were in charge of *pony lads*). This latter was an older term which disappeared from usage from the 1970s onwards. In the older systems, there were also *butties*, in the *big butty system* the main *butty* was put in charge of producing all coal by the owner or manager and then he paid the rest of the workforce himself. These butties would then manage the pit with a *stover* (also called *stever*) who was a pit top boss and could control wages and labour conditions. The term *butty* was not to be confused with its alternative meaning of *friend* in some Nottinghamshire mines.

A further issue which was raised by some of the miners interviewed was the way in which some of the men made it to these supervisory or managerial roles. Some of them started work at the very bottom and progressed over the years to higher roles where they were supervising or managing men. Although these men were still not always liked, they were generally respected and most miners reflected that these men had many years of experience working in a coal mine and tended to have good 'pit sense'. However, especially in more recent years, there was an increasing habit for men to arrive fresh at the pit in the higher positions, coming from college or university without any previous mining experience. These *16 week wonders*, referring to the time taken for additional mining training, were generally not respected and were often thought not to understand how mining or miners worked.

We can see that there are many different terms for the different work that had to be carried out at the mines and this is similar to all the different tools that were used by these workers. We do still see some regional variation, with some differentiation within the region; for example, *area production managers*, which only tended to be used in Nottinghamshire. But rather than regional variation, we see more uniformity in these terms within the East Midlands, although some of the terms used outside the region were not used or understood by the miners in this project. Some of these jobs are very specialised and some are more prestigious than others; those working directly at the coalface tend to be given the highest prestige (and tend to be paid more as well). Many jobs are initially carried out by apprentices and most miners have to carry out a variety of jobs so that they have experience of working in different areas of the mine. For those within management, there are two levels of managers and a higher level of formality is associated with those at the highest level, who also tend to be the managers who do not actually work at the mine themselves. The second level of management comprises those who work alongside the other miners and who, especially if they have worked their way up through the ranks, are treated most positively by the other miners, who often respect them for their knowledge even if they do not like them. We can see the use of some terms which are used more widely outside of the mining industry (such as *gaffer* and *sparkie*), and we can also see the influence of mechanisation, with some terms either disappearing or changing their meaning to reflect new working practices (such as *ganger*). We can also still see examples of job titles which are very descriptive, either literally (such as *sinkers* and *beltman*) as well as those which are more figurative, for example the *snakers* who were in charge of moving the conveyor.

4.2.5 Coal seams and pieces of coal

Another field in which we see considerable variation is in the names given for the seams worked in the different coal mines, which varied due to geological strata, and there are also different names for different-sized pieces of coal. For full information about all the different coal seams in the East Midlands, and also for the rest of the UK, Bob Bradley's website gives lists of all layers in every region (see the entry for Bradley in the references section at the end of this book). Coal seams varied greatly with regards not only to the height of the coal seam and therefore its very different working conditions but also in terms of the quality of the coal, and many of the interviewed miners provide extensive detail on both these aspects. DCR, who worked in Haworth, comments that the *deep soft* seam in which he worked was about

Analysis 115

16 to 18 feet high in some places, and it was very different to some of the low seams worked in other regions through which men had to crawl. As AD explains, this was the case in the yard seam where he worked which was less than three feet high, adding that when he was working on his knees his back touched the roof. With regard to the names given to the coal seams, over sixty miners give names to the seams they worked in, and all give four names or more. There are some who simply refer to *seams* or *strata*, as well as two references to *5ft* seams, and all others give names for the areas in which they worked, and how they progressed from different seams as coal extraction was exhausted in certain regions. The most commonly used seam names are *black shale*, *deep hard*, *deep soft*, *hazels* (including *high hazels*, *low hazels* and *hazels*), *low main*, *main bright/main coal*, *parkgate*, *piper*, *top hard*, *tupton*, *waterloo* and *yard seam* (also referred to as *yardy piper*). Most of these very commonly used seam names stretch through most of the East Midlands region, but there are some smaller seams which were more localised and are also named by fewer miners, for example *stockings* and *eureka* which are mainly found in the South Derbyshire region, *dunsil* which is found in North Derbyshire and *belper low* or *belper lawn* which is found in the Nottinghamshire region.

When talking about coal of different sizes, terms range from very large pieces of coal to fine dust. Coal which was sent to power stations tended to be more like dust and was known as *slack*, *slurry* or *blend*, and could be of much lower quality (a *crusher machine* which was also known as a *parrot beaked crusher* ensured coal was crushed to this consistency), whereas *house coal*, sometimes referred to as *brights*, needed to be of a much higher quality to allow it to burn well and could also be extracted by a *shearer* which would avoid crushing, although BJ mentions that coal cut by shearers was smaller than hand-cut coal, and MH notes that trepanners would give lump coal. BPS2 from Derbyshire explains how, 'when we were stinting it were all lumps, you got what you got. But when every pit used to have household coal, so then they put the power stations in, so they used to have shearers to smash it up, that went to your power stations and your trepanners cut lumpy coal, it didn't smash it and that was your household coal and that's what they sold.'

Coal was also made up of different elements including *rock* and *ironstone* which could not be sold alongside the coal and had to be extracted (see section 4.2.9 where the screening plant is discussed). Miners could be fined if their tubs were thought to contain too much waste material, which was also known as *dot* (representing the local pronunciation of 'dirt') or *bat*. Large pieces of coal were known as *lumps* most commonly but also as *battleships* or *rakers* (which tended to be the very largest pieces of coal; see Figure 4.7 for a miner hand-loading large pieces of coal). In the wider literature, Griffin (1988: 42) has mentioned the term *sammies* for large stones which fell out of the roof; however, this term is not used by our miners in this context (although we will

Figure 4.7 Miner hand-loading large pieces of coal onto a face conveyor (photo credit: Coal Authority)

see it coming up as a term for rubbish in section 4.2.9), but the term *grey lady* seems to mean something similar. Smaller lumps of coal were mainly called *cobbles* but also *nuts*, *beans*, *peas* and *fines* (in decreasing size), and pieces of coal could also be referred to as *singles*, *doubles* or *trebles* to indicate their size – these were also frequently used for *house coal*. ABS says that *cobbles* tended to be around two inches across. There are two references to *cannel/ kennel* coal which is said to have the consistency of tar, as well as *diamond brights* which burnt very well.

We can see that the mining seams themselves show regionality as they vary throughout the East Midlands, and although some seams occur in much of the region others are more localised. There are terms for large and small pieces of coal, however we see very little commentary on local pronunciation of words as we did in the previous sections. There are fewer regional patterns within the East Midlands and very little feedback on variation among miners. Perhaps these terms are more generic throughout the UK. There is some discussion in the other pit talk literature which does suggest some terms that East Midlands miners do not use, such as *kank* which has a different meaning in the East Midlands.

Analysis 117

4.2.6 Coal containers and safety devices for such containers

Once the coal had been mined from the seams it had to be transported back to the surface. This could be done in different ways, depending on whether the mine had a vertical shaft (where it would have to be taken out by lifts, discussed in section 4.2.8) which was often referred to as *skip winding*, or if it were a drift mine where coal could be transported straight out from the coalface, often by conveyor belt. There were different types of containers – which can be sub-categorised into containers (with sides), as well as different types of trolleys and flat cars (which tended not to have sides) – which were used to transport equipment. In this section we will be considering these types of containers as well as the different safety devices to stop them moving or rolling, as moving containers posed a real danger to miners (as was discussed in the section on dangers in 4.2.2, where such movement could result in trapped fingers, hands, heads, as well as a miner being crushed). There is some overlap between the terms used for different types of containers but we will combine terms for trolleys and flat cars together as they seem more similar to each other than the other containers used mainly for coal.

Almost eighty miners give different terms for coal containers and many supply multiple names. The most common are *tubs* which was the term given by almost seventy miners, followed by *mine cars* which was used by around twenty miners. In the discussion of *mine cars*, there are occasional references to size, including that some of these mine cars could hold between two to four tons of coal. Other terms which are used by far fewer interviewees include *bunkers* (which include *butterfly, inline, vertical* and *retractable bunker*), *jotties* (which we will come back to when discussing the flat transporters), *skips*, *hops/hoppers* (which are more like buckets rather than full-size containers), *bogeys, transporters* and *ring trams* and *morris* (which referred to the company who made them). Almost fifty miners give a term for different types of trolleys and forty miners mention different names for flat cars, but these will be considered together as there was considerable overlap between the terms used for both these types of containers. There appear to be three main terms for different types of containers without sides – the most common being *dannies* which was used by around twenty-five miners. There are different types of *dannies* named by the miners as well, which include forms such as *horned dannies, supply dannies, transport dannies* and *flat dannies*. The second most common term for this type of flat car is a *jotty*, and it is interesting to note that there do not appear to be any sub-types of jotties used by the miners. The term *tub* is also still used, even for a container without sides, and there is also a mention of a ½ *tub* by one miner as well as a *flat tub* and a *dolly tub*. Other terms which are used more infrequently include *beckrels, ring boats, skips, yellow peril* (which held explosives), *8-wheeler, flats* (which was used for large loads that could not be transported by normal tubs as well as for transporting ponies that died underground), *load binders* (which were round steel tubs) and *coolie cars*. We see the terms *bogey* and *hopper* being used by Griffin (1988: 87) who says that *bogeys* or *hoppers* were used to 'take the spoil up to the top of the heap'. As well as being used for transporting coal and equipment, coal containers were also needed as part of shaft sinking, see Figure 4.8.

As mentioned above, it was crucial that these different types of containers needed to be controlled, especially as they were often very heavy, and

Figure 4.8 Shaft sinking at Bevercotes Colliery in the late 1950s (photo credit: Coal Authority)

Analysis 119

there were a number of different safety devices, either to stop the containers moving, or to enable them to be derailed if they did break free. Most miners give a term for at least one safety device, and most miners mention multiple terms as well as descriptions about the appearance of such devices and how they were used. Starting with the devices used to stop tubs moving, usually by inserting something into the spokes of the tubs to stop movement, these are frequently referred to as *lockers* – which was given by over fifty of the miners – which could be made of steel or wood and it is emphasised that these were used in wheels (rather than under them as with some other devices we will examine in a moment). There are some elaborations on this term, with one miner explaining that such a locker could also be called a *fish plate*, and there are also references to *haulage lockers, pigtail lockers, wheel lockers, lockering, dobber-lockering* and using a *stop lock*. RW, who worked in Cadley Hill in South Derbyshire, said that 'a locker was a short iron rod, our term was dobber-lockering, you used to shove the lockers in the wheels on an incline to slow the wagons down before they reached the pit bottom'. A term which is used much less frequently is *dick*, which was used in some North Nottinghamshire collieries. DA tells the story of miners' confusion and fear when starting work at a North Nottinghamshire mine and when seeing a runaway tub they were told to put their *dick* in to stop it moving – their response being 'bugger that, put yourn in' (also showing the non-standard possessive pronoun). There appear to be more terms for devices that were used under wheels to stop movement, but as a result usage spreads more evenly throughout the interviewed group without any clear geographical distinctions and includes the common terms *scotch* or *scotcher* as well as *chocks* (which we will come back to when discussing hydraulic supports which also had *chocks*) and *chockblocks* (which was a large wooden block with one side at a 45 degree angle), *cheese, cheeseblocks, cleats, wedges, pinner, cleats, dumplings* (wooden wedges cut in a shape like a wedge of cheese, as explained by MH and DWN, and the description *cheeseblocks* is also used by DR) and *tub stops* (DCR from Haworth explains that *tub stops* were operated by the banksmen and were automatic brakes that were used when loading tubs into the lift). These could be placed in-between rails, and if a tub ran away it would run into these and would derail which would stop it moving. The term *jups* is said by KS to be used at Thoresby to refer to little bits of wood. Reference was also made to *keps*, which were safety devices on the lifts to stop the lift being overwound at the top of the shaft, and JHK explains that these *keps* had to be released before the lift could travel down.

There are also devices which attach to the tubs to slow them down, including *stangs, drop girders, clips, safety chains, nuddies* (although BBT explains that this term could also be used to describe small square blocks that were put on top of arches), *squeezers, drags* (which are attached to a tub with a *pig tail hook*), *double clip drags, manker/manker props*, as well as *iron drag hooks* which attached to the final tub. Other safety devices include *jazz rails* whose purpose was to derail tubs, also known as a *derail runner*, and *derricks* and *warwicks*, also known as *double warwicks* and *warwick girders*, which were long metal poles that angled down from the ceiling and stopped tubs moving. JHN2 states that you would click over a *warwick* and it would then lift up again and stop the tubs running, and GN refers to this as a *sprag*. There are also occasional references to *Manchester gates* which appear to have had a similar function but were swung across rail tracks rather than from the roof. RG describes these as gates which opened up and shut behind the tubs so if they did get away it would stop them running too far; he adds that he thinks it was named after the person who invented it. EP also uses the term *idleback* as a safety device which throws the tubs back on the road (this term was also used in section 4.2.1 to describe lazy miners, so this could be linked to these devices lying on the roadways). There is much admiration for miners who were adept at using the devices to stop tubs moving, as much skill was required to do it quickly and without injury.

It is interesting to see that such crucial items in the working day of many miners have so many different terms to describe them. Part of this might be down to the fact that some of these devices were made and adjusted by miners to fit the job they needed them to do, which is why there is likely to be great variation between mines and miners as some of the devices will not have been 'official' pieces of equipment. Many of these terms are also descriptive (*cheese blocks* and *wedges*) and suggest what these items looked like. In the same way that the safety devices were adapted for individual purposes, this also seems to be the case for the containers – other than the *tubs* themselves, which seems to be a uniform term across the East Midlands, many of the other transporters were adjusted to carry different sizes of machinery and equipment and could be made to measure. In this next chapter, we will see how some of these terms are similar, but not identical, to terms used in other regions of the UK.

4.2.7 Shafts and roadways

This section deals not only with the shafts which were used to transport men and material into and out of the mine but also with the underground roadways, including main roads as well as connecting roadways. Shafts connected the surface with the underground workings and enabled men and materials to be transported underground. There were some mines which had only one shaft, often referred to as a *shonky pit*, but most had at least two shafts (this was a safety feature to ensure that there was an extra way to exit the mine in case of accidents or fires, such a form of exit was also described as *egress*). Usually, one of these was used to transport men, material and equipment inward and one outward. Officially, the terms *downcast* and *upcast* shaft were used, where the *downcast shaft* also allowed fresh air to enter the mine workings. There are many terms for both of these shafts and there is also overlap between the words used in different pits. There are also many terms for the

Analysis 121

shafts themselves, with over sixty miners giving multiple terms for the shafts, with a maximum of six different terms given by several individuals. We see that many mines had two shafts (some more), and that often the shafts had names to do with their function, and that these names often came in pairs. As just mentioned, a mine with a single shaft was sometimes referred to as a *shonky pit/shaft*, and mines without shafts but with drifts were sometimes called *adits*. Of the paired items, nineteen miners refer to *intake* and *return*, or occasionally *outtake* (where the *intake* takes men/material into the mine and the *return* back out again). A further eleven miners refer to *inbye* and *outbye* (which were also used for the roadways), where the *inbye* refers to the shaft used for entering the mine and the *outbye* refers to the shaft for leaving. There are also the terms *downcast* (into the mine) and *upcast* (out of the mine) used by a small number of the miners. Furthermore, there are also names for the function of the shaft, such as a *manriding shaft*, which the men used, and the *coaling/coal* shaft, used for coal and equipment. The shafts could also be numbered, for example some miners who worked at Glapwell in Derbyshire explain that their three shafts were referred to as *Glapwell 1, 2* and *3*. Other numbered references include just *1* and *2*, where normally the number 1 shaft was for entering the mine and the number 2 for leaving, although EP2 who worked at Bilsthorpe in Nottinghamshire explains that the number 1 shaft was only used for men and the number 2 shaft only for coal and materials (a shaft used only for coal is also referred to as a *skip shaft* and DWN from Derbyshire notes that this term refers to a shaft that went from one seam to another seam without going to the surface).

Almost seventy miners responded with a term for the intake gate, with almost half giving a second and sometimes also a third term. The most common term, with thirty-nine occurrences, is *main gate* and there were twenty-five occurrences of *loader gate*, with one miner stating that this is where fresh air also entered the mine. There are also those who call it the *mother gate*, *supply gate* and *tail gate* (some of these terms are also used for the return shaft). There are a smaller number of terms such as *d-gate* (which only seemed to be used by miners who had worked at Teversal and Silverhill in Nottinghamshire), *feeder gate*, *inbye/intake*. Descriptions which only appear a small number of times include *air gate, centre gate, conveyor roadway* and *front end gate*. It seems some of these terms are used differently in different mines, and HH says that he had never heard of the term *feeder gate* until he met with miners from Crown Farm Colliery (near Mansfield in Nottinghamshire).

For the return gate, there is around the same number of miners who give at least one term for this gate, with sixty-five miners giving one term and many miners give a second, third and, in two cases, a fourth and fifth term. As with the intake gate, there are several terms which are used in high numbers; for example, thirty-one miners talk of the *tail gate* and twenty-seven miners refer to this gate as the *supply gate* (both of these terms are only used very infrequently for the intake gate). The term *return gate* is used by just under twenty miners and one specifically states that this is where foul air would leave the mine. This seems to contrast with the fact that three miners call this gate the *air gate*. There are also lower numbers for *feeder gate* (which was also used by some for the intake gate), *loader gate* (which was one of the most frequent terms for the intake gate) and *outbye*. There are several terms which are only used by one miner, such as *36* (which is said to be the *tail gate* at Cotgrave), *back end*, *d-gate*, *left gate* (the miner who uses this term says it could also be called the *right gate* and that the intake would be referred to as the *centre gate*), *main gate*, *mother gate* (both *main* and *mother* are used much more to define the intake gate) and *sewer gate*. There is a real variety of terms used for these two gates and the same term can be used for both gates which led to confusion for miners who moved from mine to mine. DA, who worked at Annesley in Nottinghamshire, notes that his pit was unique as the return airway was called the *feeder gate* which was very unusual, and he explains that they used this term 'as you can feed the equipment up that one' and that 'feeder gates at most other pits are either called return gates or supply gates or tail gates, but feeder gates are the same thing'.

For the roads in the mine itself, there are far fewer terms used and also fewer miners who give specific terms for these. The main roadways are tunnels from the bottom of the shafts or drifts which provide access to all working places at the colliery. From Figure 4.9 we can see how large some of these roadways are and the type of machinery that was needed underground. They are usually arched shaped, if large enough, and allowed the transport systems to pass along them. There were generally two main roadways, which was necessary for ventilation purposes, whereby one roadway carried fresh air into the mine and the other carried the stale air back out. Around thirty-five miners say that they had specific names for these roads, and the main term, which is used by ten miners, is the term *roadway*, with another four giving the term *main road*. Other miners refer to the machinery which travelled on this road, for example *car roads* (for mine cars) as well as *manrider* and *paddy roads* (we will look at the words for underground transport in section 4.2.8). Terms which are used by only one or two miners include *supply road* and *timber gate*, and there are just a few references to *inbye* and *outbye* (depending on whether the direction of travel is into the mine or back towards the main shaft to exit). Some miners also say that parts of the roads are referred to as *junctions*, which are often numbered as well as being named after the miner who started work on that particular part of the mine. For those mines without a shaft, this main roadway can also be referred to as the *drift trunk*.

The final term in this section is for the little roadways underground which connected the main roadways to each other. These were sometimes used as shortcuts and some miners note that they used them to get back to the lift more quickly at the end of the shift. Almost seventy miners give a term for these roads and the overwhelming majority (around forty-six) use the

Analysis 123

Figure 4.9 Circular tunnelling machine being assembled in a roadway in the early 1980s in Cadley Hill Colliery, Leicestershire (photo credit: Coal Authority)

same one – which is *snicket* – and many just give this one term. A few of the men clarify that they pronounce this as *snigget* and all of these miners worked in the Cadley Hill mine in the South Derbyshire minefield. The term *snicket* is widely used outside the mining industry to describe a narrow passageway between two houses, although the similar term *ginnel/gennel* which is used above ground is only given once in the interviews for such a roadway (see Braber 2015: 14). There are some other terms for these roadways which are less common than *snicket* and these are *airgates*, *crossgates*, *slits*, *shunts*, *slamps* and *sliproads*. There are also several references to *stable holes*, *manholes* and *hideyholes*, but rather than full connecting roads these refer to little inlets made at the side of the roadway which could be used when turning machines round, as well as for safety holes to escape from runaway tubs.

In this section we have seen that for the terms for shafts and roadways there is significant variation, especially for the shafts going up and down into the mine. There are multiple terms, which seem to be used more widely in the UK, and some of these are more specific to the East Midlands. We also see that the same term is sometimes used for different shafts (such as *supply gate* and *feeder gate*). This must have been very confusing when miners moved around and found different terms being used from their own home pits. For the roads, there is much less variation, and more of the focus was on air movement around the mine as this was crucial to keeping the mine ventilated and safe for the workers. For the terms used for side roads, we see more local terms, for example words such as *snicket* and the term *snigget* (only used by Leicestershire miners) which is used above ground for a passageway separating houses. However, the term *jitty* and *ginnel/gennel*, which we also see used above ground, is very rarely used underground. It would be very interesting to examine why these two words are used differently by mine workers to those outside the mine.

4.2.8 Equipment and structures

This section includes specific structures within the mine, as well as larger equipment used to shear coal and transport it back to the surface. The first structural aspect of the mine to be discussed are the steel arched supports which, in higher seams, were built to support the roof and stop it collapsing onto miners (we will deal with supports later in this section). Around fifty-five miners have a term for these supports, with just over forty miners referring to them as *rings* (with one inclusion of *German rings* and one *big rings*). These relate to the shape of the supports, and there are only two variations to this shape, where miners refer to these as *flat tops* and *kit kats* (DR who worked at Silverhill in Nottinghamshire is the only miner to mention this latter term and he explains that these particular supports looked like a chocolate kit kat bar, with a flat bottom, a piece which comes at an angle and then a square top). There are also thirteen references to *arches* (which also occasionally include reference to the fact that they are *steel arches* or *girders*). Some of the men who discuss this word explain that these arches were made up of different *component* parts, which include *olliebanks*, *bows*, *fishplates*, *hushpuppies*, *legs*, *u-bolts*, *tins*, *zings* and a *crown*. NC adds that the rippers 'set one, two or three arch girders a shift, depending on how far the coal cutter's advanced during the shift'.

Another type of support which was frequently used below ground was on a smaller scale than the steel arched supports and was used on lower seams to hold up the roof. Griffin has explained that such supports were introduced into mines during the two world wars (Griffin 1977: 115). As the area where the coal was removed advanced forwards, these supports were put up to support the roof and to allow the men to progress further forward, and

Analysis 125

sometimes these would be removed afterwards and the roof would be allowed to collapse. Much of the discussion around these supports centres around the fact that they were originally made of wood, then steel and sometimes they were powered hydraulically (they are infrequently referred to as *hydraulic supports*); hydraulic supports have replaced steel supports since 1945 (Griffin 1977: 115). Almost eighty miners give a term for these supports, and many mention several terms as they explain that such props could vary in size and structure (see Figure 4.10 for an example). The most common term is *chocks* which is given by fifty-five of the miners (and includes sub-categories such as *gate end chocks*, *dowty chocks*, *hydraulic chocks*, *anchor chocks* and *desford chocks*). Chocks are described as having two legs (whereas some of the others have four or five legs, for example the *gulicks* which are less frequently discussed). Other associated terms include *chocknogs* and *chockblocks*, which are small pieces of wood that go on top of the chocks, in-between the chock

Figure 4.10 Props (photo credit: Coal Authority)

and the roof (the term *chock* was also discussed in section 4.2.8 as it was used as a safety device to stop tubs from moving, with many of the miners using the word to describe both these things). The second most frequent word is *props* which is given by almost thirty miners (and included sub-categories of *dowty prop, dolly prop, dobby props* and *dobson's prop*, the first three of these are also simply referred to in smaller numbers as *dowties, dobbies* and *dollies*). JHK explains that *dolly props* were hydraulic at the bottom with a piston with a cap on the top and the lever could move this up and down to support the roof or bars. Other less frequently named words are *horseheads*, also known as *hossheads* (particularly for girders), *cabbage heads* (which were also used as lids on top of *props* and *chocks*; such lids were occasionally referred to as *cleats*), *sprags, gullicks, L-bars, meckers, jacks, face/shield supports, cockameg*, with one miner noting that this is called a *sniper* in the north-east. Griffin has explained that a hydraulic chock 'consists of a number of hydraulic props (called *legs*) having canopies which are steel cantilever beams, the whole being mounted on a steel platform to form one unit' (Griffin 1977: 115). JHN2 says that in Leicestershire props could also be referred to as *trees*, but none of the Leicestershire miners mentions this. PR, who worked in Bilsthorpe, which had a large influx of Geordie miners, notes that those miners used to call props *snipers* but that he had never heard anyone else use that term. JP also mentions that knocking in a steel prop could be called *thonking* but no other miners use this. We also see reference to *props* and *cabbage heads* in Brian Morley's exhibition catalogue when describing the days before hydraulic chock installation.

There are different machines and structures used for the actual coaling, where coal is removed. Traditionally this was done by hand but, over time, increased mechanisation meant that *hand-filling* by miners came to be taken over by machinery, such as coal cutting machines. Just over sixty of the miners give a name to this kind of coal cutting machine and many mention several names given that the machines used changed over time and many were known by their manufacturers' names. Some of the most common terms are *shearer*, used by thirty-seven miners, as well as *trepanner* which is given by twenty-six of the miners. Griffin (1977: 114) has described a trepanner as 'cut[ting] into the coal as the machine it sits on travels along the coal face'. Both of these terms are often used in conjunction with words which describe their usage, so there are extensive mentions of *single header* or *double headed shearers* and *trepanners* (and in fact the acronym *DERDS* is explained as meaning *double ended ranging drum shearer*). There are also *front shearers* and *overhead shearers* (see Figure 4.11 for an example of a shearer). Another common way these particular machines are described is how they are used, whether they are *floor mounted* or *conveyor mounted*, indeed the acronym *CMT* means *conveyor mounted trepanner*. Another term which occurs relatively frequently is *dosco* which is sometimes also called a *dosco roadheader* (see Figure 4.12 for an example of such a roadheader). Other words which are used less frequently

Analysis

Figure 4.11 Shearer on 93's face (Thoresby) in 1976 (photo credit: Coal Authority)

include the more generic terms *cutter* (also *longwall cutter*) as well as *ranging drum*, *stage loader*, *bunker*, *power loader*, *jib cutter*, *swan neck*, *plough* and *machine*. There are also fewer instances of those including manufacturing names, such as *Anderton*, *Meko*, *Meko Moore*, *Samson*, *AB cutter* and *BJD* (which stands for British Jeffrey Diamond). Griffin mentions an Anderton Shearer (Griffin 1977: 114) and gives the following description: 'The shearer has a horizontally pivoted drum laced with picks around the barrel of the drum. As the machine moves away from the stable hole along the face, this drum rotates at high speed, thus shearing down the coal which is then gathered up and eased onto the AFC' (this will be discussed in this section).

Once the coal had been cut it then had to be transported back to the surface. In many cases, this was done by an underground conveyor which as Griffin (1977: 114) has mentioned can be referred to in different ways, such as an *armoured flexible conveyor* (also referred to as an *AFC*) or *panzer*, another German term that is also described by many of the miners in this project (see Figure 4.13 for an example of a loaded conveyor belt). Around seventy-five interviewees give a term for this conveyor, and the term *panzer* is the most common term – used by fifty-two of the miners – with many explaining the fact that this was a German word. It is also described as a *(conveyor) belt* by around twenty-two of the miners, with one referring to it as a *cable belt*.

Figure 4.12 DOSCO roadheader (photo credit: Coal Authority)

Other common terms include *AFC* as well as the breakdown of these initials (*armoured face/flexible conveyor* and there appears to be some disagreement whether the *F* stands for *flexible* or *face*), *chain* is also relatively common (with one *scraper chain*) as are terms such as *trepanner* and *stage loader* which refer to the machines which could be mounted on these conveyors. Two final words which occur in the interviews and questionnaires are *crawley*, which is mainly used by Derbyshire miners (with the exception of one Nottinghamshire miner), and *python*, which presumably refers to its appearance as it was not a straight conveyor but could bend and be moved (and in fact as we saw in section 4.2.4, the men who moved this along were sometimes called *snakers*). ABM comments that the difference between a *panzer* and a *crawley* was to do with the number of links between the bars on them. There were less on a *panzer* and more on a *crawley* and DR adds that a *crawley* was much slower and *crawled along*. One of the miners states that the term *python* is only used at Annesley in Nottinghamshire, but we also see it used by another miner in Nottinghamshire and one in Derbyshire. In additional conversation some miners say that another name for the underground chain could also be a *sylvester*.

As well as a conveyor belt for transporting coal, there were other methods for transporting men underground. This was needed as in many mines the coalface which the miners were working at could be more than a mile from

Analysis 129

Figure 4.13 Loaded conveyor belt at Gedling Colliery (photo credit: Coal Authority)

the bottom of the shaft and it improved efficiency to get men to work faster. Travelling on the conveyor belt that we have just discussed was illegal and miners could be fined if they were found to have done so; however, many of the miners say that this did happen despite the dangers. The main ways of transporting men underground were by a conveyor belt which they were permitted to ride on and by underground train/tram. Babbington in Nottinghamshire also had underground cable cars (see Figure 4.14 and Figure 4.15 for an underground manriding train), referred to as *the hunt rider* (however, this was not mentioned by any of our miners, not even those who worked in Babbington). For the conveyor belt, there were just over fifty miners who named this as a method of getting to the coalface, and the most common name given was the *belt*, as well as *manrider*, and these terms were sometimes combined into the *manriding belt*. There are occasional references to *belt conveyor* and a *cable belt* (which is said by one miner to have been used only at Linby in Nottinghamshire, but we also find mentions of this in Moorgreen in Nottinghamshire which had a drift belt, rather than shaft). There are also just two mentions of the term *big Goliath*, both from Nottinghamshire miners. The other method of transportation underground was by train/tram, and almost seventy miners give a word for this method of transport. The most common word, which is used by fifty of the miners, is *paddy* (also used in the

Figure 4.14 The Hunt Rider cable cars at Babbington (photo credit: Coal Authority)

Figure 4.15 Underground manriding train at Thoresby (photo credit: Coal Authority)

Analysis 131

fictional mining story *Jobey* written by Leslie Williamson), usually this word is used just by itself but we also see combinations such as *paddy wagon*, *paddy transport*, *paddy cars*, *paddy mail* and *paddy train* (*paddy mail* is the term used by Williams (1962: 450) as the transport used to take men overground from one colliery to another). In additional conversation at the end of the interviews, KS comments that occasionally a *paddy* could also refer to an overground train. The next most common term is *manrider* with twenty-nine uses and other forms which are used less often are *locos* (short for *locomotives*, which itself is used only once), *monorail* and *cars*. BH2, who worked in Coalville in Leicestershire, believes that *paddy* was used more in Derbyshire than in Leicestershire where they were more likely to use the term *manrider*.

As mentioned previously, there were some drift mines which did not have a vertical shaft but the others did require a means of getting below ground. In times past, this could be done with a *hoppit* or *kibble*, which was like a bucket and was sometimes also used to transport material down, but later lifts were built that were wound down the mine (but are only very occasionally referred to as *skips* or *skip winders* by the miners). Overall, almost eighty miners say they had a word they would use for this lift and there appear to be two main words used: *cage* and *chair*. The first of these, *cage* was given by sixty-five miners, and *chair* was given by thirty-seven miners, many give both terms and BBT from Leicestershire states that he would only use *cage* and never *chair*. Some of the comments refer to the size and speed of these lifts and how many men they could hold. Some of the bigger ones were called *double-deckers* as they could hold two decks of men, one above the other, which can be seen in Figure 4.16. Most mines also used these lifts for winding coal up to the surface, and some of the common jobs discussed in section 4.2.4 were the *banksman* and the *onsetter* who would count men (and their identity tags, which will be discussed next) onto and out of the lifts. PR, who worked in Bilsthorpe and Thoresby in Nottinghamshire (of which Thoresby was one of the most modern mines and the last to close in the region), mentions that when men were on board 'chairs could only go manriding speed, they couldn't go coal riding speed', showing that the speed travelled would vary; other miners also comment on tricks played on apprentices by sending the cage down faster in their first shift to give them a fright. Miners were also asked whether there was a term for a 'lift full of men' as we were aware of the word *bantle*. Only thirty of the miners say that there was a term for this, and some just give numbers, for example *22 each deck* or *32 persons/men*, there is also one mention of a *14 inch date* as the cage would be so full, and one miner refers to the cage as being *chockablock* if full. Only six miners use the term *bantle* and a further nine used the term *draw* or *full draw* to describe a cage which was full. The term *uprider* and *a canch of men* both appear just once, but without any further reference or explanation.

When discussing lifts, it is mentioned that men had to give an identity tag to the *banksman*, this was both for safety (so it was known how many men

132 *Lexical Variation of an East Midlands Mining Community*

Figure 4.16 Double-decker cage at Mansfield (photo credit: Mansfield and Ashfield Chad)

Analysis

were underground) but also for payment. Most miners had three identity tags, one of which was handed in at the beginning of the shift, one of which was handed to the banksman and one which was kept in case of accidents and could be used for identification (see Figure 4.17 for an image of these). BBY comments that this *check* was often kept on the miners' belts so they would not lose it. These could be different shapes and included the number assigned to that miner as well as frequently the name of the pit. Many miners comment that they can still remember their number and many have these tags, for example on their key rings. In more modern pits, there were swipe card systems which took over from these metal tags. More than seventy miners give specific names to these identity tags and many mention more than one name, which makes it harder to see if there was particular geographic variation as is suggested by some of the miners. The three most common terms are *motties* which is used thirty-eight times, *checks* which is used thirty-five times and *tallies* which is given twenty-five times (and is said to be typically Yorkshire by one miner). There are only a handful of miners who specifically state that there are particular terms they did not use (for example, one miner says he would use *checks* rather than *motty*, two would use *tallies* not *motty* and one would use *checks* and not *motties* or *tags*). The four miners who do this are all from Derbyshire or Leicestershire pits. There are only a very few other terms which are used infrequently and these include *ID* and *swipe card*.

Figure 4.17 Motties, tallies or checks (photo credit: Suzy Harrison)

In fact, many of the miners who worked in mines that have a swipe card system explain that they continued to use *checks/motties/tallies* even when they were no longer used. These tags therefore seem to hold a very strong bond to their mining heritage and are also often featured at different mining heritage centres and museums.

Another common structure in the mine were the gate end boxes which were flameproof enclosures mainly used near the coalface and which formed a control board. They contained electric bars, isolators, switches, transformers and protective devices which controlled motors, lighting and other equipment in the mines. As this was a structure which many miners did not have any contact with, fewer miners supply any other terms for it; however, still just over thirty miners say that they would use different words for it. Half of those miners would use the word *panel* (and one mentions *switch panel*) and eight would use *switch* (including one occurrence of *switch panel* and *switchgear*). There are other words which only appear once or twice, including *latches*, *tension end* and *transformers* as well as *baldwin* and *francis*, the last two presumably being manufacturing names.

When discussing job descriptions in section 4.2.4, quite a number of miners mention one specific job, often held by someone at a higher level, namely the person who carried the explosives (*powder monkey*) as well as the person who conducted the explosions and who was often referred to as the *shot firer*. Miners were asked about different terms for explosives and sixty of them give other words for it, with *powder* (given by fifty miners, as well as one occurrence each of *powder bags* and *pit powder*) and *dets* (used by twenty-five miners, with only two occurrences of the full term *detonator*) being the two most common (and many miners gave both these terms). Words which appear very infrequently include *jelly*, *tnt*, *semtex*, *bobbins*, *polar ammon*, *penabel*, as well as descriptions of size such as *4oz* or *5oz* stick (two miners explain that a *bobbins* is a *4oz stick*). BG also mentions a particular tool related to explosives, known as a *waffler* which he explains is a cutting machine, 'like a shark with a long nose, a long pointy nose with teeth … that you put the powder in to get it going'. DR comments that an important safety device to control explosions was *stone dust* and he explains that if there was an explosion, the fire would leap from one piece of dust to another and this would cause the explosion. When there was stone dust in the mine, it could control the explosion by acting as a neutral element between the dust specks and stopping the explosion. Brian Morley describes the *shot firer detting the powder* in his exhibition catalogue which was taking place in the *stable hole*.

The last words in this section concern something which is intrinsically linked with being a miner: the flame safety lamp and later the helmet cap lamp which not only allowed miners to see what they were doing but in the case of the flame safety lamp also allowed deputies to measure dangerous levels of gas. For the flame safety lamp, just over forty miners say they had particular words to describe this and the majority of them give only one term

Analysis 135

for the item. The word *oil lamp* or *oiler* is used by eighteen miners and twelve miners mention the term *davey* or *davey lamp*, which is named after the inventor Humphrey Davey who first came up with this type of lamp which was specifically designed to be used underground without causing methane explosions by encasing previous open flames with gauze. As a result, this lamp is also called a *safety lamp* by six miners. BC explains that deputies' safety lamps were relightable (so could be relit after being extinguished by gas) whereas ordinary workers' lamps could not. There are infrequent references to other names for this lamp, including *ring nose*, *GR6*, *garforth*, *relightable* and *clanny/clony* which is said to be a very old term (BDM comments that he thinks *clanny lamp* was exclusively used in Moorgreen). For the lamps worn on helmets, there are just over fifty participants who give a term for this, the majority are *lamp* or *cap lamp* and there are only a few other terms which are used once or twice, such as *ring rose*, *black box*, *torch*, *flasher*, *GR6* and *spotter* (this last term is used for a supervisor's helmet whose light would be brighter than the other miners' helmets).

This section has dealt with a large number of different structures and equipment found as part of everyday mining life. We can see there is a large amount of variation in terms used. For example, the identity disks carried by miners vary between the three main terms of *motties*, *checks* and *tallies*. These are a very important part of mining heritage even today and the terms seem to be tied to particular mines, with some miners stating that they would only use some of the terms and not others. There does not seem to be a particular geographical pattern though. The same occurs for both *cage* and *chair*, the term 'lift' is never used and many miners give both of these terms as possible for the mines they worked in. Here there seems little variation with most miners agreeing that both terms can be used interchangeably and we also see the terms being used in other regions of the UK. The terms for the hydraulic supports are also universal, with *props* being a very common term. Any other terms are only used by much smaller numbers but these are likely to be more regional in nature. Much of the large-scale machinery is referred to by manufacturers' names or their construction (for example *floor-mounted* or *conveyor-mounted trepanner*) and these are also likely to be used more widely across the larger coalfield. As with some of the tools examined in section 4.2.3, manufacturing names often feature on the objects, so it seems logical that such terms are then used to name these items. In the terms for the conveyor, we see some more localised terms, with *crawley* and *python* seeming to be used more specifically in certain areas of the East Midlands whereas *AFC* and *panzer* appear to be the more widely recognised terms. Finally, the miner's lamp seems to have relatively little variation although a clear distinction is made between lamps used by the deputy and those used by all other miners. In the next section, we will examine the names given to locations found above and below ground to see how they vary.

4.2.9 Locations above and below ground

There are a number of areas above and below ground which were important in the working lives of miners and where they carried out much of their work. We were interested to know what different words they used for some of these locations. The first of these concerns the area in the mine where the active coal work was being carried out and where coal was being extracted. In this chapter, we have so far referred to this area several time as the *coalface* and it is the most common terms used by these miners. Of the seventy-three miners who gave a response to this question, fifty mention either *face* or *coalface* (this also includes individual references to *longwall face*, *pit face* and *mother face*). Another relatively common term, used by twenty-three miners is either *bank* or *benk*. This a confusing term, as *pit bank* or *bank* also refers to the area known as the *pit top* on the surface of the earth. Quite a number of miners, including RCH, comment on the use of the word *bank* and how its meaning varies throughout the East Midlands. There does not seem to be a geographical link, because miners from all three counties use this term. Many point out that it is a term that has two meanings, but no one provides a reason for why the word means almost opposite places in the mine. ABS from Gedling comments that *bank* had different meanings which were confusing to miners and that this is also reflected in the fact that *banksman* referred to the man who put miners on the lift and a general worker on the surface. There are a few other names given for this area of the mine which are used by individual miners and these are *pick point*, *panel*, *face line* and *district* – some of these faces were numbered (as junctions and roadways also could be).

Although mining conditions varied greatly, most mines had issues with water, whether water had to be pumped out, leaked in or was standing underground. In section 4.2.1 on bonuses, there was mention of *watter money* which would be paid for working in wet conditions. Almost fifty miners give terms for water, mainly below ground, but there are also mentions of water on the surface, and it seems that some terms could refer to both. The most common terms are *sump* which is given by nineteen miners and includes *sump* by itself, as well as *sump hole*, *sump lodge* (*lodge* also appears by itself and also in the compound *water lodge* but both are far less frequent) and *water sump*. BC explains that the sump was 'a hole in the ground at the lowest level to catch water and from there a pump would be used to clear it'. The term *swilley* is given by twelve miners and is explained by BC as meaning 'small roadway areas catching or holding water'. There is also the term *resa* (presumably from 'reservoir'), mentioned by nine miners. These terms mainly seem to refer to collections of water underground which collected at the pit bottom. Other terms which appear infrequently are *acid water*, *Belper lawn*, *roof drips*, *lake*, *lagoons* (mainly on surface), *pit pond*, *puddle* (HH explains that this term was used even if it was a lot of water), *nuisance water* and having to work *int wet*.

Another area mentioned by a large number of miners was the area used for waste material. Once the coal had been extracted, there was an empty area which was often used to deposit waste, such as stone or other rubbish, and miners were asked what they would call this area as well as what their names for such waste material would be. To start with the names for rubbish, there are around ten miners who refer to this as *rammel* and a slightly smaller number who refer to it as *waste*. Other terms which occur infrequently are *sammies* (which was discussed in light of what Griffin has said in section 4.2.5 meaning stone), *bear*, *pyries*, *iron stone*, *grey lady* (which was also discussed in section 4.2.5), *dinosaur/dog bollock* (both referring to big round stones found within the coal), *ball knackers*, *fools gold*, *iron pyrite*, *gummins* and *clunch* (both of which seem to refer to soft waste material found under the seam or conveyor belt) and *fault stones*. For the most common terminology – it is hard to know whether the term refers to the waste or the waste area as they are the same – the names are *gob/gobbins* and *goaf*. The words *gob* and *gobbins* are used by fifty-five of the miners (and also included *gob area*, *gob hole* and *gob side*). Many of the miners also note that the word *gob* could also be used to mean 'to throw' something, particularly in the sense of throwing it out. The word *goaf*, which some miners state was the official term, was used by just six miners, and we see it applied by Williams (1962: 795) when talking about withdrawing props from the goaf and how dangerous this could be. The words *packing/packs* are also used infrequently to describe this waste area.

As well as waste areas, there were also unworked areas of the coalface. These included areas to support the roof or areas which had not yet been coaled. Overall, there were thirty-four miners who responded to this question with around half giving two different terms for what this area was called. The most common word given is *pillar* (including one comment for *shaft pillar* and one for *reserve pillar*). This term is very likely linked to an earlier system of coal mining, which came before the more contemporary 'longwall' system, where pillars of coal were left to support the roof (like a chessboard, see also references to this system in Lewis (1971: 42) and for full details see chapter 4 in British Coal (1989)). This term still seems to be in common use for coal left underground. A further eleven miners refer to this area as *virgin*, *virgin coal* or *virgin ground*. This suggests that it could be an area to be mined next, which the terms *next face* or *reserves* indicate – given by one and two miners respectively. Other terms used by just one or two miners include *churchyard* (if the area was particularly near the surface), *robbing heads*, *face rib sides*, *cannel coal* (which also seems to suggest particularly hard coal or rock), *untapped* and *block of coal*. Another miner says that these areas were also numbered (as other areas of the mine were).

Moving to above ground level, there were several structures which feature as part of daily mining life. The first of these was the union office, where the union representative could work and be visited by other miners. As mentioned in Chapter 2, relations with unions were very strained following the strike of

1984–1985 and the new union, the UDM, caused much friction which continues to this day. In fact, feeling runs so strong that on one of the consent forms for the questionnaire, one miner includes the note, 'I will withdraw approval if any of my submitted material is used to promote the UDM'. Almost thirty miners give a word for this office, the most common of which is *union box*, used by nine miners, and a further three refer simply to *box* and one each to *union cabin* and *union office*. Another description is *NUM office*, used by six miners, and one gives the term *UDM office*. Words which are used by single miners include *den of thieves*, *bangers office*, *union cabin*, *the den* and *nacods* (which is an acronym which refers to the National Association of Colliery Overmen, Deputies and Shotfirers).

The second overground structures were the *headstocks* found above the shaft mouth which often include a winding wheel and engine that powered the lifts travelling up and down the shafts. These carried the pulleys over which passed the winding ropes from the winding engine to the lifting gear. In many places these headstocks have come to symbolise the mining industry as they are so visible, even from a very long way away. The headstocks at Clipston are said to be some of the highest in Europe and work is being carried out to incorporate them in future planning of the area (see Figure 4.18). The term *headstocks* is the most common term used by the interviewed miners, with fourteen out of thirty mentioning this word, and there are also three

Figure 4.18 Headstocks and winding gear at Clipstone

who refer to this structure as *headgear*. Other words which are used include *winding gear*, *winder*, *shaft top*, *pit top*, *towers*, *shaftside (winding) wheels* and *heapstead* which is believed by some to be more traditionally from the north-east. A particular reference is from JS who worked in Annesley in Nottinghamshire who noted that miners in this pit referred to the headstocks as *the big A*, which reflected both the shape of headstocks as well as the first letter of their pit. A conversation follows with MH, his fellow miner who carried out the interview, together with the joke 'what does the A stand for?', to which he replies, 'to remind the blacksmith's to put their 'arness on', which reflects local dialect with the h-dropping as well as the teasing between miners who worked below ground and those who worked on the surface. DCR and PB, who worked at Haworth, explain that the *towers* at their mine were called *number 1 Haworth Castle* and *number 2*, as well as *big tower* and *little tower*, and they explain that the structures were called castles because they had turrets on. These apparently were added to ensure that they were the tallest standing concrete structures in Europe (the tower at Maltby near Rotherham in South Yorkshire was higher, which is why the turrets had to be added in Haworth).

Once the coal had left the mine, it was cleaned, sorted and prepared to be shipped out, depending on whether it was house coal or used for power plants (in section 4.2.5 it was noted that house coal tended to be pieces of coal, whereas power stations could function with *slack* as well). As well as cleaning and sizing the coal it also had to be separated from stone and other waste material. This was done in the coal preparation plant (see Figure 4.19). We asked our miners if they had alternative words for this place. In all, fifty-four miners responded to this question. From the answers, we can immediately see a distinction between the mines where the coal was only sized and those where it was also cleaned. In the mines where the coal was also cleaned, it was frequently referred to as a *washer* or *washery*, which are the words given by twenty-six miners, with one additional *wash box* and *washy*. A further seventeen miners give the word *screens* as the place where sorting would happen with a further twelve miners using the word *coal prep plant* or *prep plant* and a further three just using *plant*. One miner says the acronym *CPP* was used. The only other word was *shaker* which is used by one miner for the machine that did the sorting as it would shake to move the coal of different sizes into different containers. GN from Leicestershire says that to sieve small bits of coal could be called *to riddle the slack*. If large pieces of coal had to be made smaller, this would be done with a *lump wrecker*.

The final overground structure was the spoil heap which would be made up of all the waste material discarded by the coal preparation plant. As Dennis et al. have written, 'The dominant feature of the landscape is the spoil or slag heaps. There is no point in the town from which they are not visible. Houses and mine-workings crouch under their shadow' (1969: 11). These spoil heaps frequently now are the last remaining indications that a mine

Figure 4.19 Coal preparation plant at Mansfield Colliery (photo credit: Coal Authority)

used to be located in a certain place and in many areas these spoil heaps have been landscaped and made part of local parks. In fact, the highest point in Nottinghamshire is Silverhill, which is the old spoil heap of the Silverhill mine that closed in the 1990s. A bronze statue of a kneeling miner holding a Davey lamp, entitled 'Testing for Gas' and created by Anthony Dufort, stands as a tribute to Nottinghamshire miners, and the plinth of the sculpture contains the names of the principal collieries in the region from 1819 to 2005 (see Figure 4.20). In fact, the spoil heap had to be elevated by five metres to ensure it was the highest peak in the county. Overall, forty-four of the miners give an alternative name for the spoil heap, with about a third of these miners giving two terms and one miner giving four alternative words. Only one miner gives the term *spoil heap* but sixteen miners describe it being called a *slag heap*. Other common terms are *(pit)tip* or *dirt tip* which is used by twenty-one miners, and the similar *pit hill* is used by a further three miners. It is also called

Analysis 141

Figure 4.20 Testing for gas

a *dot hill* (local pronunciation for the word 'dirt', which is also discussed in section 4.2.3 for a *dot shovel*). This term came to form the basis of a Heritage Lottery Funded project that I carried out with local mining heritage groups and schoolchildren, creating an art and sound installation around the language and heritage of local coal miners as it reflected mining language as well as local pronunciation. The term *bonk* or *bank* is also given by five miners (*bank* was also discussed as being a term used for the coalface earlier in this section). Wright has described how miners avoided using 'official terms' and has given this word as an example. He has noted (Wright 1972: 44) that the National Coal Board in 1965 ordered that *slag heaps* should from then on be referred to as *spoil heaps*, but our findings indicate that many miners continued using their own terms. We can also see that such terms vary, as Wright has added that the terms he has come across vary from *pit tips*, *pit hills* and *pit heaps* to *batches*, *bengs*, *bonks* and *dirt heaps*, while Gibbs (personal communication, but also see Gibbs 2021) has stated that in Scotland slag heaps are referred to as *bings*. We can conclude therefore that the term *dot hill* is used by a small number of East Midlands miners and not elsewhere in the country.

The words discussed in this section also highlight differences between the amount of variation to be found. One example of variation is related to a word used by some miners to describe the coalface; where some miners used *bank* to describe it, this term can also be used to mean the pit surface, the area around the headstocks. There does not seem to be any immediate geographical link to this usage, but only variation among mines themselves. We find further references to animal terminology as well as taboo language, both frequently used by miners in the terms *dog/dinosaur bollock* for large round stones found within the coal. There are different terms used to describe such lumps and also other rubbish. Where *goaf* seems to be accepted as the official term, many miners report that they would use *gob* instead, which seems to be linked more closely to the East Midlands than other terms which are used more widely, including *waste* for example. For terms describing the headstocks, we see references to terms used outside the East Midlands such as *heapstead*, which is believed to come from the north-east, and we also see very local terms, such as the *Big A*, which is only used for the headstocks at Annesley-Bentinck, which have a capital A painted on them. These types of local terms are also often associated with local jokes and stories as we also found in other sections on nicknames and different types of workers. There are also examples of local language influencing pit talk, with examples such as *dot hills* which represent local pronunciation and seem to signal localness as they are specifically mentioned by some of these miners.

4.2.10 Other words

At the end of the interviews and questionnaires the miners were asked whether there were any terms that they felt had been important to their work which had not been covered in the interview or questionnaire. In their responses some of the words they give have to do with categories already covered, and these have already been dealt with in the relevant sections, but there are some words and explanations which will be discussed individually here. One of these words is *stinting*, which LM describes as being used in the

Analysis 143

days before armoured face conveyors, where a coalface could be around 200 yards long and each man would have a ten-yard *stint* to work –referring to an individual section of the coalface which would be worked. NC, who was employed in Rainworth in Nottinghamshire, notes that he worked in the pits before mechanisation and explains, 'I used to chuck coal on by hand with a shovel. I used to have 22 yards, 6 feet high, and 6 feet deep, and we used to have to blast it and chuck it on by hand. Then that were your stint, as we'd call it.' There are also several references to the word *kank* which could mean stone in coal, particularly hard coal, and so had the connotation of being particularly bad coal. This term is also said to mean *crap* as in bad quality. There are other terms for hard coal, including *musselbed*. In earlier sections we have seen that there were different terms which include animal names – some additional ones are *elephant's feet* (which JHN explains are like stilts which fasten onto the bottom of the legs, pushed down by the weight) and *elephant's blocks* (also referred to as *footblocks*, which were used to place on the leg of a prop), which were placed above and below props.

There are additional terms to describe events in the mine or particular states. JP, who worked at Whitwick, mentions *jaffnagged* as being very tired, but no other miners have heard of this. RCH also mentions that some tools were not always easy to get hold of, so miners would sometimes hide tools so that only they knew where to find them if they needed them, and he refers to this as *fobbing*. In section 4.2.1, there was mention of *rodding up*, which was used by Leicestershire miners to say that they were going home at the end of a shift. Related to this, JP mentions that if two miners fell out, they would be *off the rod* as they would no longer hang up their tools next to each other. RR from Shirebrook in Derbyshire mentions that saying goodbye at the end of a shift could be *see you on brushes* and explains that this was the place to 'have a quick fag before the start of the shift, sitting on the brush guard, where the brushes were kept to clean boots'. As the men were not allowed to smoke underground, quite a few of them mention that they chewed *baccy*, which could be referred to as *a screw of baccy*. A worker who had to work on the pit top for the day instead of his usual underground job is said to have been a *flat capper*. DR from Nottinghamshire mentions that miners could say they were *up to 't bollocks in it* if they were 'particularly rammed with work', whereas *teking a rack off* (with the non-standard FACE vowel) means to slow down. Something else which could happen is that coal could build up on the conveyor and therefore block more coal from coming in, which is referred to as *swamping the loader*. This was not seen as a good thing as it could slow down the process of coal being removed from the mine and lead to a back-up on the conveyor, which would have to be stopped, and miners would say *why we standing* or *why are we stood*? If the miners had to go to the toilet underground, they could either bury it or use the *thunderbox*, which was the underground toilet available in some mines. A final term discussed at the end of the interview by BH is *total cave*, which describes the way in which, as the face progressed, the open area is eventually left standing and caves in –called *total cave* – which can cause subsidence above ground and cause cracks in houses and pavements.

4.3 Conclusion

In this chapter we have examined and investigated many of the words and expressions which miners used in their everyday life. In the next chapter there will be an attempt to draw together some of the themes and findings to see which patterns have emerged. The examination of lexical items to investigate how they were used and how they varied among miners is fascinating but there is another aspect which should first be considered. As Wright has mentioned: 'It is in the customs, superstitions and folklore intermingled with miners' language that much of its fascination lies' (Wright 1972: 48). Our work does not just collect language but also discusses an important way of life, and one which is fast disappearing. One of the most common themes raised by the miners is the *camaraderie* or *brotherhood* they felt with those they worked with. GB explains that in the showers they stood in a circle and washed each other's backs, and that they had to do this because if they did not they would end up with a *diamond back*, an unwashed area of the back that they could not reach themselves, illustrating that these miners relied on each other for their work and safety. KC adds that, 'life down the mine was rough, it was depressing. The only thing that actually kept you going down the pit was the camaraderie with your friends and your workmates down the pit. Apart from anything else, it was horrible.' SF is one the miners who worked in Thoresby, which closed the day before we interviewed him, and he noted that the relationships with colleagues were 'closer than family', and that the previous day had been very difficult as some of the miners had wanted to leave quickly while others had wanted to hug everybody, so everyone wanted to say goodbye in their own way and it had been highly emotional.

Many of the explanations of the lexical items we asked the miners about contain extensive stories about their way of life and the connection they felt with each other. They discuss how the danger of their work meant that they had to be able to rely on one another. This has also been found by Bell (2006: 48 and 2008: 118) in his interviews with Derbyshire and Nottinghamshire miners who noted that this was the best thing about working underground. BBT says that miners always helped each other out and would 'never see anybody struggle'. To this, BH adds that the work was exceptionally hard and dangerous, and that the camaraderie didn't finish outside the pit but that these men were more like brothers to him. Adding that miners do not carry grudges, he says, 'I've seen people go down the road, have an argument, go down the road and knock three bells out of one another and come back and that's it, passing a prop, job done. Miners never ever carry stones, because you never know what's going to happen tomorrow.' Although this sentiment is frequently echoed during the interviews, it is also worth noting that many miners spoke of the divisive results of the Miners' Strike, which ended this feeling between different groups of miners. EP says that this sense of community has disappeared now that the pits have gone. Many of the interviewees spoke of their working days as being the best days of their life, regardless of the work they had to do. GB comments that he would return to this work immediately if he could – even though it has made him deaf and he has emphysema, with white finger and arthritis in his knees as a result – because they were the best days of his life.

In addition to this working camaraderie, the sense of belonging and community also spread outside of the mine and to families. Much of the social life of miners was caught up with their work – football clubs, cricket teams, outings and holidays, allotments, galas and brass bands all form the basis of much discussion in these interviews. AD, who worked in Clipston in Nottinghamshire, says: 'It was a community. Everybody worked down the pit, I mean when I first started in 1966 there was 1,400 men employed at the pit, then on a night time you'd all go to the welfare. So you would see the same people that you had been working with all day, but it was socialising, it wasn't working.' DJH comments that the pit provided everything in relation to social activities and that many of their clubs and societies would not have run without financial support from the pit.

Much of the language discussed as part of being a miner also reflects the local language used in the various regions of the East Midlands. We see many local words (such as *tab* for *ear* as in *elephant's tab* and *mashin'* for tea making) as well as local pronunciations reflected in the language of these miners. With more 'traditional' dialects disappearing, some of the language used by the miners reflects older pronunciations which may not continue to be used by younger speakers. Some of the patterns we found can be compared to data collected for the *Survey of English Dialects*. For example, Lewis notes that 'the mythologies, superstitions and survival at the coal face emphasise tradition' (Lewis 1971: 31), and this is also reflected in the language, which continues to be used underground while it is lost above ground. He has given the example of 'gata', an Old Norse term meaning 'road', which has continued to be used in the sense of *gate* below ground, as we have noted in discussions of different terms for underground roadways in section 4.2.7. Dave Douglass (personal communication) has added that he thinks miners used dialect terms which were disappearing above ground and that miners' language could be examined for linguistic features that may be declining in 'everyday' language. Some of the language discussed in this chapter can also be found in books describing the East Midlands coalfield. For example, the three books on the Nottinghamshire, Derbyshire and Leicestershire coalfield by Bell (2006, 2007, 2008) include many stories about life as a coal miner, and many of the words discussed here also appear in those books; in fact, the book on Nottinghamshire includes a two-page glossary at the front of the book explaining some of these terms. KC, who worked at Clipston, says that 'Nottinghamshire language, I mean is part and parcel, because it was such a big industry and in Nottinghamshire I should say it was the biggest industry and the Nottinghamshire accent curtails with pit talk, it's all linked into one.'

We asked the miners whether they are aware of differences in language used by miners from different regions, and we can see from the comments throughout this chapter that certain terms were associated with miners from other regions. Some miners also talk about the difficulty of understanding other miners, either those who moved into the region or if they themselves moved. BH, who moved within the East Midlands, says that he found 'much of their terminology alien' when he first moved to Whitwick and had difficulty understanding the terminology they used there. To this, DJH adds that, 'we had these men and of course they all brought a different dialect. We called a tool a sylvester, they called it a nanny. We called a boring machine aurora, they called it a jap, because it was the firm that made it. We had all these different names.' SF, who had been a deputy, explains that gates having different names in different mines was difficult: 'you are a deputy and you're trying to phone a report out and you tell them what you think it is and he goes what's that then. It were difficult at first but you get used to it.'

Many of the miners noted that the pits they worked in had large numbers of miners from other regions, from inside the East Midlands, from around the UK and from abroad. There were large numbers of Eastern European miners and also some miners with African Caribbean heritage (Norma Gregory has carried out extensive work with these miners in Nottinghamshire and this work can be found on her website). Gedling, in Nottinghamshire, was even known as the 'pit of nations' because of the large number of different nationalities who worked there (although BJ mentions that Bilsthorpe was also sometimes referred to in this way), and EP2 mentions that these men were 'all good lads'. ABS, who worked in Gedling, explains that this mine was very cosmopolitan because of all the miners from different backgrounds, but that some of the North Nottinghamshire pits were very 'clannish' and less open to outsiders. LL2 adds that mines also differed and said that Clifton was 'like a family pit' but that in other mines, such as Cotgrave, which had many outsiders, 'the comradeship wasn't very good'. Miners who moved from Derbyshire to Nottinghamshire were referred to as having come *from ovver 't brook*, referring to the River Erewash, and this was the source of much teasing and name calling. PS, who worked in North Nottinghamshire mines, commented that there could be differences in language used by miners who worked just a few miles away. BPN from Bilsthorpe notes that there is 'definitely a language difference between Derbyshire and Nottinghamshire but it's strange because [in] each coalfield 30 per cent of the miners are Geordies'. JS from Nottinghamshire notes that Derbyshire miners bringing in their own terms 'brightened things up a bit'. MH comments that miners from other regions, such as the north-east, would use their own terms when talking to each other, but would use the East Midlands terms when talking to the other miners, and DJ adds that those who moved to a mine tended to adopt the terms used there, rather than the other way around. However, SF thinks that when he worked at Calverton (where a lot of north-eastern miners worked) they used to speed up their speech deliberately and use certain words so that you could not understand them. BBY comments that many of the Nottinghamshire pits were known as *life-long collieries* as they were believed to have the longest reserves and to be most profitable and many miners moved to these mines when other regions around the UK were closing. LM says that Markham was referred to as 'the dustbin of the area' as miners were moved there when other pits in the region closed (many regions provided housing and other facilities to entice miners to move and to bring along their families).

Miners were also asked whether language changed over time. During the interviews there are discussions of words which were no longer used and how certain terms continued to be used even though working practices did change. SF notes that older miners sometimes had different words that no one else would understand. AB from Nottinghamshire says that many terms were passed down from generation to generation, and he also adds that being from Derbyshire and working in Nottinghamshire meant that his pronunciation of certain words changed over time in order to fit in. For example, his pronunciation of Linby (one of the mines at which he worked) changed from Linby to Linbeh (which is a feature referred to as happY tensing which we have noted increasingly in certain parts of the East Midlands (see Braber and Robinson 2018: 49–51)) and this was something he was teased for. Many of the miners mention teasing, and this also ties in with the nicknames that are mentioned throughout this chapter. It was part and parcel of the job and DH notes that, 'if you work at pit you've got to take a ragging or you don't work at pit, it's as simple as that'. RG adds that there was lots of banter and miners had to be able to take it because otherwise it would be a waste of time trying to work down there. He explains that this kind of talk was necessary 'because of the fear factor, it took away the fear of what you were doing because you knew you was under strain, you was under pressure, there was a danger there as well so you still had to be semi-serious in what you were doing. You're not just looking after your life, you're looking after somebody else's life at the same time.' Cave has also noted that in his South Yorkshire mining community teasing, nicknames and sharing of stories can be a release of aggression and tension and an aid to building a strong sense of solidarity (Cave 2001: 283).

Many of the miners we interviewed as part of this project were concerned that their way of life would soon be forgotten, and certainly the language used as part of this everyday work is no longer known or recognised by younger generations. GB says that the children he now works with as a teaching assistant have no idea that there was a coal mine right across the river and that they have no awareness of the mining way of life. Although it may seem that the loss of this industry means this language is no longer needed, recording and preserving this way of life is valuable and is an important aspect of local heritage. In this chapter, only limited extracts have been included, but more detailed extracts of recordings can be found on the Coal and Dialect website, under the section entitled 'oral histories' (see https://coalanddialect.wixsite.com/coaldialect/oral-histories which includes recordings for all different aspects of work and social life).

Finally, it would be fascinating to compare the East Midlands variety – or indeed, varieties – to the language of miners from other regions to examine to what extent there are similarities and differences. In the next chapter, some ways forward will be considered and also how the work carried out for this research project can be applied to other projects.

5 Conclusion: Preserving Pit Talk

This book set out to record the work carried out during our pit talk project and its results. The project work involved interviewing and sending questionnaires to a wide range of former coal miners around the East Midlands. This included different stages of data collection from just over ninety former miners. It also examined how mining language differed in the East Midlands from other coal mining regions and to what extent language moved around with miners. As well as individual words and descriptions, the interviews and questionnaires collected additional information about a way of living and working which is now past. This collection took place in order to catalogue, record and preserve a language which is in danger of disappearing in the near future.

This discussion and conclusion makes general and specific comments about our findings. We discuss these findings to determine the variation found among the project participants. We question whether specific links can be made to variation found within these groups and with other coal mining varieties. We also consider the role of language as heritage and how this study can be used as a testing ground for future work with other industrial languages. It emphasises the importance of working with local communities in order to carry out the most effective linguistics studies. The conclusion finishes by suggesting possible avenues for further research and how the findings of this project can be applied elsewhere.

5.1 Coal miners and their language – general comments on findings

To start with some general findings, we have found clear examples of a distinct coal mining lexicon used by miners. There are words and phrases which are distinctive to this particular field of work. Due to the nature of this work, specialised words were needed to describe the processes of work, the tools and equipment used, and the structures found above and below ground. We found attitudes surrounding pit talk, which included swearing and taboo words, but also opinions that these should not be used outside the mine and not when women and children were around. There was much discussion around teasing and nicknames and these were an integral part of a miner's daily life and identity. Many interviewees talk about the camaraderie and brotherhood they felt with their colleagues and how often they depended upon each other for safety and survival. It seems that the teasing and nicknames were a coping mechanism for working in such dangerous conditions as well as a way of building strong connections between individuals. We have seen this attitude reflected not just in our interviews, but also in other literary work written about miners. In *Jobey*, a book which is set in a small Nottinghamshire mining community during the General Strike of 1926, we hear how, 'If a man perpetrated a little act of kindness he had to cover it up by a rough tongue or an abrupt action. It was part of the rules. Otherwise he displayed a chink in the armour of tough exterior they all affected' (Williamson 2002: 61). As well as many mentions of senses of community and belonging, we have also recorded much discussion about language used, as well as individual words about which we asked the miners.

We have found that some words were used by a very wide group of our participants, for example when they discuss words relating to food and drink, particularly the word *snap* and all the compounds it formed a part of. It appears to be a universal word among most of the East Midlands miners, whereas other words are used by smaller groups of participants and there is extensive variation and often lack of agreement on which words were used. This is also a word which we see being used in the wider community and it would be interesting to investigate to what extent this word is associated with miners for those who use this term. On the other hand, some words are used less widely. For example, *dudley* – for the metal water container – is a word used by some, with others claiming never to have heard of it. There is also disagreement among the miners who do use it on where the term comes from, although most seem to think it is linked either to the company who made it or the location at which the company was based. Many words which illustrate the dangerous nature of the work carried out have been found (for example, relating to the different gases found underground, such as *firedamp* and *blackdamp*), relating both to the physical nature of the work and the injuries that could be result from such work. The words for the different gases are quite universal among the miners and it would seem to have been important to have agreement and understanding of what these words are, in case miners found themselves in a scenario with gas, as different types of gas require different reactions. We have also established that the many different jobs in the mines were represented by specific job descriptions, some of which changed over time as mines modernised and mechanised. Terms such as *hostler* or *ostler* disappear as pit ponies were gradually phased out of mines, whereas other terms, such as *ganger*, which was initially used to describe haulage using ponies, came to be used for mechanised haulage instead. Finally, these different jobs necessitated the use of different tools and many words were used throughout the mines to describe the hammers, spanners and other equipment needed for the miners to carry out their job. Some tools, such as hammers and shovels, have a great variety of words used to describe them. This is due to the fact that there is much variety in the shape and function of these particular tools. Also, many of the terms describe what these objects look like or what they are used for. So we find lots of hammer terms related to the weight of the hammer (*7lb*, *14lb*, *28lb* for example) as well as words which describe the shape of the shovel, for example *elephant's tab* or *banjo* as well as descriptions such as *dirt shovel* and *coal shovel*.

The participants' knowledge of this mining lexicon was affected by several different factors: how long they had worked in the mines, what types of jobs they had done and, to some extent, the amount of contact they still had with other miners. Those who had worked in mines the longest had the most extensive vocabulary and could remember many terms while those who had worked there for a shorter time frequently forgot the words for specific items. Furthermore, particularly with job descriptions and tools, we have found that miners' knowledge very much depends upon their own jobs and roles within the mine as they often know very specific vocabulary for particular jobs that others do not know. When talking about their lives, the miners tend to focus specifically on what they had done and therefore this influences the vocabulary discussed during the interviews. It has also become clear that some terms were specific to certain mines, and therefore where the miners had worked could further influence the words they use for particular lexical fields. This also accounts for the knowledge they have of other linguistic mining varieties; those miners who worked in mines with many men from other regions are often aware of the words used by these men, even though they did not use these them themselves. For example, miners who worked in pits such as Ollerton and Calverton, which had large numbers of miners from the north-east, comment on words such as *bait* (where East Midlands miners would use *snap* to describe their food) and also the typically northeast term *marra* for friend or work colleague. Most often, these miners say that they themselves would be unlikely to use these terms, but that the incoming miners often still used them even if they stopped using other terms that originated in the region from where they came. It seems that the two terms *bait* and *marra* were particularly important aspects of local identity for the miners who had come from the north-east. We have not found similar words in mines which had large numbers of Scottish miners (for example Thringstone in Leicestershire) even though such local terms must also have existed. We have found that some miners are still part of their local mining communities and some are part of local mining heritage groups and local museums, and this also keeps their knowledge alive to a much greater extent. These miners in particular have the most detailed knowledge of the mining lexicon. On the whole, these are the miners who took part in the second stage of interviewing – once we had covered initial information from the first set of interviews – which varied much more in terms of knowledge of a wide range of terms.

In some cases, certain words can also be linked to a sense of being a miner and belonging to a close-knit community group (for example, using the word *collier* or *hewer* rather than the word *miner* which is seen as being used by outsiders). This also refers to the word *mine* itself, where miners are far more likely to refer to the *pit* they worked in. Dennis et al. have noted that this sense of belonging is also due to the fact that miners feel no one else could do their job, they are proud of it and they know they have been looked down upon by outsiders in the past (1969: 73). As Wales has written, what we see in some communities in the north is that some traditional features of northern English may be recessive, so we may see certain pronunciations, grammatical constructions and lexical items disappearing, but others will remain as 'salient markers' of identity (Wales 2006: 180). It could be that certain words and expressions come to be seen to be associated with being a miner and continue to be used to signal affiliation with this group. Perhaps words like *snap* will come to be associated with miners and index a sense of such identity. We also saw extensive discussions by the miners to illustrate the way that certain words were pronounced which also reflect local varieties of language, so we saw miners saying and spelling words in non-standard ways, such as *watter*, *ovver*, *grandfaither*, *dot*, *in 't tin*, and they were very keen to emphasise this. Such pronunciations also make these words more local to the miners and seem to index a strong sense of local identity and belonging to these communities. In some ways, there were even distinctions within the East Midlands, with Leicestershire miners using different pronunciations such as *peck* and *denting*, where miners from Derbyshire and Nottinghamshire would say *pick* and *dinting*. Again, these pronunciations were focused on by miners as being different.

We can also see from the data we collected that changing working practices and conditions in the mine also led to language change. Many of the miners discuss words which were no longer used or had changed their referent (such as *ganger*, which changed usage from moving materials by pit pony to equipment, whereas other words such as *hostler* or *ostler*, which described the men in charge of the pit ponies, disappeared as these animals were slowly replaced by mechanised forms of transport). Wright has written '[C]hanging conditions have meant, sadly, the gradual disappearance of traditional expressions ... [A]s the mining environment changes, so do its words' (Wright 1972: 48). He has added that when miners from different regions meet, they can still communicate because they are aware of the concepts of each other's work. However, problems and dangers can arise when they have to move permanently to other coalfields and have to adapt to new terminology. We can see, for example, that the Kent branch of the National Union of Mineworkers brought out a 'Glossary of Pit Terms' in 1965 as they were bringing in miners from all over the country.

5.2 Variation among miners

Within our data, we have collected information from a range of miners. They vary in the regions they worked in – mainly the Nottinghamshire coalfield but there were also a selection of miners from the Derbyshire and Leicestershire coalfields, some miners also have experience from other regions around the UK, and one miner had worked in Australia for a short time. Most of the miners had moved around mines but worked within one of the East Midlands regions. The men also range in their ages, from early fifties to late eighties at the time of interviewing. They also differ in how long they had worked in the coal mines, ranging from just a few years to their entire working life. There is also divergence in how long it was since they had worked in the mines; one miner had finished his last shift the day before his interview and some men had finished working or had retired more than twenty years ago. In the first set of interviews, we relied on snowball sampling and on people who made contact with us after hearing about the project, and therefore in the second set of interviews we tried to focus specifically on miners who were still active in the coal mining heritage as this implied a much wider knowledge and memory of the different words. We have also found that the majority of the miners who took part in the project were from Nottinghamshire. This is significant as the last coalfields were mainly found in this area and many men moved to Nottinghamshire when other pits closed. We did try to ensure we interviewed and questioned miners from North and South Derbyshire and Leicestershire to give as wide a range of East Midlands mining lexicon as possible, but as we can see from Table 3.1 in section 3.3 the overwhelming majority of participants in our project were Nottinghamshire miners. However, because of the quantity of data, we have been able to compare the different regions to examine lexical variation.

Our aims were to examine the variation among miners and their awareness of this variation as well as the influence of miners from outside the region, in particular miners from the north-east as they made up a large majority of migrating miners to the East Midlands coalfield. The miners were asked about terms used in their everyday working life, including terms surrounding wages and money, dangerous conditions and injuries, different job titles and levels of management, tools and equipment, coal seams, different-sized pieces of coal, containers and safety devices, and structures above and below ground. Not all miners give words for every item and some topics are not touched upon in the interviews. As a result the analysis carried out in Chapter 4 was qualitative rather than quantitative, but it enables a review of words used.

As expected, we found that not all miners agree with each other, and some of the words they used can also be found in other industries outside of coal mining.

There was certainly regional variation, with particular examples where miners in Leicestershire (and to some extent South Derbyshire) were found using different terms from the other miners. This relates to words such as *doddy* for overtime, *rodding up* for the end of shift and *'ommer* for hammer, which are not used in the other regions. Moreover, it seems that miners from around the region are aware that terms used in Leicestershire were different to terms used elsewhere in the East Midlands, and this includes the words *denting* (levelling out floors after a floor lift) and *peck* for *dinting* and *pick* respectively. Even in cases where the Leicestershire miners do not actually mention these terms themselves, it seems that there is an awareness that the Leicestershire mining area was somehow a bit different to that of North Derbyshire and Nottinghamshire. From the maps in sections 2.3.1–2.3.3 (Figures 2.2, 2.3, 2.4, 2.5 and 2.6), we can see that the smaller South Derbyshire/Leicestershire coalfield is removed from the larger coalfield which runs along the Derbyshire/Nottinghamshire border, and linguistic differences could be a result of this geographic distance from the main coalfield. There are also many examples where words were said to be used specifically by miners of a particular mine, rather than being linked to a larger geographic region. Many specific words are only mentioned by miners who worked in the same pit; for example, the term *feeder gate* being used for the return airway rather than the main intake only seems to be used by miners who worked in Annesley in Nottinghamshire, and *mortek* for hammer is used in a mine with many Eastern European miners.

Where possible, we have tried to examine mining lexis discussed in other works to investigate to what extent some of these mining terms were national rather than regional. There is a real lack of contemporary research from around the country (which was discussed in section 2.6), but some publications describe other regional varieties, including Yorkshire, the north-east and the South Midlands. The publication related to Yorkshire (Redmonds 2016) is historical in nature, covering the time period from 1250 to 1850, and thus is not relevant to our project as practices and tools changed extensively. The literature on the north-east and South Midlands (Douglass 1973; Forster 1969; Griffiths 2007) was more recent, and we also asked some of our miners about knowledge of some of these words mentioned in those works. Due to time constraints, we were unable systematically to go through other mining terms. Nevertheless, we have found that many of the terms covered in this literature were not known to our miners; for example, *tokens* – where the East Midlands miners would use *tallies*, *motties* or *checks* for their identity tags. For those miners who completed the questionnaire, we also added some terms used in Wright's questionnaire on the last page of our questionnaire to allow for direct comparison between his findings and our miners. As Wright's survey included miners from around the UK, we expected his questionnaire to show results not used by our miners. In work which examined the life of a Yorkshire mining community (Dennis et al. 1969), there is some discussion of employment terms, and we see that some are similar to the terms used by

Conclusion: Preserving Pit Talk

our interviewees, but others differ. For example, the job title *drawers off* for the men who removed the timber supports was not used in the East Midlands, where *back rippers* was used instead. The term *panners* – which was used by Yorkshire miners to describe the men who left the workplace safe for the workers on the next shift – was also not used by our interviewees. Some terms are the same and we see references to *day workers* and *haulage men* in both. Where the Yorkshire men call the men in charge of the coal cutters *machine men*, these tend to be called *machine drivers* in the East Midlands.

Wright's questionnaire showed much variation, but we have also found variation within the East Midlands, and our findings can be compared with Wright's results as two of his miners are from the East Midlands, albeit both from Nottinghamshire (Warsop and Clifton pits) as well as allowing comparison with other coal mining regions in the UK. His responses also include IPA transcriptions of individual words, so these can also be used to examine any variation from the words used in our interviews. Of Wright's original questionnaire, which included just over eighty questions, twenty-nine of his terms were included after the end of our questionnaire to allow for direct comparison. These were the words that many of the miners in the earlier interviews refer to and were most likely to elicit responses. In his analysis, Wright does not include a breakdown for all eighty questions, so just those which have been completed by both his miners and our miners will be compared. For question 2, the part of mine above ground (official term *pit head*) shows variation, with Wright's participants giving *pit head, pit top, pit bank* and *heapstead*, and both Nottinghamshire miners using *pit top*, whereas ours use either *pit top* or more predominantly *surface*, with one example of *headstocks* and one mentioning *spull*, which does not appear in any of the other East Midlands interviews. None of Wright's participants refer to this as *surface* so this seems either a typical East Midlands term or a newer term. Question 7 refers to the big mounds of material dug up and left near the mine (official term *slag heaps*) and these are referred to as *bing, pit hill, bank, spoilbank and dirt tip* by Wright's participants, with the two Nottinghamshire miners using either *tip* or *dirt-heap* and ours using *pit tip, spoil heaps, slag heaps, dirt tip* and one mention of *heap*. So although there are some similarities, there are certain terms which are not used in the East Midlands which are used in other areas.

Question 11 in Wright's questionnaire refers to the chief passage in the mine (official term *main road*) and this shows relatively little variation for Wright's miners, who use *main road, road, main roadway, main girder road* or *gate*. The two Nottinghamshire miners use *main road* and *road*. The majority of our miners use predominantly the same terms, which are *main road/gate* or *roadway*, although we see individual mentions of *spineroad* and *motorway*, neither of which appears in Wright's list. So these terms seems quite universal for most miners. Question 13 is related to the safety holes which are built for miners to go into when machines or other equipment are passing (official term *manhole*); almost all miners use a version of *manhole* (some with varying pronunciation as Wright gives IPA for all his responses). All of our miners give the term *manhole* and a few additionally add *refuge hole*, so this is a term without any real variation used throughout the UK mining industry. Question 15 asks about the side roads which go off the main passageway underground and Wright's miners use the term *heading, stall gate* and *gate*, with the two Nottinghamshire miners using *stall-gate* and *gate*. Here we see a great difference with our miners, with real variation in the terms used, ranging from *gate road, slits, junction, roadway, snicket* and *gates*. There are no miners who give *heading* – which is frequent in Wright's responses. We do see two miners give the term *snicket* which we will also see in the discussion of question 16, which asks about the small connecting passages underground. Wright's participants give *througher, board, slip road, stall road* and also *snicket* (which is the term used by the two Nottinghamshire miners). For our East Midlands miners, the predominant response is *snicket*, which is rarely given by Wright's miners. There are one or two miners who give other terms, such as *side roads, slit gate, crossgate/crosscut* and *junction*, but these only appear once. This is an interesting term as it is also found in use in the wider community and so may be closely linked with the region.

The next question Wright analyses is what the man at the pit bottom in charge of loading cages is called (official term *onsetter*). Most of the miners questioned give *onsetter* (including the two Nottinghamshire miners) but there are some other variations that only appear once, such as *hanger-on, hitcher* and *pit-bottomer*. All of the miners except for two use *onsetter* in our questionnaire, and the two who do not use *banksman* instead, which is a term mainly used for the man who works at the top of the shaft controlling the men and material going down underground. In the rest of our questionnaires and interviews we also find that this term is used almost universally by all men as this is the man who most miners would be in contact with on every shift. The next term, question 31, asks about food which is taken to work. Here we see a big difference between Wright's responses and our responses. Although both of the Nottinghamshire miners use *snap* (and this is also used by some miners in other parts of the country), there is much variation, ranging from *piece, jock, tommy* and *tommy-box, bait, crowdy* and *grub*. The miners in our project almost universally respond with *snap* (the only exception is that one miner uses *sandwich*, and one additionally gives *bait*, explaining that this comes from the north-east). As we saw in section 4.2.1, the term *snap* appears to be a real East Midlands term and is associated with being a local word. During the rest of the interviews, most references are given to *snap* and any miners using other terms say that Geordie miners used *bait*. This word appears to be very closely linked with an East Midlands coal mining identity.

For the next question, there seems to be very little overlap with Wright's findings and our findings. Question 40 asks for the name given to a small bit of wood which gives support while coal is cut (for example like a *small chock*). Wright's miners respond with *stale, chocker, sprag* (which is the word used by one of the Nottinghamshire miners, the other does not respond to this question), *clog, cog, postin, head-tree* and *cog*. So we can already see from Wright's results that there is great regional variation for this term. Our miners use *split bars, locker, sprag, cleat, chock, chock nog, sprag* and *pinner*, and there are multiple references to *props* (which we will return to in a moment) and *wedges*. It is not clear why a term such as this should show so much individual variation, as it suggests that most mines used their own words for this piece of wood. This could be because such bits of wood did not exist as pre-made entities but were made by miners as and when they were needed, and, as they were more makeshift than other equipment, they were given individual names by those who made them. Question 43 asks about vertical props and most of Wright's miners use either *long prop, leg, puncheon* or *upright*. In this case, both Nottinghamshire miners use *leg*. Our miners predominantly use *prop* and only one miner uses *leg* which appeared to be the term used by the East Midlands miners in Wright's study. There are also individual references to *uprights* and *post*. As well as a vertical prop, there is also a horizontal prop, which is question 44 in Wright's study. There is a relatively small number of terms, including *bar*, which are used by the majority of miners (although Wright does show variation between use of the northern and southern BATH vowel), as well as individual occurrences of *crown, puncher, collar* and *flat*. Most of the miners from our study use the term *split bars* or *bars* and there are also references to *struts, cross-member, beam, board* and *coverboard*. It seems that for this type of prop there is much more variation than for the vertical prop that tends to be used much more universally by miners across the country. The last term related to such props and supports is question 45, which asks about the small piece of wood used to support the roof, presumably placed on top of the props. Wright's miners use either *wedge, lid* or *pad* and there is one instance of *capping*. The overwhelming majority of our miners use *lid* with only occasional other words such as *pinner, wedge, cleat* and *chockwood*. In this case, *lid* seems to be used very widely by miners across the country and throughout different time periods.

Wright also asks for the name given to the waste area in the mine and both Nottinghamshire miners use *gob*, which is also used by quite a number of the other miners, as well as terms such as *goaf, cundy* and *waste*. Quite a number of our miners leave this question blank, but for those who do answer, *gob* is the most common occurrence, with a few examples of *goaf* and *waste*. It was discussed in section 4.2.9 that *goaf* was seen as the official term but it does not appear to be used by many miners, who prefer their own local versions of this word. Miners were also asked in question 49 about the term used to fill a hole ready for firing, and Wright's miners give either *stem* or *ram*, with the only exception being one of the miners from Nottinghamshire who gives the term *gob in*. In our study, both *ramming* and *stemming* are also the most common terms given, with only three miners giving *packing* and one *charging*. So there seems to be little variation for this particular job which needed to be done. Another question is about the terms given for the upheaving of the floor which can take place underground. For the miners Wright asked, *floor lift* is the most common (and is used by both Nottinghamshire miners) and there are also a few other terms such as *floor blow*, *floor lift* and *heaving* that are only used by a very small number of miners. Thirteen of the East Midlands miners in our project give *floor lift* and there are only two occurrences of *heave* and one each of *floor blow* and *floor rise*. So this term appears to be universal throughout the UK's mining regions. On the other side of the mine, question 52 asked about a depression in the roof, which can result in a fall of parts of the roof. Many of the responses given by Wright's participants are compounds including the adjective *bad*, such as *bad stone*, *bad hole* (given by one Nottinghamshire miner) and *bad ground*. Other examples include *potash*, *slip*, *pothole* (given by one Nottinghamshire miner), *welver*, *bellmould* and *roll*. For our miners there is almost no consistency, with most miners who give a response giving a different term, including *bad top*, *inner roof*, *ironstone*, *fault*, *dirt lump*, *grey lady*, *widowmaker*, *bad roof* and *pothole*. This appears to be another term which varies greatly from pit to pit without any apparent pattern, and it the same for both Wright's and our data. The next term is related to the previous one and asks what name can be used for coal that sounds as if it is not solid. Wright's participants give the terms *boss*, *drummy*, *drawn*, *baggy* and *nesh*. The two Nottinghamshire miners use *drummy* and *drawn*. It is interesting to see that the word *nesh*, which is often associated with the East Midlands and is used to mean someone who feels the cold or is a bit weak, is used by the Welsh miner. About half of our miners do not give a term for this, but of those who do there is very little similarity in the terms they use. They give the terms *spelch*, *empty*, *hollow*, *flaky*, *ringing*, *undercut*, *mudstone*, *hollow face* and *friable*. This is a term which does not show any consistency in the region and is used very variably by miners throughout the region.

Wright also asks in question 56 for the term that miners favour for the containers used to transport coal and the most common term given is *tub* (both with /ʊ/ and /ʌ/ which differentiates between northern and southern speakers), and also *tram* and *corf*, with the additional word *chumman*, which is only used for an empty container. For the East Midlands miners in our data we can see two main terms, *tubs* as well as *on belt* or *on conveyor*, which shows that many of the miners must have worked in drift mines where coal was transported directly out of the mine and did not have to travel up a vertical shaft. There are also some references to *mine cars* and *skips* although these are given less frequently. These results are similar to the rest of the interviews and questionnaires, although fewer miners talked about transporting coal by belt or conveyor during the interviews. Following this, the miners were asked in question 62 how such tubs could be stopped or slowed down and there is a great amount of variation found in Wright's responses, ranging from *snibble*, *cow*, *lashing chain*, *drag*, *lounge*, *shackle*, *sprag*, *locker*, *coupling* and *clivvis*

Conclusion: Preserving Pit Talk

(which is used by one of the Nottinghamshire miners; the other does not give a term). Here we see great variation with the miners from the East Midlands who overwhelmingly use *lockers* (eleven out of the twenty-three). The other terms which are given are used only by individual miners and include *rope haulage*, *switch off* and *crusher*. The term given by the Nottinghamshire miner in Wright's study is not given by any of our miners (and this also includes the interviews and questionnaires) and it seems that the main term used in the East Midlands is *lockers*.

The last two words discussed in Wright's study are the words used for small bits of coal and also debris (including stones and rubbish) found in the mine. Small bits of coal are most commonly referred to as *cobbles* and there are also singular references to *smalls*, *nuts* and *duffy*. The two Nottinghamshire miners use different words, with one giving *cobbles* and one using *smalls*. In our comparison, we do see the term *cobbles* being used frequently, but also *slack* and to a lesser extent *fines*. There are also occasional references to *small stuff*, *singles* and *conny*. It seems that the term *slack* is either a more modern term or is used mainly by East Midlands miners, although it would seem to be a term that is used more widely for fine material. The final term in question 69 asks about different words for debris and Wright's miners have three terms which seem to be used roughly equally – *dirt*, *muck* and *rip* (with both *dirt* and *muck* showing phonological variation among speakers). Our miners show a much larger range of variation, with terms including *spoil(s)*, *rubbish*, *rubble*, *waste*, *pack waste*, *slack*, *slag*, *gob*, *gummings*, *bat*, *spillage* and *dot/dirt*. Here there seems to be much more variation and it seems that many mines had their own terms for rubbish materials found in the mine. So from Wright's study we can see that there is a large amount of regional variation found across the different mining areas. In some of these examples, the Nottinghamshire miners give similar words to the miners in our study but there is also still a large amount of variation where the miners in our study use different words to Wright's Nottinghamshire miners. This seems to suggest that rather than larger-scale similarity, there is much variation among mines themselves, with many local terms being used in individual mines. This does make it harder to make any large-scale generalisations about specific mining terms.

Douglass's work on the pit talk of County Durham includes sections on language, pit songs and pit clothes as well as information about the daily life of a miner. There is also a glossary of terms, some of which are not familiar to our miners, for example, *canteen* for water bottle, where many East Midlands miners use the term *dudley*, or *jowl* for sounding the roof and checking for safety, which is never used by our miners. However, there are other terms, such as *loco* for the underground train or *mell* for a particular type of hammer, which are the same as the East Midlands terms. There are also terms which are not exactly the same but are clearly linked. Douglass writes about *horny trams* for flat tubs without sides, our miners give terms such as *horned dannies*. Also, Douglass gives the term *pick-windy* for a small pneumatic drill, which East Midlands miners refer to as a *windy pick*. Because a large number of miners from the north-east moved to the East Midlands, there are many terms that the East Midlands miners are aware of, but would not use themselves, such as the already mentioned *bait* where the local word would be *snap* for lunch, and *marra* for a work mate. These terms are seen as belonging to the north-east and seem to give a strong sense of that local identity.

A more recent publication is Griffith's (2007) work on the north-eastern coalfield. This publication is a mixture of poems, anecdotes and extracts from interviews which are given alongside local words for such terms. The book is ordered around different areas of the mine, such as the pit surface and shaft, as well as job titles, work practices and coal itself. Griffiths has said (2007: 14) that, '[W]hile there is reasonable consistency in technical terms between coalfields, there is also marked variation in familiar terms'. With this, Griffiths has given examples of words from other coalfields, one of which is the word *kank* to describe a twist in a rope, as being typical of the Midlands. Many of our miners were specifically asked about this term, and none of them had come across its meaning; for most of them it meant either stone or coal which was very hard, or it was used to describe something of poor quality. Griffiths has also noted that there is much outside influence in mining language, with words coming from Germany (which we have seen in the use of *damp* from *Dampf* for gas and also *panzer* for the underground conveyor), and he has said that the word *shaft* also comes from the German *Schacht*. He has also explained that, although new terms did increase with mechanisation, many older terms also continue to be used. Similarly, we have found examples of miners who had swipe cards still referring to them as *motties*, *tallies* or *checks*. Griffiths's terms for job descriptions are also used by our miners, including *banksman* and *onsetter* for those who put men and materials into and out of the cages. We have also seen terms that differ slightly in meaning, for example the term *rammel* for a thin layer of stone, where for East Midlands miners this means rubbish more generally.

The last chapter of Griffiths's book is entirely about everyday terms which were used at the pit and which have a more general meaning in wider communities outside the mine. We have made an attempt to examine to what extent pit talk has moved outside the mines and also how it is affected by the local dialects found in the East Midlands. In this, we have noticed the influence of local variation in the ways words are pronounced, and some terms used in mines, such as *snicket*, may also have other meanings outside the mines. We have also confirmed that some words used in the mine, such as *snap*, have spread outside mining communities, although it is hard to establish whether *snap* was used originally by miners or by the wider community. Griffiths has said that the important role coal miners played in the north-east also meant that the language they used was treated as being of importance. He has written: 'Though Pitmatic in the narrower sense is the talk of miners at work, a male dialect in effect, and the preserve of a working pitman, yet the importance of coal mining to the region and the consequent status of the miner was reflected in the status of the dialect' (Griffiths 2007: 18), adding that the pitman seems to have left a special mark on the region's dialect, for example the phrase 'dropping off at the keps' to mean 'feeling tired' from the term for the safety clips on top of the lift which stopped it from free-falling down the shaft.

The work carried out by Forster on the South Midlands is most closely linked to our work on the East Midlands, as some of the colliers in that book were from mines in South Leicestershire (for example, Cadley Hill, Snibston, Ellistown, South Leicester). And as Forster's study was conducted in the late 1960s there should be some overlap with the dates our miners were working. Forster has stated that miners developed their own language, 'a mixture of local dialects and technical mining terms' (Forster 1969: 1). His aim was to collect words in contemporary usage only, but that proved very difficult due to extensive reminiscing. He has therefore concluded that miners are keeping old words alive when they describe the processes and tools of the 1930s in their discussions. Second, Forster wanted to define words, but he has said that this was rather difficult and compromises had to be made. We have found similar issues in our interviews, where there is frequent disagreement about the definition and usage of particular words and expressions, such as the large variation for the shafts transporting men and material into and out of the mine. Forster has also discussed the effect of migration extensively. Miners who moved individually had to adopt new terms and may have been confused initially by these new terms and may have felt uncomfortable using them. When miners moved in large groups, they may have retained certain aspects of their language and associated proudly with them as being their own local terms. Finally, there was the case (for example in Kent) where new mines were opened and miners from all over the country started work there, which must have resulted in much confusion. Other issues which Forster has mentioned as being important to mining language are the process of mechanisation and the standardisation of terms since nationalisation. The rest of Forster's book is a glossary of terms, providing their definitions and at times explanations about where such terms are used. There are terms in his glossary which are familiar to the miners in the East Midlands, such as *banjo* for a large, round shovel and *tadge* to describe a tool that can be used as an axe or a pick. However, there are some terms which are unfamiliar for our miners, even when the glossary states they are local to Derbyshire or Leicestershire (and therefore likely to have been given by miners who worked in the same pits); for example, the word *box* is said to mean tub in Derbyshire, but it is not mentioned by any of our miners, also *pitcher* – said by Forster to be used by Leicestershire miners to describe the miner loading the tubs, but not used by any of our miners. Forster has also stated that the term *jacks* is used by East Midlands miners to refer to a band of dirt just under the coal seam, where our miners use this term to describe the *prop support* found underground.

So it is clear to see that there are some terms which are used solely or differently by East Midlands miners and this language changed over time and was also used differently depending on the jobs carried out by the miners involved. Lewis has also discussed the variability of mining terminology regionally and says, 'it is not only apparent that a glossary of terms is needed but also that regional differences make generalisations extremely dangerous' (Lewis 1971: ix). So variability is not unexpected, but some patterns can be detected in the way in which East Midland coal miners use such language. Many of the miners we interviewed and questioned note that their mines had lots of outsiders, while others say they did not, and this also influenced how language was used in the mines. When asked whether the language used by miners varied within the East Midlands, many of the miners say this was the case but then often find it hard to give examples. It seems as if, rather than claim a simple geographical divide (for example, Leicestershire miners have a different mining lexicon to Nottinghamshire miners), it is more accurate to say that there is variation between mines. There are terms used outside the East Midlands mines which are not known in the region. Some terms are local to the East Midlands, some are local to specific mines and/or miners. There are some 'home terms' which are used only in a single mine. Some terms belonged to specialised areas of work and were only used by those in a particular occupation. All this – in addition to other features such as danger, which affected all miners – contributed a to a lexicon used by these miners and gave them a greater sense of belonging to their community.

5.3 Language as heritage

As discussed in section 1.9, language is a part of heritage which is frequently neglected when considering the cultural and heritage aspects of particular community groups. Furthermore, there is no systematic approach to preserving intangible heritage and it is not always clear how language fits within such a system. UNESCO has included language in its 2003 Convention of Intangible Cultural Heritage, but it is not always clear exactly what is meant by the protection of 'Living Heritage and Mother Languages' as listed on their website. The case studies given on its web pages seem to point to the languages of endangered minorities who have particular traditions of song or poetry which are in danger of disappearing, thus projects work to preserve such languages and the customs that are associated with it. UNESCO says that:

> Constituting an essential part of an ethnic community, mother language is a carrier of values and knowledge, very often used in the practice and transmission of intangible cultural heritage. The spoken word in mother language is important in the enactment and transmission of virtually all

Conclusion: Preserving Pit Talk

intangible heritage, especially in oral traditions and expressions, songs and most rituals. Using their mother tongue, bearers of specific traditions often use highly specialized sets of terms and expressions, which reveal the intrinsic depth [and] oneness between mother tongue and the intangible cultural heritage. (UNESCO: Intangible Cultural Heritage)

This means that there are several issues for the coal mining communities studied in this book. First, the UK has not signed this Convention, so currently we have no way of officially or formally protecting languages in this country. Second, even if the UK did decide to sign up, the cases that are covered concern languages and not particular registers or lexicons that are in danger of disappearing. Pit talk is a variety of language and is not an official language as such. It is mainly a highly specific lexicon, which could be referred to as a register or jargon, but still a variety which is in danger of disappearing due to changes in the industrial landscape. This lexicon is closely tied to the lives of miners and a loss of their vocabulary is also, in a sense, a loss of a particular way of life. I feel that the documentation of this type of language is also important for linguistic preservation. Documenting mining heritage and recognising mining language are crucial.

Third, many mining communities are now fragmented following the closures of the coal mines and very soon knowledge of this lexicon will be resigned to the past. By studying this particular community (and as Millar and colleagues have done with Scottish fishing communities), we can find a way of preserving this knowledge. It can help to provide a much-needed framework or methodology which would allow this work to be carried out with other communities, industrial and otherwise, around the UK and beyond. Wales has cited Widdowson who has said that we need to ensure there is pride in the industries and ways of life which in turn will help to preserve such dialects (Wales 2006: 208–209). Wales has given the example of turning factories, mills and coal mines into museums and galleries rather than them being obliterated from the landscape. This is a very good point, but even within such museums which do exist about coal mining, the language used by the workers is very rarely documented or exists as an aside that many people are unaware of. For example, interesting linguistic features can be found in oral history collections and used to describe particular objects in a museum, but such opportunities are rarely taken. We will come back to this point in the next section.

Fourth, we need to involve local communities in the preservation of language such as pit talk. Many of the institutions involved with intangible heritage state that heritage is threatened by industrialisation, the movement of people from rural to urban settings, and the abandonment of traditional employments and practices (Alivizatou 2012: 11–12) but I am interested in how such symbols of industrialisation can also be in danger of becoming lost and how they should be preserved and passed on to future generations (see Kearney 2009: 210). As a result, what needs to be considered is what can be done to create such a framework for collecting this type of language from particular community groups. A very important factor of this kind of work is that it is crucial to engage with local communities and ensure public engagement. Czaykowska-Higgins (2009: 34) notes that: 'Linguistic research is [...] at the very least a social act and not simply an isolated intellectual act.' In other words, our research takes place in the community and would be impossible without collaboration. This collaboration can take the form of public engagement through community projects. Our research has enabled individuals, community groups and interest groups to get involved in learning about and understanding their heritage, while recording and preserving it for future generations. It has encouraged learning, conservation and participation among those involved. By comparing and contrasting language and cultural traditions from the region, for the first time we have been able to demonstrate how this pit talk is distinctive from other areas around the UK and how it is influenced by and influences local language (see Braber forthcoming, which focuses on the importance of community projects). We can see how some of these terms come to symbolise belonging to a coal mining community; in the coal mining anthology we put together not only did the miners who wrote these poems and stories use this vocabulary, but many of the contributions were from family members, and some of these continued to use some of this lexis to describe the work and lives of their fathers (Braber and Amos 2021).

5.4 Future work

Although the research described in this book has helped us know and understand the language of East Midlands coal miners, there is still much work to be done. As far as I am aware there are no contemporary studies being carried out with other mining communities in the UK, and, as with the East Midlands coal miners, many of these men are the last who will be able to shed light on such vocabulary. Furthermore, such work would also allow us to compare in more detail the pit talk of different regions. We also do not currently have full information about the movement of miners around the country. Nor do we understand the extent to which certain features of pit talk are used outside miners' families and what we can expect from the future of miners' families (will words such as *snap* and *mashing* continue, and will they be associated with coal miners or not?). The loss of such language could also be dangerous; for example, there are particular dangers associated with the underground mining systems (such as flooding and subsidence) and much information held by different authorities, such as the Coal Authority, needs experts who understand the language of particular reports made by surveyors and managers to describe conditions below the ground. One possibility of future work would be to examine Wright's data in more detail to break down the geographical variation found in his data and compare this with additional interviews and discussions with miners from around the UK in order to understand whether this geographical variation of the 1970s was still found in later years.

Future work could include closer examination of the migration patterns of miners within regions and how this could relate to specific lexical patterns. It would also be interesting to examine how many miners worked across the region in different mines and investigate whether this led to changing language practices. More work is also needed to examine the extent of differences between the East Midlands coal regions and other coal mining regions in the UK. Some of the words in this lexicon may also be found in other regions, and that is to be expected, as we know that many miners and their families moved around the country following work. However, there are many terms which are distinctive to the East Midlands, and these words add to the distinct identity of 'miner' held by many who formerly worked in the pits.

Other comparative work could be carried out with vocabulary found in the *Survey of English Dialects* (*SED*) or the *English Dialect Dictionary* (*EDD*). Do the words of the East Midlands miners appear in these historical texts and do they give us any more information about the etymology of such words? Wright has said that considering that mining is an old industry, there is 'a surprising number of hitherto unrecorded words. Yet most of these must have existed, at least in speech, for a long time' (Wright 1972: 44). He has also highlighted that the *EDD* notes words coming from particular areas, but he finds these words being used in other regions. Miners may also not recognise words that are given in the *EDD* or *SED*, even though they are said to be used in their region.

A contemporary version of Wright's questionnaire could be carried out with miners from across the UK to examine whether knowledge of words has changed since the early 1970s, and to allow an examination of more modern technology and the influence of that on mining language. And of course this work need not be limited to the UK; there are mining communities in other countries and a systematic analysis of those varieties could also be carried out to examine whether we see similar variation and links to local dialect in those words.

Wright has also said that he 'left a gap' for grammatical patterns (1972: 47). This is also the case for this book. Due to its focus, I have mainly looked at lexical variation, but the interviews also contain extensive information about local morpho-syntactic and phonetic features that can be found with these speakers. There are many examples of non-standard preposition usage, non-standard verb agreement, non-standard plural marking and definite article reduction that are also of interest to linguists and could form the focus of future work. Furthermore, these interviews contain extensive information about local accent features, and the different ages of the miners as well as the fact that they come from across the East Midlands mean that some comparative work could also be done to examine particular phonological or phonetic features of the region. Some of these features have been discussed in the previous chapter, mainly in the examples in which the miners point out how their pronunciation is different from Standard English, but there are many other features that could be examined in more detail.

Finally, as mentioned earlier, the work undertaken in this project can be transformed into a framework for collecting data from particular industrial groups, or other communities of practice, which would allow for a robust methodology to record and conserve changing varieties that may be in danger of disappearing following industrial or societal changes. Particularly as there is no support from bodies such as UNESCO which may have policies in place, certain linguistic communities in the UK are in danger of leaving no trace of the varieties they use, and these can be important aspects of their linguistic and heritage identity.

5.5 Conclusion

Although this may sound dramatic, we need to grasp every opportunity to record speakers of different linguistic varieties and people who use such specialised industrial registers, because it may be our last chance to do so. As Moore has said, 'Vestiges of the past are still there in the community. For example, old miners do not just disappear overnight although they will gradually fade away over a period of time' (Moore 1995: 81). Very soon these last miners will not be able to tell us about their language and we will have lost a valuable opportunity to record it. It is important to engage communities and not work within an academic vacuum. Interest in local variation can be very beneficial and can lead to greater engagement with language varieties. Pearce (2020: 488) has noted that when there is a fear of a sense of place being eroded, then interest in that place can grow and this can lead to an increased interest in language issues, through awareness raising and the increased availability of local merchandising (such as tea towels and mugs with local expressions). Pearce's work also examined other metalinguistic awareness such as online discussions and social networking sites which can express the diversity of language that linguists examine. As far as I am aware there are no online mining groups, but that is not to say they do not exist nor cannot be used within other communities. Understanding how people use language is important, and to use Wright's words:

> It is in the customs, superstitions and folklore intermingled with miners' language that much of its fascination lies. One feels that one is not just collecting words but learning more important matters impossible to convey without speech, because the word patterns have always to be related to the society using them. (Wright 1972: 48)

Conclusion: Preserving Pit Talk

By interviewing these miners and examining their language usage, we have learned more; not only about the language but also about a way of life and what it meant and felt like to be a miner. Griffin has said that 'the history of the miner is a continuous and continuing struggle; and those who forget this do so at their peril' (A. R. Griffin 1981: 1). As Cave has said about this variety of language, 'it is a trade argot with a long history. It connects people to a local industrial landscape, above and below ground, most of which is now invisible' (Cave 2001: 186). Such a lexicon allows for many shared connotations between miners, it requires a double insider-ness, not only being regional in nature but also a tie to their occupation. The sense of 'being' a miner and belonging to a mining community was a very important aspect of life for many of the miners we interviewed, and the language they used formed an important aspect of this sense of belonging and identity.

References

Adams, Michael. 2014. Vocabulary analysis in sociolinguistic research. In Janet Holmes and Kirk Hazen (eds), *Research Methods in Sociolinguistics*, pp. 163–176. Oxford: Wiley Blackwell.

Agha, Asif. 2003. The social life of cultural value. *Language & Communication* 23: 231–273.

Alivizatou, Marilena. 2012. The paradoxes of intangible heritage. In Michelle L. Stefano, Peter Davis and Gerard Corsane (eds), *Safeguarding Intangible Cultural Heritage*, pp. 9–21. Woodbridge: Boydell Press.

Álvarez López, Laura. 2019. The dialect of São João da Chapada: Possible remains of a mining language in Minas Gerais, Brazil. *International Journal of the Sociology of Language* 258: 143–170.

Amos, David and Natalie Braber. 2017. *Images of Coalmining in the East Midlands*. Sheffield: Bradwell Books.

Asprey, Esther. 2007. *Black Country English and Black Country Identity*. Unpublished PhD thesis, University of Leeds.

Baugh, Albert, C. and Thomas Cable. 2002. *A History of the English Language*. London: Routledge.

BBC News. 2012. Cromarty fisherfolk dialect's last native speaker dies. https://www.bbc.co.uk/news/uk-scotland-highlands-islands-19802616 (last accessed 6 October 2020).

Beal, Joan. 1993. The grammar and Tyneside and Northumbrian English. In James Milroy and Lesley Milroy (eds), *Real English. The Grammar of English Dialects in the British Isles*, pp. 187–213. London: Longman.

Beal, Joan. 2006. *Language and Region*. London: Routledge.

Beal, Joan. 2009. Enregisterment, commodification and historical context: 'Geordie' versus 'Sheffieldish'. *American Speech* 84(2): 138–156.

Beal, Joan. 2010. *An Introduction to Regional Englishes*. Edinburgh: Edinburgh University Press.

Beal, Joan. 2018. Dialect as heritage. In Angela Creese and Adrian Blackledge (eds), *The Routledge Handbook of Language and Superdiversity*, pp. 165–180. London: Routledge.

Beal, Joan and Lourdes Burbano-Elizondo. 2012. 'All the lads and lasses': Lexical variation in Tyne and Wear. *English Today* 28(4): 10–22.

Beatty, Christina, Steve Fothergill and Tony Gore. 2019. *The State of the Coalfields 2019*. Sheffield: Centre for Regional, Economic and Social Research, Sheffield Hallam University.
Beeching, Kate. 2011. Sociolinguistic aspects of lexical variation in French. In Timothy Pooley and Anthony Lodge (eds), *On Linguistic Change in French: Sociohistorical Approaches*, pp. 37–54. Chambéry: University of Savoy Press.
Beeton, John. 1999. *Nottingham as it is Spoke*. Four volumes. Nottingham: JB Enterprises.
Bell, David. 2006. *Memories of the Derbyshire Coalfields*. Newbury: Countryside Books.
Bell, David. 2007. *Memories of the Leicestershire Coalfield*. Newbury: Countryside Books.
Bell, David. 2008. *Memories of the Nottinghamshire Coalfield*. Newbury: Countryside Books.
Berger, Stefan (ed.). 2020. *Constructing Industrial Pasts. Heritage, Historical Culture and Identity in Regions undergoing Structural Economic Transformation*. Oxford: Berghahn.
Boberg, Charles. 2005. The North American regional vocabulary survey: New variables and methods in the study of North American English. *American Speech* 80(1): 22–60.
Braber, Natalie. 2015. *Nottinghamshire Dialect*. Sheffield: Bradwell Books.
Braber, Natalie. 2020. Nottingham: City of Literature – dialect literature and literary dialect. In Patrick Honeybone and Warren Maguire (eds), *Dialect Writing and the North of England*, pp. 75–102. Edinburgh: Edinburgh University Press.
Braber, Natalie. Forthcoming. Community projects. In Hazel Price and Dan McIntyre (eds), *Communicating Linguistics: Language, Community and Public Engagement*. London: Routledge.
Braber, Natalie and David Amos. 2021. *Coal in the Blood. An East Midlands Coal Mining Anthology*. Nottingham: Five Leaves.
Braber, Natalie and Nicholas Flynn. 2015. The East Midlands: Nottingham. In Raymond Hickey (ed.), *Researching Northern Englishes*, pp. 369–392. Amsterdam: John Benjamins.
Braber, Natalie and Jonnie Robinson. 2018. *East Midlands English*. Berlin: Mouton de Gruyter.
Braber, Natalie, Claire Ashmore and Suzy Harrison. 2017. *Pit Talk of the East Midlands*. Sheffield: Bradwell Books.
Bradley, Bob. Seam names and codes. http://www.healeyhero.co.uk/rescue/individual/Bob_Bradley/Bk-8/Seam-Names.html (last accessed April 2021).
Britain, David. 2000. The difference that space makes: An evaluation of the application of human geographic thought in sociolinguistic dialectology. *Essex Research Reports in Linguistics* 29: 38–82.
Britain, David. 2005. The dying dialects of England? In Antonio Bertacca (ed.), *Historical Linguistic Studies of Spoken English*, pp. 35–46. Pisa: Edizione Plus.
Britain, David (ed.). 2007. *Language in the British Isles*. Cambridge: Cambridge University Press.
Britain, David. 2009. One foot in the grave? Dialect death, dialect contact, and dialect birth in England. *International Journal of the Sociology of Language* 196/197: 121–155.

Britain, David. 2013. Space, diffusion and mobility. In Jack Chambers and Natalie Schilling (eds), *Handbook of Language Variation and Change* (second edition), pp. 471–500. Oxford: Wiley-Blackwell.

British Coal. 1989. *British Coalmining. An Introduction.* Burton-on-Trent: British Coal Technical Department.

Burbano-Elizondo, Lourdes. 2008. *Language Variation and Identity in Sunderland.* Unpublished PhD thesis, University of Sheffield.

Burland, Kate. 2017. Where the Black Country meets 'Black Barnsley'. Dialect variation and identity in an ex-mining community of Barnsley. In Emma Moore and Chris Montgomery (eds), *Language and a Sense of Place*, pp. 234–257. Cambridge: Cambridge University Press.

Cameron, Deborah. 2000. Styling the worker: Gender and the commodification of language in the globalized service economy. *Journal of Sociolinguistics* 4(3): 323–347.

Carr, Geoffrey. 1990. *Tales from the Mines.* Matlock: J. N. M. Publications.

Carswell, Jeanne and Tracey Roberts. 1992. *Getting the Coal. Impressions of a Twentieth Century Mining Community.* Oxford: The Alden Press.

Cave, Andrew. 2001. *Language Variety and Communicative Style as Local and Subcultural Identity in a South Yorkshire Coalmining Community.* Unpublished PhD thesis, University of Sheffield.

Chambers, J. K. 1994. An introduction to dialect topography. *English World-Wide* 15: 35–53.

Coates, Ken and Michael Barratt Brown. 1997. *The Struggle for Survival in the Coalfield Communities of Britain.* Nottingham: Spokesman.

Coleman, David. 2017. *A Nottinghamshire Pitman's Story.* Nottingham: Dayglo Books.

Collins, Brian T. 1975. *Coalmining in Nottinghamshire – A Summary.* Nottingham: Department of Planning and Transportation.

Colls, Robert. 1977. *The Collier's Rant. Song and Culture in the Industrial Village.* London: Croom Helm.

Cornips, Leonie and Pieter Muysken. 2019. Introduction: Language in the mines. *International Journal of the Sociology of Language* 258: 1–11.

Cornips, Leonie and Vincent de Rooij. 2019. Katanga Swahili and Heerlen Dutch: A sociohistorical and linguistic comparison of contact varieties in mining regions. *International Journal of the Sociology of Language* 258: 35–69.

Coupland, Nikolas. 1984. Accommodation at work: Some phonological data and their implications. *International Journal of the Sociology of Language* 46: 49–70.

Court, W. H. B. 1945. Problems of the British coal industry between the wars. *The Economic History Review* 15(1–2): 1–24.

Cresswell, Helen. 2008. *The Secret World of Polly Flint.* Nottingham: Five Leaves.

Critcher, Chas, Klaus Schuber and David Waddington (eds). 1995. *Regeneration of the Coalfield Areas. Anglo-German Perspectives.* London: Pinter.

Czaykowska-Higgins, Ewa. 2009. Research models, community engagement, and linguistic fieldwork: Reflections on working within Canadian Indigenous communities. *Language Documentation and Conservation* 3(1): 15–50.

Dennis, Norman, Fernando Henriques and Clifford Slaughter. 1969. *Coal is our Life. An Analysis of a Yorkshire Mining Community.* London: Tavistock Publications.

Dent, Susie. 2013. Mapping the word. Local vocabulary and its themes. In Clive Upton and Bethan Davies (eds), *Analysing 21st-Century British English. Conceptual and Methodological Aspects of the Voices Project*, pp. 110–123. London: Routledge.

Deumert, Ana and Anne Storch. 2019. Language as world heritage? Critical perspectives on language-as-archive. In Natsuko Akagawa and Laurajane Smith (eds), *Safeguarding Intangible Heritage*, pp. 102–117. London: Routledge.

Devlin, Thomas. 2014. *Sociophonetic Variation, Orientation and Topic in County Durham*. Unpublished PhD thesis, University of York.

Devlin, Thomas, Peter French and Carmen Llamas. 2019. Vowel change across time, space, and conversational topic: The use of localized features in former mining communities. *Language Variation and Change* 31: 303–328.

Docherty, Gerard and Paul Foulkes. 1999. Derby and Newcastle: Instrumental phonetics and variationist studies. In Paul Foulkes and Gerard Docherty (eds), *Urban Voices*, pp. 47–71. London: Arnold.

Douglas, Fiona. 2017. Using archives to conduct collaborative research on language and region. In Emma Moore and Chris Montgomery (eds), *A Sense of Place*, pp. 128–146. Cambridge: Cambridge University Press.

Douglass, David. 1973. *Pit Talk in County Durham*. Oxford: TruExpress.

Drew, Paul and John Heritage (eds). 1992. *Talk at Work*. Cambridge: Cambridge University Press.

DuPree McNair, Elizabeth. 2005. *Mill Villagers and Farmers: Dialect and Economics in a Small Southern Town*. Durham, NC: Duke University Press.

Durkin, Philip. 2012. Variation in the lexicon: The 'Cinderella' of sociolinguistics? *English Today* 28(4): 3–9.

Dury, George. 1963. *The East Midlands and the Peak*. London: Thomas Nelston and Sons.

Dyer, Judy. 2002. 'We all speak the sound around here': Dialect levelling in a Scottish-English community. *Journal of Sociolinguistics* 6(1): 99–116.

Emery, Jay. 2020. Urban trauma in the ruins of industrial culture: Miners' welfares of the Nottinghamshire coalfield, UK. *Social & Cultural Geography*. DOI: 10.1080/14649365.2020.1809011.

Fareham, J. C. Date unknown. *Clipstone Colliery Village 1922–1972. Recollections of Village Life in a Nottinghamshire Mining Community*. Publisher unknown.

Fennell, Barbara. 2001. *A History of English. A Sociolinguistic Approach*. Oxford: Blackwell.

Ferguson, Rebecca, Rodney Harrison and Daniel Weinbren. 2010. Heritage and the recent and contemporary past. In Tim Benton (ed.), *Understanding Heritage and Memory*, pp. 277–315. Manchester: Manchester University Press.

Flynn, Nicholas. 2007. *A Sociophonetic Comparison of Adolescent Speech in Two Areas of Nottingham*. Unpublished MA thesis, University of Essex.

Flynn, Nicholas. 2012. *A Sociophonetic Study of Nottingham Speakers*. Unpublished PhD thesis, University of York.

Forster, William. 1969. *Pit-Talk: A Survey of Terms used by Miners in the South Midlands*. Leicester: Vaughan Papers in Adult Education.

Fox, Alan. 2012. Regional differentiation in farming technology, 1500–1720. In Sam Turner and Bob Silvester (eds), *Life in Medieval Landscapes. People and Places in the Middle Ages*, pp. 166–180. Oxford: Oxbow Books.

Francis, E. H. 1979. British coalfields. *Science Progress* 66(261): 1–23.
Franks, Angela. 2001. *Nottinghamshire Miners' Tales*. Keyworth: Reflections of a Bygone Age.
Freese, Barbara. 2003. *Coal. A Human History*. London: Arrow Books.
Friends of Thringstone. 2013. *Scottish in Thringstone. The Story of People Coming to the Village in the 1960s*. Loughborough: Teamprint.
Friends of Thringstone. 2014. *Memories of Durham Miners*. Loughborough: Teamprint.
Gibbs, Ewan. 2021. *Coal Country. The Meaning and Memory of Deindustrialization in Postwar Scotland*. London: University of London Press.
Griffin, Alan R. 1962. *The Miners of Nottinghamshire 1914–1944. A History of the Nottinghamshire Miners' Unions*. London: George Allen & Unwin Ltd.
Griffin, Alan R. 1971a. *Mining in the East Midlands, 1550–1947*. London: Cass.
Griffin, Alan R. 1971b. *Coalmining*. London: Longman.
Griffin, Alan R. 1977. *The British Coalmining Industry. Retrospect and Prospect*. Ashbourne: Moorland Publishing.
Griffin, Alan R. 1981. *The Nottinghamshire Coalfield 1881–1981. A Century of Progress*. Ashbourne: Moorland Publishing.
Griffin, Colin P. 1981. *The Leicestershire and South Derbyshire Miners, Vol. I, 1840–1914*. Coalville: NUM Leicester Area.
Griffin, Colin P. 1988. *The Leicestershire Miners, Vol. II, 1814–1945*. Coalville: NUM Leicester Area.
Griffin, Colin P. 1989. *The Leicestershire Miners, Vol. III, 1945–1988*. Coalville: NUM Leicester Area.
Griffin, Colin P. 1990. *The Nottinghamshire Miners' Industrial Union. 'Spencer Union'. Rufford Branch Minutes 1926–1936*. Nottingham: The Thoroton Society of Nottinghamshire.
Griffin, Colin P. 1993. 'Three days down the pit and three days play': Underemployment in the East Midland coalfields between the wars. *International Review of Social History* 38(3): 321–343.
Griffiths, Bill. 2007. *Pitmatic: The Talk of the North East Coalfield*. Newcastle: Northumbria University Press.
Harrison, Rodney. 2010. Heritage as social action. In Susie West (ed.), *Understanding Heritage in Practice*, pp. 240–276. Manchester: Manchester University Press.
Hennessy, Kate. 2012. From intangible expression to digital cultural heritage. In Michelle L. Stefano, Peter Davis and Gerard Corsane (eds), *Safeguarding Intangible Cultural Heritage*, pp. 33–45. Woodbridge: Boydell Press.
Herold, Ruth. 1997. Solving the actuation problem: Merger and immigration in eastern Pennsylvania. *Language Variation and Change* 9: 165–189.
Hollows, Derek. 2010. *Voices in the Dark. Pony Talk and Mining Tales*. Marston Gate: Amazon.
Honeybone, Patrick and Kevin Watson. 2013. Salience and the sociolinguistics of Scouse spelling. *English World-Wide* 34(3): 305–340.
Hooson, William. 1747. *The Miners Dictionary*, reprinted in 1979. Ilkley: The Scholar Press.
Hornsby, David. 2018. A new dialect for a new village: Evidence for koinéization in East Kent. In Laura Wright (ed.), *Southern English Varieties. Then and Now*, pp. 74–109. Berlin: Walter de Gruyter.

Hudson, Ray and David Sadler. 1990. State policies and the changing geography of the coal industry in the United Kingdom in the 1980s and 1990s. *Transactions of the Institute of British Geographers* 15(4): 435–454.

Hughes, Arthur, Peter Trudgill and Dominic Watt. 2005. *English Accents and Dialects*. London: Hodder Arnold.

Jansen, Sandra and Natalie Braber. 2020. Foot-fronting and foot–strut splitting: Vowel variation in the East Midlands. *English Language and Linguistics*, 1–31. DOI: 10.1017/S1360674320000325.

Jencks, Clinton E. 1967. Social status of coal miners in Britain since nationalization. *The American Journal of Economics and Sociology* 26(3): 301–312.

Johnstone, Barbara. 2010. Indexing the local. In Nikolas Coupland (ed.), *Handbook of Language and Globalization*, pp. 386–405. Oxford: Blackwell.

Karpf, Anne. 2014. The human voice and the texture of experience. *Oral History* 42(2): 50–55.

Kearney, A. 2009. Intangible cultural heritage. Global awareness and local interest. In Laurajane Smith and N Akagawa (eds), *Intangible Heritage*, pp. 209–225. London: Routledge.

Kerswill, Paul. 2018. Dialect formation and dialect change in the Industrial Revolution: British vernacular English in the nineteenth century. In Laura Wright (ed.), *Southern English Varieties. Then and Now*, pp. 8–38. Berlin: Walter de Gruyter.

Kerswill, Paul, Carmen Llamas and Clive Upton. 1999. The first SuRE moves: Early steps towards a large dialect project. *Leeds Studies in English* 30: 257–269.

Keyworth and District Local History Meeting Report. 2003. Available online: http://www.keyworth-history.org.uk/about/reports/0310.htm (last accessed December 2020).

Kirby, M. W. 1977. *The British Coalmining Industry 1870–1946. A Political and Economic History*. London: The Macmillan Press.

Kortmann, Bernd and Clive Upton (eds). 2008. *Varieties of English 1: The British Isles*. Berlin: Mouton de Gruyter.

Lawrie, Susan H. 1991. A linguistic survey of the use and familiarity of Scottish dialect items in north east Fife. *Scottish Language* 10: 18–29.

Leach, Hannah. 2018. *Sociophonetic Variation in Stoke-on-Trent's Pottery Industry*. Unpublished PhD thesis, University of Sheffield.

Lee, Peter. Forthcoming. *Dialect of a Lesser Known Variety of English in the East Midlands: Dialect and Sociolinguistic Variation of Traveller English in the East Midlands*. Unpublished PhD thesis, Nottingham Trent University.

Leeman, Adrian, Marie-José Kolly and David Britain. 2018. The English Dialects App: The creation of a crowdsourced dialect corpus. *Ampersand* 5: 1–17.

Lewis, B. 1971. *Coal Mining in the Eighteenth and Nineteenth Centuries*. London: Longman.

Llamas, Carmen. 1999. A new methodology: Data elicitation for social and regional language variation studies. *Leeds Working Papers in Linguistics and Phonetics* 7: 95–118.

Llamas, Carmen. 2001. *Language Variation and Innovation in Teesside English*. Unpublished PhD thesis, University of Leeds.

McIvor, Arthur. 2020. Where is 'Red Clydeside'? Industrial heritage, working-class culture and memory in the Glasgow region. In Stefan Berger (ed.), *Constructing*

Industrial Pasts. Heritage, Historical Culture and Identity in Regions undergoing Structural Economic Transformation, pp. 47–67. Oxford: Berghahn.

Mapping UK Mining Heritage. Available online: http://www.mininghistorythehumanjourney.net/edu/EastMidlandsIntro.shtml (last accessed December 2020).

Marzo, Stefania. 2019. From flamano to urban vernacular. Linguistic and metalinguistic heritage of first generation miners in Flemish Limburg. *International Journal of the Sociology of Language* 258: 99–119.

Mesthrie, Rajend. 2019. Fanakalo as a mining language in South Africa: A new overview. *International Journal of the Sociology of Language* 258: 13–33.

Miethaner, Ulrich. 2000. Orthographic transcriptions of non-standard varieties: The case of earlier African-American English. *Journal of Sociolinguistics* 4(4): 534–560.

Millar, Robert McColl. 1999. Some geographical and cultural patterns in the lexical/semantic structure of Scots. *Northern Scotland* 18: 55–65.

Millar, Robert McColl. 2016. Dialect death? The present state of the dialects of the Scottish fishing communities. In Cinzia Russi (ed.), *Current Trends in Historical Sociolinguistics*, pp. 143–164. Warsaw: de Gruyter Open.

Millar, Robert McColl, William Barras and Lisa Bonnici. 2014. *Lexical Variation and Attrition in the Scottish Fishing Communities*. Edinburgh: Edinburgh University Press.

Milroy, James. 1996. A current change in British English: Variation in (th) in Derby. *Newcastle and Durham Working Papers in Linguistics* 4: 213–222.

Milroy, Lesley. 1987. *Language and Social Networks*. Oxford: Blackwell.

Milroy, Lesley and Matthew Gordon. 2003. *Sociolinguistics: Method and Interpretation*. Oxford: Blackwell.

Montgomery, Chris. 2007. *Northern English Dialects: A Perceptual Approach*. Unpublished PhD thesis, University of Sheffield.

Moore, Roger. 1995. *Community and Conflict in Eastwood: A Study from the Nottinghamshire Coalfield before 1914*. Nottingham: University of Nottingham.

Morley, Brian. No date. *Mining Artist. Exhibition Catalogue*. Nottingham: Nottinghamshire Mining Museum.

Muysken, Pieter. 2019. Multilingualism and mixed language in the mines of Potosí (Bolivia). *International Journal of the Sociology of Language* 258: 121–142.

National Coal Mining Museum for England. Nationalisation Timeline. Available online: https://www.ncm.org.uk/library/nationalisation-timeline (last accessed 4 December 2020).

Northern Mine Research Society. Available online: https://www.nmrs.org.uk/ (last accessed 6 October 2020).

Nottinghamshire County Council. 1986. *The Coal Industry in Nottinghamshire*. Nottingham: Nottinghamshire County Council.

Orton, Harold, Stewart Sanderson and John Widdowson. 1978. *The Linguistic Atlas of England*. London: Croom Helm.

Orton, Harold, Eugen Dieth, Willfrid Halliday, Michael Barry, P. M. Tilling and Martyn Wakelin. 1962–1971. *Survey of English Dialects A and B: Introduction and The Basic Material, Introduction and 4 Volumes, Each of 3 Parts*. Leeds: E. J. Arnold and Son.

Paterson, Harry. 2014. *Look Back in Anger: The Miners' Strike in Nottinghamshire 30 Years On*. Nottingham: Five Leaves Publication.

Pearce, Michael. 2009. A perceptual dialect map of Northeast England. *English Language and Linguistics* 37(2): 162–192.

Pearce, Michael. 2020. The survival of traditional dialect lexis on the participatory web. *English Studies* 101(4): 487–509.

Pecht, Nantke. 2019. Grammatical features of a moribund coalminers' language in a Belgian *cite*. *International Journal of the Sociology of Language* 258: 71–98.

Petyt, K. M. 1985. *'Dialect' and 'Accent' in Industrial West Yorkshire*. Amsterdam: John Benjamins.

Pietikäinen, Sari. 2019. Discussion: Language in nature resource economies. *International Journal of the Sociology of Language* 258: 171–176.

Power, Rosemary. 2008. 'After the black gold': A view of mining heritage from coalfield areas in Britain. *Folklore* 119: 160–181.

Price, Brian P. 1971. *The Yorkshire, Nottinghamshire and Derbyshire Coalfield*. London: MacDonald & Co.

Redmonds, George. 2016. *The Vocabulary of Coal Mining in Yorkshire, 1250–1850*. Lancashire: Northern Mine Research Society.

Rickford, John R. 1986. The need for new approaches to social class analysis in sociolinguistics. *Language and Communication* 6(3): 215–221.

Robinson, Colin. 1995. Privatisation: Saving the British coal industry? *Surrey Energy Economics Discussion Paper Series* 83: 1–22.

Robinson, Colin and Eileen Marshall. 1985. *Can Coal be Saved? A Radical Proposal to Reserve the Decline of a Major Industry*. Hobart Paper. London: The Institute of Economic Affairs.

Robinson, Jonathan. 2015. *Evolving English Wordbank. A Glossary of Present-Day English Dialect and Slang*. Sheffield: Bradwell Books.

Robinson, Jonnie. 2012. Lexical variation in the *BBC Voices* recordings. *English Today* 28(4): 23–37.

Robinson, Justyna. 2012. A *gay* paper: Why should sociolinguistics bother with semantics? *English Today* 28(4): 38–54.

Robinson, Mike. 2018. Talking of heritage. The past in conversation. In Angela Creese and Adrian Blackledge (eds), *The Routledge Handbook of Language and Superdiversity*, pp. 194–207. London: Routledge.

Rosetta Project. 2012. Available online: https://rosettaproject.org/blog/02012/oct/31/cromarty-dialect-learning-from-death-of-language/ (last accessed 6 October 2020).

Sandow, Rhys. 2020. The Anglo-Cornish dialect is 'a performance, a deliberate performance'. *English Today* 36(3): 77–84.

Sandow, Rhys. 2021. *Anglo-Cornish Dialect Lexis: Variation, Change, and Social Meaning*. Unpublished PhD thesis, University of Sussex.

Scollins, Richard and John Titford. 2000. *Ey up mi duck! Dialect of Derbyshire and the East Midlands*. Newbury: Countryside Books.

Shaw, Katy. 2012. *Mining the Meaning: Cultural Representations of the 1984–5 UK Miners' Strike*. Cambridge: Cambridge Scholars.

Simmelbauer, Andrea. 2000. *The Dialect of Northumberland. A Lexical Investigation*. Heidelberg: Winter.

Simpson, Katherine and Robin Simmons. 2019. Social haunting or reclaiming the past? Education and the working class in a former mining community. *Journal for Critical Education Policy Studies* 17(3): 1–23.

Smith, Laurajane. 2020. Industrial heritage and the remaking of class identity. In Stefan Berger (ed.), *Constructing Industrial Pasts. Heritage, Historical Culture and Identity in Regions undergoing Structural Economic Transformation*, pp. 27–46. Oxford: Berghahn.

Stennett, Alan and Richard Scollins. 2006. *Nobbut a Yellerbelly!* Newbury: Countryside Books.

Stocker, David. 2006. *England's Landscape. The East Midlands.* London: Collins.

Thesing, William B. (ed.). 2000. *Caverns of Night. Coal Mines in Art, Literature and Film.* Columbia, SC: University of South Carolina Press.

Tonge, J. 1907. *Coal.* London: Archibald Books.

Trinder, Barrie. 2000. Coming to terms with the 20th century: Changing perceptions of the British industrial past. *The Journal of the Society for Industrial Archaeology* 26(2): 65–80.

Trudgill, Peter. 1986. *Dialects in Contact.* Oxford: Blackwell.

Trudgill, Peter. 1989. Contact and isolation in linguistic change. In Leiv Egil Breivik and Ernst Håkon Jahr (eds), *Language Change. Contributions to the Study of its Causes*, pp. 227–237. Berlin: Mouton de Gruyter.

Trudgill, Peter. 1999. *The Dialects of England.* Oxford: Blackwell.

UNESCO. 2003. *Intangible Heritage: Text of the Convention.* Available online: https://ich.unesco.org/en/convention (last accessed November 2020).

UNESCO. Intangible cultural heritage. Available online: https://ich.unesco.org/en/ich-and-mother-languages-00555 (last accessed May 2021).

Upton, Clive. 1995. Mixing and fudging in midland and southern dialects of England: The *cup* and *foot* vowels. In Jack Windsor Lewis (ed.), *Studies in General and English Phonetics*, pp. 385–394. London: Routledge.

Upton, Clive. 2012. The importance of being Janus. In Manfred Markus, Yoko Iyeiri, Reinhard Henberger and Emil Chanson (eds), *Middle and Modern English Corpus Linguistics*, pp. 257–268. Amsterdam: John Benjamins.

Upton, Clive. 2013. Blurred boundaries. The dialect word from the BBC. In Clive Upton and Bethan Davies (eds), *Analysing 21st-Century British English. Conceptual and Methodological Aspects of the Voices Project*, pp. 180–197. London: Routledge.

Upton, Clive and Bethan Davies (eds). 2013. *Analysing 21st-Century British English. Conceptual and Methodological Aspects of the Voices Project.* London: Routledge.

Upton, Clive and J .D. A. Widdowson. 1999. *Lexical Erosion in English Dialects.* Sheffield: National Centre for English Cultural Tradition.

Upton, Clive and J. D. A. Widdowson. 2006. *An Atlas of English Dialects. Second Edition.* London: Routledge.

Waddington, David, Chas Critcher, Bella Dicks and David Parry. 2001. *Out of the Ashes? The Social Impact of Industrial Contraction and Regeneration on Britain's Mining Communities.* London: The Stationery Office.

Wain, Ken. 2014. *The Coalmining Industry of Sheffield and North-East Derbyshire.* Stroud: Amberley Publishing.

Wales, Katie. 2000. North and South: An English linguistic divide? *English Today* 16(1): 4–15.

Wales, Katie. 2006. *Northern English. A Social and Cultural History.* Cambridge: Cambridge University Press.

Wallace, Kate. 2007. *Social Variation in the English of the Southampton Area.* Unpublished PhD thesis, University of Leeds.
Waller, Robert J. 1983. *The Dukeries Transformed: The Social and Political Development of a Twentieth-Century Coalfield.* Oxford: Clarendon Press.
Watt, Dominic and Carmen Llamas. 2017. Identifying places. The role of borders. In Emma Moore and Chris Montgomery (eds), *A Sense of Place*, pp. 191–214. Cambridge: Cambridge University Press.
Wells, J. C. 1986. *Accents of English 2. The British Isles.* Cambridge: Cambridge University Press.
Williams, J. E. 1962. *The Derbyshire Miners: A Study in Industrial and Social History.* London: Allen and Unwin.
Williamson, Leslie. 2002. *Jobey*. Leicester: Ulverscroft.
Wolfram, Walt and Natalie Schilling-Estes. 1995. Moribund dialects and the endangerment canon: The case of the Ocracoke Brogue. *Language* 71(4): 696–721.
Wright, Peter. 1972. Coal-mining language: A recent investigation. In Martyn F. Wakelin (ed.), *Patterns in the Folk Speech of the British Isles*, pp. 32–49. London: William Clowes & Sons.
Wright, Peter. 1975. *The Derbyshire Drawl. How it is Spoke.* Whitehaven: Dalesman Books.
Wright, Peter, 1979. *The Notts Natter. How it is Spoke.* Whitehaven: Dalesman Books.
YouTube Tangier Tidewater Dialect. Available online: https://www.youtube.com/watch?v=AIZgw09CG9E (last accessed 6 October 2020).
Zhang, Qing. 2005. A Chinese yuppie in Bejing: Phonological variation and the construction of a new professional identity. *Language in Society* 34: 431–466.

Web sources

(All accurate in 2021 – this is not an exhaustive list and there may be others)

Anglo American Mining Terms
https://www.angloamerican.com/futuresmart/stories/our-industry/mining-explained/mining-terms-explained-a-to-z

Coalmining History Resource Centre Mining Terminology
https://web.archive.org/web/20150530001906/http://www.cmhrc.co.uk/site/literature/glossary

Earth Science Partnership
https://www.earthsciencepartnership.co.uk/newsfeed/useful-glossary-of-coal-mine-terms/

Engole Coal Mining Terms
https://engole.info/coal-mining-terms/

Forest of Dean Mining Terms
https://www.forestofdeanhistory.org.uk/assets/Uploads/Dave-Tuffleys-Mining-Glossary.pdf

Glossary of Coal Mining Terms
https://www.hoodfamily.info/glossary/glossaryindex.html
https://www.sec.gov/Archives/edgar/data/1165780/000116578003000001/glossary.htm
https://link.springer.com/content/pdf/bbm%3A978-94-010-0610-1%2F1.pdf

Glossary of Mining and Geordie Terms
http://www.dmm.org.uk/pitwork/html/defs.htm

Glossary of Scotch Mining Terms
http://www.scottishmining.co.uk/Indexes/Barrowman.html

Government of Canada Glossary of Mining Terminology
https://www.aadnc-aandc.gc.ca/eng/1100100028056/1100100028058

Hanna Basin Museum, Coal Miner Jargon
https://www.hannabasinmuseum.com/uploads/6/5/9/5/6595987/coal_miner_jargon.pdf

Healey Hero
http://www.healeyhero.co.uk/rescue/glossary/glossary.htm

Kentucky Coal Education
http://www.coaleducation.org/glossary.htm

Legends of America
https://www.legendsofamerica.com/we-miningterms/

Scottish Mining Words
http://www.scottishmining.co.uk/3.html

Welsh Mining Terms
http://www.welshcoalmines.co.uk/Glossary.htm

Index

African-Caribbean, 146
agriculture, 13, 105
Annesley colliery, 46, 49, 92, 122, 128, 139, 142, 154
argot *see also* jargon: register, 13, 18, 167
Asfordby colliery, 41
attrition, 1, 6–9, 12, 14, 22

Babbington colliery, 46, 129, 130
Bagworth colliery, 36, 37, 41
BATH vowel, 5, 62, 93, 157
Bentinck colliery, 47, 142
Bestwood colliery, 47, 48, 67
Bevercotes colliery, 48, 118
Bevin, Ernst, 30, 88
Bevin boys, 30, 88
Black Death, 26
Bolsover colliery, 41, 43, 44, 47
Brexit, 3, 16
British Coal Corporation (BCC), 32
British Library, 6, 66, 80
brotherhood *see also* camaraderie, 55, 71, 144, 150

Cadley Hill colliery, 39, 119, 123, 161
Calverton colliery, 48, 49, 147, 151
camaraderie *see also* brotherhood, 18, 52, 55, 65, 71, 81, 83, 87, 95, 144, 145, 150
canals, 28, 33, 34, 43, 47
carbon dioxide, 101
carbon monoxide, 28, 101
Chesterfield colliery, 41, 42, 43, 44

Church Gresley, 39
Cinderhill colliery, 45
Clifton colliery, 146, 155
Clipstone colliery, 2, 47, 49, 50, 89, 138
Coal Authority, 32, 81, 164
Coalville colliery, 2, 37, 41, 50, 67, 131,
Coleorton, 38, 39, 40
colliery closures, 2
Conservative Party, 3, 16,
Cornwall, 15
Cotgrave colliery, 48, 122, 146
COVID-19, 64, 76
Creswell colliery, 43, 44
Cromarty, 15
Cumberland, 25, 50

deprivation, 2, 16, 43, 53
Derwent, 43
Desford, 39, 40, 125
Devon, 25
dialect levelling, 6, 7
dialect literature, 56, 63
diffusion, 6, 7, 16
Donisthorpe colliery, 37, 39, 41
Dukeries, 34, 47, 48, 50
Durham, 25, 35, 48, 50, 55, 58, 84, 106, 159

education, 6, 32, 52
Ellistown colliery, 39
English Dialect App, 10
English Dialect Dictionary, 7, 165
English Dialect Grammar, 7
English Heritage, 19

180   *Index*

FACE vowel, 88, 143
First World War, 23, 29, 30, 33, 34, 40, 52
folklore, 51, 144, 166

Gedling colliery, 47, 129
Glapwell colliery, 44, 121
Gloucester, 25, 50
GOAT vowel, 18

happY vowel, 6, 63, 147
Haworth colliery, 49, 99, 114, 119, 139
Heanor colliery, 41, 42, 43
Hucknall colliery, 46, 47
Huddersfield, 43

Ibstock colliery, 41
ill health, 2
industrial language, 1, 4, 13–19, 22, 149
Industrial Revolution, 6, 23, 24, 25, 27, 41, 43
intangible heritage, 19, 20, 21, 162, 163
isogloss, 11, 14, 76

jargon *see also* argot: register, 13, 83, 84, 163

Kent, 17, 25, 58, 152, 161

Labour Party, 2, 16, 29, 30, 31, 88
language as heritage, 20, 149, 162–4
Langwith colliery, 44, 95
Leen Valley, 34, 46, 47
legacy, 3, 79
Leicestershire Miners' Association, 40
lettER vowel, 62
lexical diversity, 9
Linby colliery, 46, 129, 147
London, 34, 43,
l-vocalisation, 5, 95, 100

job losses *see also* unemployment, 2, 31, 32

Manchester, 5, 43, 120
Mansfield, 1, 3, 47, 50, 53, 121, 132, 140
Markham colliery, 36, 44, 92, 147

mass media, 8
Measham colliery, 37, 39, 41
mechanisation, 8, 14, 16, 29, 35, 57, 85, 109, 110, 114, 126, 143, 160, 161
memorabilia, 3, 20, 63
methane, 28, 101, 102, 135
migration, 1, 39, 48, 49, 50–1, 56, 59, 70, 84, 161, 165
Miners' Federation, 24, 30
Miners' Welfare, 51, 52
mobility, 7, 8, 12, 60
Moira colliery, 37, 39, 40
museums, 20, 81, 134, 151, 163

National Coal Board (NCB), 23, 30, 31, 32, 35, 40, 43, 44, 48, 55, 57, 66, 77, 85, 97, 142
National Coal Mining Museum of England, 3, 30, 66, 81, 84
National Miners' Association of Great Britain, 29, 40
National Union of Mineworkers (NUM), 30, 31, 36, 40, 44, 49, 58, 80, 138, 152
nationalisation, 30, 31, 40, 66, 85, 161
New Lount colliery, 37
Newstead colliery, 46, 93
nicknames, 18, 59, 94, 95, 98, 112, 142, 147, 150
north-east, 3, 9, 16, 17, 24, 26, 36, 39, 41, 48, 49, 54, 55, 58, 63, 66, 75, 84, 85, 90, 93, 94, 95, 98, 103, 107, 109, 126, 139, 142, 147, 151, 153, 154, 156, 160
Northumberland, 25, 48, 58, 84
Nottingham Miners' Industrial Union, 36

Ollerton colliery, 47, 50, 89, 151
oral history, 15, 21, 55, 79, 80, 163
Ormonde colliery, 43

pitmatic, 58, 85, 160
Pleasley colliery, 2, 44, 67, 107
positionality, 80–1
pottery, 15, 16
pride, 15, 21, 60, 84, 163

Index 181

railways, 28, 29, 34, 39, 43
Rainworth colliery, 47, 143
register *see also* argot: jargon, 3, 60, 163, 166
Renishaw Park colliery, 41, 44
Romans, 25, 26, 33, 37
rural dialects, 7

Salop, 25
Sankey Commission, 29
scabs, 36
Scargill, Arthur, 31, 49
Scotland, 3, 10, 12, 17, 24, 25, 27, 49, 50, 63, 84, 90, 142
Second World War, 2, 19, 30, 31, 34, 40, 43, 48
Sense Relation Networks (SRN), 12, 64, 65, 69, 70, 71–5, 76, 86
Sheffield, 5, 12, 43,
Shirebrook colliery, 41, 44, 104, 143
Silverhill colliery, 47, 99, 121, 124, 140
Snibston colliery, 37, 39, 40, 161
Snibston Discovery Centre, 2
social media, 12, 79
social mobility, 12
Somerset, 17, 25
South Derbyshire Amalgamated Miners' Association (SDAMA), 40
South Leicester colliery, 37
South Midlands, 40, 57, 58, 66, 75, 83, 154, 161
Spencer, George Alfred, 36, 48
Staffordshire, 3, 25, 47, 50, 63, 84
Standard English, 4, 7, 8, 67, 166
standardisation, 8, 12, 57, 85, 161
Stanton Ironworks, 41, 47
steam engine, 27
STRUT vowel, 5, 58, 62
superdiversity, 6
Survey of English Dialects (SED), 4, 7, 8, 11, 56, 67, 72, 145, 165
Swannington colliery, 37
swearing, 90, 94, 149

taboo language, 142, 149
tangible heritage, 3
Tangier Tidewater dialect, 15
teasing, 59, 98, 139, 146, 147, 150
Teversal colliery, 44, 47, 49, 99, 121
t-glottalling, 5
Thatcher, Margaret, 31, 36
th-fronting, 5
Thoresby colliery, 1, 23, 34, 36, 47, 49, 52, 68, 69, 119, 127, 130, 131, 144
Thringstone colliery, 50, 55, 151
tin mining, 15
trade union, 24, 29, 84, 87
transition zone, 6, 14, 62
Trent, 33, 43
Trent Valley, 33, 44
turnpikes, 34

unemployment *see also* job losses, 2, 16, 29, 32, 36, 40, 41, 53
UNESCO, 20, 162, 163, 166
Union of Democratic Mineworkers (UDM), 31, 36, 41, 81, 138
urban dialects, 6

velar nasal plus, 5, 62
voices study, 6, 12, 65, 72

Wales, 3, 17, 25, 27, 36, 50, 63
Warsop colliery, 44, 89, 155
Warwickshire, 25, 84
Welbeck colliery, 46, 49
Westmorland, 25
Whitwick colliery, 37, 39, 88, 103, 143, 146
Wollaton colliery, 33, 44, 47
Worcestershire, 25

yakka, 85
yod dropping, 5, 62
Yorkshire, 15, 17, 18, 25, 27, 32, 33, 35, 41, 44, 49, 50, 59, 66, 84, 96, 97, 133, 139, 147, 154, 155

EU representative:
Easy Access System Europe
Mustamäe tee 50, 10621 Tallinn, Estonia
Gpsr.requests@easproject.com

www.ingramcontent.com/pod-product-compliance
Lightning Source LLC
Chambersburg PA
CBHW071846230426
43671CB00012B/2084